nato

a beginner's guide

RELATED TITLES FROM ONEWORLD

Democracy: A Beginner's Guide, David Beetham, ISBN 1–85168–363–1

Political Philosophy: An Historical Introduction, Michael J. White,
    1–85168–328–3

Terrorism: A Beginner's Guide, Leonard Weinberg, ISBN 1–85168–358–5

The Palestine–Israeli Conflict: A Beginner's Guide, Dan Cohn-Sherbok and
    Dawoud El-Alami, ISBN 1–85168–332–1

nato

a beginner's guide

jennifer medcalf

ONEWORLD

OXFORD

nato: a beginner's guide

Oneworld Publications
(Sales and editorial)
185 Banbury Road
Oxford OX2 7AR
England
www.oneworld-publications.com

ISBN 1–85168–353–4

Typeset by Jayvee, Trivandrum, India
Cover design by the Bridgewater Book Company
Printed and bound in India by Thomson Press Ltd

contents

five   **an expanding alliance: nato's post-cold war
        enlargement process**   127

six   **outreach and partnership: nato's relations
        with its neighbours**   150

conclusion: an alliance revitalized? future challenges for nato 178

illustrations

diagrams

maps

acknowledgements

Writing a book is a daunting prospect and I could not have begun this endeavour, let alone have completed it, without the support of colleagues, friends and family. Their contribution to the writing of this book and the set of circumstances that went with it has been invaluable and more than deserves recognition.

I would like to thank Victoria Roddam of Oneworld for giving me the opportunity to write this book and for her encouragement and guidance as it progressed. Roger Eatwell provided the initial introduction to Oneworld and continues to be a constant source of support and good advice. Three anonymous reviewers provided helpful suggestions on the initial concept of this book and on the draft version. Their comments and input were greatly appreciated. I would also like to thank Ann Grand for editing the final manuscript.

I would like to thank Christopher Bennett and Alison Smith at NATO HQ for organizing a very productive visit there. I am also grateful to the NATO officials that agreed to be interviewed and took time out of their schedules to answer my questions. The maps and illustrations used in this book are adapted from the NATO website. Figures for defence expenditure and information presented in 'Member Profiles' are adapted from *The Military Balance 2003–04*, produced by the International Institute for Strategic Studies.

I am grateful to my friends and colleagues at the University of Bath who have contributed in different ways to this project. Jill O'Brien and Ann Burge deserve particular thanks for continuing to be a cheerful presence 'next door' and I am very grateful to them for always being ready to help in whatever way they can. I would also like to thank Kara Bosworth for her willingness to share her knowledge of NATO–Russia relations.

I count myself very lucky to have a group of friends who distracted me from this project when I needed distracting and helped me knuckle down when I needed to. Pete and Chris Barton, Luke and Maxine Harty, Andy Price and Helen Whitnell deserve particular thanks in this respect.

Special thanks go to my family for their support, encouragement and enthusiasm for this project, which kept me going when I thought I could not do it and to Pappy who operated his own 'open door' policy and welcomed me whenever I needed a break.

This book is for Pappy with my love and affection.

abbreviations

AAP-6	Allied Administrative Publication 6
ACE	Allied Command Europe
ACO	Allied Command for Operations
ACT	Allied Command for Transformation
AEW	Airborne Early Warning
AFSOUTH	Allied Forces Southern Europe
AMF-A	ACE Mobile Force – Air
AOR	Area of Responsibility
AWACS	Airborne Warning and Control Systems
C2	Command and Control
C³I	Command, Control, Communications, Intelligence
CAOC	Combined Air Operations Centre
CBR	Chemical, Biological, Radiological (Weapons)
CBRN	Chemical, Biological, Radiological, Nuclear (Weapons)
CC-Air/-Mar/-Land	Component Command-Air/-Maritime/-Land
CDP	Charter on a Distinctive Partnership
CENTCOM	Central Command (United States)
CEP	Civil Emergency Planning
CFE	Conventional Armed Forces in Europe
CFSP	Common Foreign and Security Policy
CJTF	Combined Joint Task Force
CSCE	Conference on Security and Cooperation in Europe
CTBT	Comprehensive Test Ban Treaty

DCAOC	Deployable Combined Air Operations Centre
DCI	Defence Capabilities Initiative
DPC	Defence Planning Committee
EAPC	European-Atlantic Partnership Council
EC	European Community
ESDI	European Security and Defence Identity
ESDP	European Security and Defence Policy
ESS	European Security Strategy
EU	European Union
FYROM	Former Yugoslav Republic of Macedonia
HG	Headline Goal
ICC	International Criminal Court
IFOR	Implementation Force
IMS	International Military Staff
IPAP	Individual Partnership Action Plan
IPP	Individual Partnership Programme
ISAF	International Security Assistance Force
JCS	Joint Chiefs of Staff
JFC	Joint Force Commander
JOIC	Joint Operational Intelligence Centre
KFOR	Kosovo Force
MAD	Mutual Assured Destruction
NAC	North Atlantic Council
NACC	North Atlantic Co-operation Council
NAEW	NATO Airborne Early Warning
NATO	North Atlantic Treaty Organization
NAVOCFORMED	Naval On-Call Force Mediterranean
NBC	Nuclear, Biological, Chemical
NPG	Nuclear Planning Group
NRC	NATO-Russia Council
NRF	NATO Response Force
NSS	National Security Strategy (United States)
NUC	NATO–Ukraine Commission
OSCE	Organization for Security and Co-operation in Europe
PACCOM	Pacific Command (United States)
PAP	Partnership Action Plan
PARP	Planning and Review Process
PfP	Partnership for Peace
PJC	Permanent Joint Council
PRT	Provincial Reconstruction Teams
QMV	Qualified Majority Voting

RMA	Revolution in Military Affairs
RRF	Rapid Reaction Force (EU)
SACEUR	Supreme Allied Commander Europe
SACLANT	Supreme Allied Commander Atlantic
SACT	Supreme Allied Commander Transformation
SALT	Strategic Arms Limitation Talks
SFOR	Stabilisation Force
SHAPE	Supreme Headquarters Allied Powers Europe
STANAVFORMED	Standing Naval Force Mediterranean
START	Strategic Arms Reduction Treaty
TMD	Theatre Missile Defence
UN	United Nations
UNMIK	United Nations Mission in Kosovo
UNPROFOR	United Nations Protection Force
UNSC	United Nations Security Council
USEUCOM	United States European Command
USJFCOM	United States Joint Forces Command
WEU	Western European Union
WMD	Weapons of Mass Destruction

introduction

Europe[1] and North America have been linked for centuries. A combination of cultural, demographic, economic, military and political components has produced a unique relationship that is not found in other regions of the world. The dynamic of these components is both one-way – historically from Europe to North America – and two-way – increasingly, in recent decades, from North America to Europe. To these, the identification of a significant number of common interests can be added. Two elements – a combination of diverse integrative forces and a coincidence of interests – have therefore traditionally underpinned the transatlantic relationship and have shaped and consolidated a comprehensive bilateral relationship between North America and Europe.

The origins of the contemporary transatlantic relationship are found in two strategic objectives: the need to integrate Western Europe politically and economically after the Second World War to prevent further conflict, hence the implementation of the Marshall Plan and the need for collective defence against the Soviet threat during forty years of Cold War, hence the establishment of the North Atlantic Treaty Organization (NATO) in 1949. These two strategic objectives illustrate two elements that have constituted the foundation of the transatlantic relationship: the importance of Europe to the United States and European recognition of the necessity of American involvement to ensure the security of the European continent.[2]

1

the origins of nato

Of all the areas of transatlantic interaction, NATO is the instrument through which the relationship has found greatest expression and meaning. It is therefore in the realms of security and defence that the transatlantic link is most profound.

NATO was formed in April 1949, though its origins can be found as early as December 1947 when the British Foreign Secretary, Ernest Bevin, privately commented to the US Secretary of State, George Marshall, that 'the Soviet Union will not deal with the West on any reasonable terms in the foreseeable future [...] the salvation of the West depends upon the formation of some sort of union, formal or informal in character, in Western Europe, backed by the United States and the Dominions – such a mobilisation of moral and material force will inspire confidence and energy within, and respect elsewhere'.[3] However, in spite of a growing threat from the East, negotiations over the founding of a transatlantic military alliance did not begin until 6 July 1948. A key reason for this delay was the United States' wariness of becoming embroiled in future European conflicts. There was clearly support for temporary military and economic assistance for the Europeans, yet there was also strong opposition, particularly in the State Department and the Department of Defense, to the concept of forging a formal military alliance in a time of peace.[4]

The parameters of the debate changed over the course of 1948, due to the seizure of Czechoslovakia by the Soviet Union on 25 February, the perceived Soviet threat to Norway and the beginning of the Berlin blockade in June. Moreover, the perceived inadequacies of the Western European Union (WEU), which was composed of European powers only, for the defence of Western Europe, made arguments for the full participation of the United States compelling. These influences, in conjunction with pressure exerted by Britain and Canada on the United States, paved the way for the forging of a military alliance between North American and West European allies. These negotiations eventually resulted in the signing of the North Atlantic Treaty on 4 April 1949, which brought NATO into being.

nato's cold war functions

The need for a credible defence against the Soviet Union during forty years of Cold War cemented the relationship between the

Allies. NATO's primary function of collective defence was expressed by Article 5 of the North Atlantic Treaty, which states:

> The Parties agree that an armed attack against one or more of them in Europe or North America shall be considered an attack against them all and consequently they agree that, if such an armed attack occurs, each of them, in exercise of the right of individual or collective self-defence recognised by Article 51 of the Charter of the United Nations, will assist the Party or Parties so attacked by taking forthwith, individually, and in concert with the other Parties, such action as it deems necessary, including the use of armed force, to restore and maintain the security of the North Atlantic area.
>
> Any such armed attack and all measures taken as a result thereof shall immediately be reported to the Security Council. Such measures shall be terminated when the Security Council has taken the measures necessary to restore and maintain international peace and security.

From its very beginning, NATO was not simply about defending the Allies against the Soviet threat. NATO also became the institutionalization of the relationship between North America and Western Europe and served to provide a framework within which West Germany could be safely reconstructed and eventually re-armed without risking a resurgence of its power. This last function was reassuring for West Europe as a whole but in particular for France and the Low Countries. For these three reasons, the role of NATO during the Cold War was, in the words of Lord Ismay, NATO's first Secretary General, to keep 'the Russians out, the Americans in, and the Germans down'.

In addition to performing these three crucial functions, NATO was also widely regarded as a community of like-minded nations that shared common values as well as facing a common threat. This was demonstrated by part of the preamble to the North Atlantic Treaty, which states:

> The Parties to this Treaty reaffirm their faith in the purposes and principles of the Charter of the United Nations and their desire to live in peace with all peoples and all governments.
>
> They are determined to safeguard the freedom, common heritage and civilisation of their peoples, founded on the principles of democracy, individual liberty and the rule of law.

NATO can therefore be distinguished from other military alliances, as it embodies the concept of a transatlantic community based on shared values. Sloan comments, in this respect, 'because NATO included a much narrower, more like-minded, mostly democratic set of nations than did the United Nations, it was possible to see the [transatlantic security] relationship as some sort of community of common values as well as shared interests – more than just an alliance'.[5] During the Cold War, this concept was compromized by the imposition of martial law in Turkey and the existence of non-democratic regimes in Portugal and Greece, yet NATO was still seen to be part of a wider attempt to create an environment in which common values and co-operative institutions could thrive.

Throughout the Cold War, NATO played an irreplaceable and unrivalled role in Western Europe's security architecture. However, the collapse of Communism and the disintegration of the Soviet Union in the period from 1989 to 1991 called into question NATO's future role and even its continued existence. The end of the Cold War was a double-edged sword for NATO: it had clearly 'won' it, by outliving the Warsaw Pact, yet at the same time, the disappearance of its *raison d'être* called into question its future relevance in the post-Cold War world. The realization that the Cold War *status quo* was not sustainable in the post-Cold War context therefore provided the impetus for the Allies to reform NATO, the results of which can be seen in the process of adaptation that NATO has undergone since the early 1990s.

nato's post-cold war adaptation

NATO's post-Cold War adaptation has been multi-dimensional. The first change that NATO has undergone is functional, which has enabled it to perform non-Article 5 crisis management, peacemaking and peacekeeping operations, initially under the authority of the United Nations (UN) but eventually as a self-authorizing force. The second change is geographic, illustrated by the execution of non-Article 5 missions outside the territory of NATO's members (as defined by Article 6 of the Washington Treaty). This functional and geographic change therefore illustrates how NATO has made the transition from being a defensive alliance focused on Western Europe, to one that contributes to global security whilst retaining a defensive role. The third concerns internal adaptation, which can be demonstrated by the emergence and consolidation of the European 'pillar' through the European Security and Defence Identity (ESDI), a measure that was designed to increase the role and capabilities of

the European NATO Allies. Since the ESDI programme was introduced in the mid-1990s, NATO has also initiated and concluded a set
of agreements with the European Union (EU) in order to facilitate
co-operation between NATO and the EU's European Security and
Defence Policy (ESDP). The fourth is the emergence and consolidation of outreach programmes to NATO's former Warsaw Pact adversaries, through the North Atlantic Cooperation Council
(NACC)/Euro-Atlantic Partnership Council (EAPC) initiative, the
Partnership for Peace (PfP) programme and initiatives involving
countries to the south of NATO, through the Mediterranean
Dialogue. Special partnership agreements with Russia and Ukraine
have also featured in this area of NATO reform. The fifth is the
enlargement of NATO's membership. The Czech Republic, Hungary
and Poland joined NATO in 1999 and there was agreement at
NATO's November 2002 Prague Summit to issue invitations to seven
more Central and East European countries – Bulgaria, Estonia,
Latvia, Lithuania, Slovenia, Slovakia and Romania. This resulted in
the growth of NATO's membership to twenty-six on 29 March 2004.
The last and most recent change is NATO's response to the 'new'
threats of international terrorism and weapons of mass destruction
(WMD), which increased dramatically in importance after the terrorist attacks of 11 September 2001 on New York and Washington,
DC.[6] This area of reform is currently the most pressing and prominent of all NATO's activities.

The implications of 9/11 have caused NATO to re-examine,
and in some cases give added momentum to, each of the areas of
post-Cold War adaptation outlined above. The decisions subsequently reached at the Prague Summit, which was heralded as a
'transformation' summit, as well as at the Istanbul Summit in
June 2004, therefore ensure that NATO will continue to evolve in
order to attempt to meet the challenges of the post-9/11 strategic
environment.

nato's ongoing military strengths

In addition to the rapid adaptation of NATO to the post-Cold War
environment, one of the main reasons NATO endured after the end
of the Cold War was the comparative advantage it continued to
possess as a military alliance. NATO, Roper comments,

> brings together virtually all the Western countries who collectively
> possess an overwhelming preponderance of military, economic and
> political power. In particular, it builds on the traditional patterns of

military cooperation between the United States, Canada and Western European countries [...] If force has to be used and our armed forces have to be placed in harm's way, countries want to know that the risks to them will be minimised because the command and control systems are tried and trusted. This, NATO, with its half century of experience of cooperation, provides in a way which no other international military structure does.[7]

NATO has an additional military role that directly relates to the patterns of military co-operation described above. NATO is not only the institutionalization of the transatlantic security and defence relationship; it can also provide the military framework for coalition operations involving NATO Allies. Operation Desert Storm, for instance, was clearly not a NATO operation. None the less, US-led coalition forces utilized NATO structures and procedures in a way that enhanced the coalition's ability to bring the conflict to a swift end. These structures and procedures can therefore be employed in non-NATO operations, enabling NATO to exist in a military sense, even when it is not involved politically. This kind of 'virtual' operation demonstrates that two kinds of NATO can be identified: a formal NATO that institutionalizes the transatlantic security relationship and an informal NATO that facilitates coalition operations involving both NATO and non-NATO Allies. Fear of losing the benefits of NATO's formal and informal roles has therefore been a key factor in ensuring its survival.

The comprehensive agenda of adaptation that NATO initiated at the end of the Cold War, in conjunction with its ongoing military strengths, has ensured that in the absence of a threat that justifies a purely collective defence posture, NATO has become an organization whose diverse activities relate mainly to political or military issues occurring in or emanating from beyond its members' borders. At the same time, NATO has continued to institutionalize the transatlantic security and defence relationship and embody a community of like-minded nations. These achievements have taken place even in the absence of NATO's *raison d'être* and principal unifying force, the Soviet Union. In view of NATO's adaptation and expansion and the sustained benefits of half a century of transatlantic co-operation, it is not hard to see why NATO has been termed 'the pre-eminent security organization for 21st century Europe'[8] and the most successful military alliance in history.

continental drift?

Unquestionably, NATO has been remarkably successful in many areas. However, in the early part of the 21st century, there is evidence to suggest that the transatlantic relationship – in all its different forms – is increasingly showing signs of strain. Although it is a contested thesis, many analysts have pointed to a process of 'continental drift' – a divergence between the United States and European states – that can be demonstrated in each of the areas that have traditionally served as unifying forces.[9] Culturally, for example, some consider that a values gap is emerging, as differences between the United States and European states become increasingly profound. Politically, many argue the significance of, and attention accorded to, developments in Europe by America's political élite is decreasing, whilst members of NATO that are also members of the EU have focused on the process of European integration rather than the enhancement of transatlantic relations. In addition to divergence in areas such as culture and politics, a whole host of geographic, generational and demographic factors that have traditionally strengthened the transatlantic link are seen by some to be losing significance and to have arguably weakened ties. NATO has also shown signs of strain, partly as a result of these broader changes in the transatlantic relationship, but also because of influences unique to the security and defence context. In the post-Cold War environment, NATO has been exposed to two areas of change – one external and one internal – that emerged as a result of the end of bipolar confrontation. These areas of change have challenged NATO and presented a test for its future vitality.

internal change: the nature of the nato relationship

The debate about the transatlantic relationship institutionalized in NATO has traditionally concentrated on two inter-related aspects: the extent, durability, and reliability of American involvement in European security and the specific relationship between the United States and the NATO Allies, that is, their relative roles and weight in foreign policy and security issues in Europe.[10] In the first instance, the commitment of the United States and its willingness to intervene in European security during the Cold War was not in doubt, even though isolationist forces in the United States periodically sought to question the rationale for, and degree of, American commitment to Europe. In the second instance, the Cold War NATO relationship was a 'partnership of unequals' between the United States as senior and the remaining NATO Allies as junior partners, which was reflected in the relative weight of the Allies in NATO's decision-making processes. During the Cold War, significant divergence from the norms of these two inter-related aspects was largely prevented by the constraints of bipolarity. The durable, yet asymmetric, nature of NATO was consequently maintained. The end of bipolar rivalry, however, presented the NATO Allies with a far wider range of options and brought the Cold War *status quo* into question.

The outbreak of conflict in the former Yugoslavia was the first indication that the role of the United States in European security could no longer be guaranteed in the same way that it had been during the Cold War. The initial reluctance of the United States to intervene gave the remaining NATO Allies sufficient grounds to question the extent, durability and reliability of the United States' post-Cold War commitment to European security. For some, the United States' ambivalence about intervening in situations in which there were no vital American interests demonstrated that the commonality of interests which had traditionally underpinned NATO had been undermined. The former US Secretary of State, James Baker's, comment, with respect to Bosnia, that 'we don't have a dog in this fight' perhaps best illustrates the changed context of NATO's debate in the early part of the 1990s. Doubts about American commitment to European security underscored the need for the European Allies to be able to take a more coherent and assertive role in the management of European security, an objective that had been prevented by the imperatives of bipolar confrontation.

In terms of the specific relationships between the NATO Allies, the conflict in the Balkans soured things considerably. This does not presuppose that during the Cold War there was always transatlantic consensus, as the Allies clashed over the best way to deal with the unifying threat of the Soviet Union, as well as other security issues not directly related to East-West confrontation, for example, the Vietnam War. France even left NATO's integrated military command structure in 1966, because it harboured doubts about the reliability of the United States and had concerns about US dominance. Following Charles de Gaulle's request that it remove its headquarters, forces and facilities from French territory, this Cold War crisis eventually resulted in NATO HQ moving from Paris to Brussels. Over the course of the post-Cold War period, damaging debates about NATO interventions, particularly in the former Yugoslavia, have on occasion brought relations between the Allies to breaking point. The controversy surrounding the United States' 'lift and strike'[11] policy in Bosnia in 1994 and Operation Allied Force, NATO's first self-authorized campaign, was particularly divisive.

Acrimonious debates about military interventions have not been restricted to NATO operations in the Balkans. The intra-Alliance crisis in February 2003, which was provoked by French, German and Belgian opposition to Turkey's request that NATO begin defensive measures to protect it in the event of a war with Iraq, has been described, even by some NATO officials, as a 'near-death experience'. Although the disagreement between the Allies was eventually resolved and NATO was able to begin planning for the defence of Turkey, the discussions between the Allies about the case for war outside the NATO context and the discussions within it about NATO's response were undoubtedly damaging.

NATO's military strengths have also been brought into question in the post-Cold War context. During the Cold War, NATO had a 'virtual' military capability because although it had a major battle plan, bipolar confrontation never resulted in military conflict and so NATO was never called upon to act. In contrast, responding to post-Cold War security challenges has required real operations and real deployments by NATO. Although it could be argued that the operational demands placed on NATO in the post-Cold War context have simply exposed long-standing weaknesses, its missions have provided clear evidence of the impact of a military capability gap between the Allies. In spite of efforts to reduce this gap, acrimonious debates about insufficient European defence spending, divergent force-planning, inadequate capabilities and increasing problems of inter-operability have been key characteristics of NATO interventions in the post-Cold War context. NATO's future as a military instrument has been called into question, as one of its perceived traditional strengths – military power – appears to be gradually eroding. This also means that the value of NATO's procedural and co-ordinating mechanisms for non-NATO operations has perhaps lessened.

external change: the international security environment

Changes in the internal dynamics and military capabilities of NATO have been matched by equally important external changes. The first concerns the focus of the Allies' attention. During the Cold War, the European theatre was the focal point of bipolar confrontation. Even though the United States, as a global power, always possessed global interests, the stakes of the Cold War meant that Western Europe assumed particular importance in the United States' strategy and planning. Post-Cold War, the relative strategic importance of Europe to the United States has decreased, demonstrating an erosion of one of NATO's traditional pillars. In Europe's place, 'rogue' states, rising regional powers and potential superpowers have absorbed increasing amounts of the United States' attention as long-term influences and potential rivals in the international system. In contrast, the end of bipolar confrontation enabled the European members of NATO that are also members of the EU to increase the existing momentum with respect to the process of European integration and the various areas that this encompasses, including security and defence policy. Inevitably, most of the European Allies have continued to accord greater attention to developments on the European continent than those beyond. Subsequently, there has been an increasing potential for divergence in focus between the NATO Allies.

The second source of external change is the nature of the security threats facing NATO. During the Cold War, there were two clearly defined threats: massive, conventional military invasion of Western Europe by Warsaw Pact forces and nuclear war. The break-up of the Warsaw Pact greatly diminished the likelihood of conventional military threats and a diverse range of security threats, from conflict resulting from religious or ethnic enmity, to the proliferation of WMD, to international terrorism, has increased in prominence and significance. The greater number and more diverse nature of post-Cold War security threats to the Allies has posed significant problems, as the Allies are now presented with strategic choices that stand in marked contrast to the strategic constraints of the Cold War. Although the Allies agree that all these threats need attention, the existence of choice has meant that the Allies have struggled to prioritize them in the same way. Moreover, they have often disagreed about the precise role NATO should play in addressing certain post-Cold War threats, particularly WMD and international terrorism.

The element that underpins these illustrations of internal and external change is the loss of the unifying Soviet threat, which, throughout the Cold War, acted as a stabilizing mechanism, guaranteeing that the Allies focused on and prioritized the same threat and making sure that the impact of intra-NATO conflict was minimized. The existence of internal and external change, since the end of the Cold War and most recently since 9/11, has therefore ensured that NATO has both seen very great change and faces equally significant challenges in the future.

aims and objectives of this book

The purpose of this book is to analyse the main areas of reform that NATO has embarked upon since the end of the Cold War, in order to assess its current position in the Western security architecture and its prospects for the future. Through presentation of each of NATO's main areas of activity and analysis of its most pressing issues, the reader will gain an insight into the challenges facing NATO in the 21st century.

The first part of the book provides a brief guide to NATO: what it is; what is does; how it works; how it is organized, and so on. Chapter One provides an overview of developments in the 1990s and early part of the 21st century, to put into context the five thematic chapters that address each of NATO's main areas of reform. Chapter Two deals with the changing functional and geographic scope of NATO's post-Cold War missions and the most important issues to have emerged as it has taken on a more proactive role in the management of European and wider security. Chapter Three discusses attempts to equip NATO to perform these new missions and also to rebalance the roles of the Allies. Chapter Four examines the new emphasis placed by NATO on combating international terrorism and the proliferation of WMD. Chapter Five examines the evolution of NATO's post-Cold War enlargement process. Chapter Six addresses NATO's partnership programmes with Central and Eastern European countries through the NACC/EAPC and the PfP, the changing nature of NATO–Russia and NATO–Ukraine relations and NATO's outreach programmes to Mediterranean and North African countries. The conclusion assesses the impact of the 2003 Iraq War on NATO, analyses the main obstacles that lie in its way as it redefines itself to meet the challenges of the post-9/11 era and considers its prospects for the 21st century.

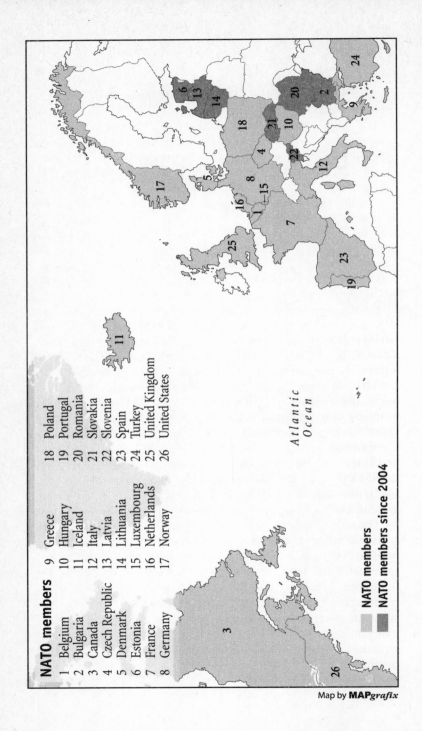

NATO members

1	Belgium	9	Greece	18	Poland
2	Bulgaria	10	Hungary	19	Portugal
3	Canada	11	Iceland	20	Romania
4	Czech Republic	12	Italy	21	Slovakia
5	Denmark	13	Latvia	22	Slovenia
6	Estonia	14	Lithuania	23	Spain
7	France	15	Luxembourg	24	Turkey
8	Germany	16	Netherlands	25	United Kingdom
		17	Norway	26	United States

Atlantic Ocean

NATO members
NATO members since 2004

Map by **MAP***grafix*

basic information

NATO is an alliance of twenty-six countries: Belgium, Bulgaria, Canada, the Czech Republic, Denmark, Estonia, France, Germany, Greece, Hungary, Iceland, Italy, Latvia, Lithuania, Luxembourg, the Netherlands, Norway, Poland, Portugal, Romania, Slovakia, Slovenia, Spain, Turkey, the United Kingdom and the United States. At NATO's founding in 1949 twelve states were members: Belgium, Canada, Denmark, France, Iceland, Italy, Luxembourg, the Netherlands, Norway, Portugal, the United Kingdom and the United States. Greece and Turkey subsequently became members in 1952, West Germany in 1955 and Spain in 1982. Following the end of the Cold War, the Czech Republic, Hungary and Poland joined in 1999 and Bulgaria, Estonia, Latvia, Lithuania, Romania, Slovakia and Slovenia in 2004.

The term 'alliance' can be employed to describe many different sorts of arrangement. Alliances can be formal or informal, defensive or offensive in nature, temporary or permanent, symmetrical or asymmetrical in terms of states' capabilities and commitments to one another, formed between states with similar values or be expedient arrangements, highly institutionalized or loosely co-ordinated and can involve two or many more states. Although many different configurations are clearly possible, alliances generally have the following three characteristics. First, they are formal and institutionalized, a characteristic that differentiates alliances from coalitions, which are generally much looser military configurations.

Second, most alliances are formed as the response to a threat, whether actual or anticipated. Alliances are therefore sustained primarily by a common perception of the threat that they were originally formed to counter, which ensures a commensurate level of cohesion. Agreement about the threat need not be total, but there must be sufficient concern to persuade alliance members to co-ordinate and perhaps even forgo national policy priorities. Due to the importance of a threat in alliance formation, the disappearance of the threat the alliance was formed to counter usually signals its end. Joffe has described this relationship between the disappearance of a threat and the demise of an alliance as the 'First Law of Alliances: Alliances die when they win'.[1] Third, the purpose of alliances is to combine members' capabilities so that states are stronger in an alliance than they would be as individual nation-states. NATO clearly meets the criteria outlined above: it is a formal, highly institutionalized military alliance, founded as a response to a commonly perceived threat (the Soviet Union), which sustained it throughout the Cold War by ensuring a high level of alliance cohesion.

Two factors differentiate NATO from other military alliances in history and the present. The first is the concept of NATO being an Atlantic community based on common values, as discussed in the introduction. The second is the way in which NATO has outlived the threat that it was designed to counter, thus defying the 'first law of alliances'. There are several theories as to why NATO did not collapse following the end of the Cold War and the disappearance of the Soviet threat. One explanation challenges the relationship between threat and alliance longevity by arguing that it is not simply the threat that is important but that institutions and organizations have value beyond this. Applied to NATO this approach explains its survival in the post-Cold War context, because of its achievements as an institution and because it was founded on shared democratic norms and values. A second explanation is that an alliance will persist because it is costly to create but less costly to maintain. From this perspective, retaining NATO was therefore in the interest of its members, even in the absence of the Soviet threat, because this was most cost-effective. A third explanation focuses on the influence of actors pursuing their own interests within organizations. When applied to NATO, this approach would identify NATO's large, multi-national staff as a key influence on NATO's response to the end of the Cold War. Cornish comments in this respect, 'NATO is a complex bureaucracy, composed of individuals and interest groups who must be expected to have an interest in their incomes and careers and therefore in the "survival" of the organization in which they are employed [...] NATO has avoided oblivion through the strength of its organizational "survival instinct".[2]

NATO's post-Cold War survival should be seen as a combination of the different theoretical explanations outlined above. However, as Chapter One demonstrates, the most important influences on NATO's survival have been its ongoing military benefits (discussed in the introduction) and its ability to adapt in order to fulfil a number of different security tasks.

nato's fundamental security tasks

Since its inception in 1949 the essential objective of NATO, as outlined in the preamble to the North Atlantic Treaty, has been to 'safeguard the freedom, common heritage and security of all its peoples, founded on the principles of democracy, individual liberty and the rule of law, to promote stability and well-being in the North Atlantic area and to unite their efforts for collective defence and for the preservation of peace and security'. In addition to retaining its Cold War functions, NATO has expanded its tasks since the end of the Cold War and now has several 'fundamental security tasks', which are defined in its current Strategic Concept; a statement of NATO's objectives agreed by members in 1999. NATO's fundamental security tasks, as outlined in the Strategic Concept, are:

- Security: to provide one of the indispensable foundations for a stable Euro-Atlantic security environment, based on the growth of democratic institutions and commitment to the peaceful resolution of disputes, in which no country would be able to intimidate or coerce any other through the threat or use of force.
- Consultation: to serve, as provided for in Article 4 of the North Atlantic Treaty, as an essential transatlantic forum for Allied consultations on any issues that affect their vital interests, including possible developments posing risks for members' security, and for appropriate co-ordination of their efforts in fields of common concern.
- Deterrence and Defence: to deter and defend against any threat of aggression against any NATO member state as provided for in Articles 5 and 6 of the Washington Treaty.

And in order to enhance the security and stability of the Euro-Atlantic area:

- Crisis Management: to stand ready, case-by-case and by consensus, in conformity with Article 7 of the Washington Treaty, to contribute to effective conflict prevention and to engage actively in crisis management, including crisis response operations.
- Partnership: To promote wide-ranging partnership, co-operation and dialogue with other countries in the Euro-Atlantic area, with the aim of increasing transparency, mutual confidence and the capacity for joint action with the Alliance.[3]

decision-making

NATO makes decisions on the basis of consensus and therefore only acts when members have consulted, discussed and reached a decision that is acceptable to all. This means that if even one member disagrees with the remaining twenty-five NATO cannot act. This principle of consensus decision-making applies at every level, from the smallest committee to meetings of Heads of State and Government. In addition, members are not prevented from making their own decisions on national security or defence policy.

For military responses to decisions reached by NATO the armed forces of its member states are engaged. NATO does not possess its own armed forces and members retain command and control of their forces until they are assigned to NATO to perform the full range of military missions.

nato's principal bodies[4]

NATO's political headquarters is in Brussels, Belgium and houses political and military staff from NATO members and Partners.

NATO's effective political authority and decision-making power lies with the North Atlantic Council (NAC), which consists of the Permanent Representatives of each member state. The Permanent Representatives are supported by National Delegations of different sizes, comprising military and political staff from member states. The Permanent Representative and National Delegation represent the interests of and act for their respective states. The NAC meets at least once a week and is chaired by the Secretary General of NATO. The NAC also holds meetings involving the Foreign Ministers and

ORGANIGRAM OF THE STRUCTURE
OF THE INTERNATIONAL STAFF

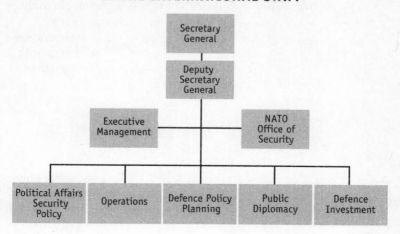

Defence Ministers of member states, which take place at least twice a year and there are also summits between Heads of State and Government of each member state.

The International Staff supports the work of the NAC and comprises officials from NATO member states who work on behalf of NATO rather than in a national capacity. The International Staff is divided into six divisions that have different responsibilities: The NATO Office of Security; Political Affairs and Security Policy; Operations; Defence Policy and Planning; Public Diplomacy; Defence Investment.

organization chart international staff

In addition to the NAC, there are two other main senior level committees in NATO: the Defence Planning Committee (DPC) and the Nuclear Planning Group (NPG). The DPC's mandate is to provide direction to NATO's military authorities and to manage the force planning process. All NATO members participate except France, which withdrew from the integrated military structure in 1966. The NPG has authority over all issues concerning NATO's nuclear policy. As with the DPC, all members except France participate. These two

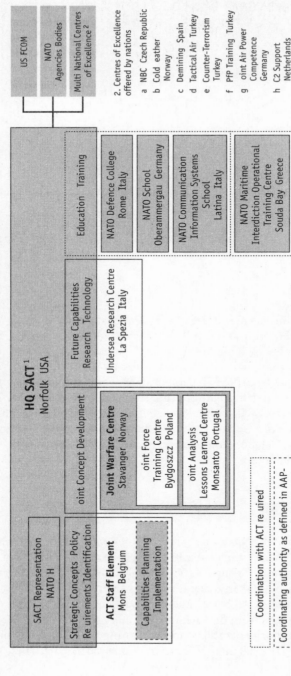

ALLIED COMMAND TRANSFORMATION

US FCOM

NATO Agencies Bodies

Multi National Centres of Excellence [2]

2. Centres of Excellence offered by nations

a NBC Czech Republic
b Cold eather Norway
c Demining Spain
d Tactical Air Turkey
e Counter-Terrorism Turkey
f PfP Training Turkey
g oint Air Power Competence Germany
h C2 Support Netherlands

HQ SACT [1]
Norfolk USA

SACT Representation NATO H

Strategic Concepts Policy Re uirements Identification

ACT Staff Element Mons Belgium

Capabilities Planning Implementation

oint Concept Development

Joint Warfare Centre Stavanger Norway

oint Force Training Centre Bydgoszcz Poland

oint Analysis Lessons Learned Centre Monsanto Portugal

Future Capabilities Research Technology

Undersea Research Centre La Spezia Italy

Education Training

NATO Defence College Rome Italy

NATO School Oberammergau Germany

NATO Communication Information Systems School Latina Italy

NATO Maritime Interdiction Operational Training Centre Souda Bay Greece

Coordination with ACT re uired

Coordinating authority as defined in AAP-

1. This diagram does not depict the internal organisation of the H SACT.

ALLIED COMMAND OPERATIONS

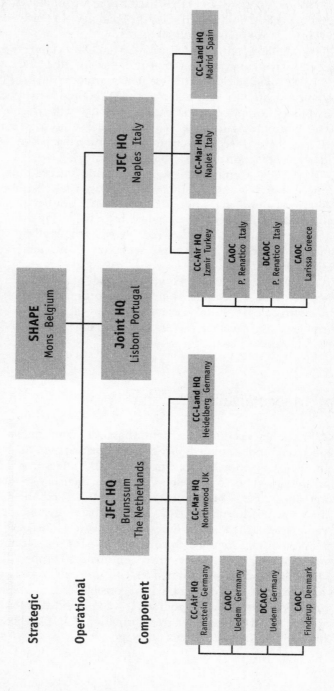

Strategic

Operational

Component

SHAPE
Mons Belgium

JFC HQ
Brunssum
The Netherlands

Joint HQ
Lisbon Portugal

JFC HQ
Naples Italy

CC-Land HQ
Heidelberg Germany

CC-Mar HQ
Northwood UK

CC-Air HQ
Ramstein Germany

CAOC
Uedem Germany

DCAOC
Uedem Germany

CAOC
Finderup Denmark

CC-Air HQ
Izmir Turkey

CAOC
P. Renatico Italy

DCAOC
P. Renatico Italy

CAOC
Larissa Greece

CC-Mar HQ
Naples Italy

CC-Land HQ
Madrid Spain

senior level committees meet in Brussels or in the capitals of NATO member states and can also involve the Foreign or Defence Ministers and Heads of State and Government.

The Military Committee is the highest military authority in NATO and works under the authority of the NAC, the DPC and the NPG. Each member state is represented by senior military officers, who serve as Military Representatives to NATO and as members of the Military Committee, supported by national staffs. The main role of this committee is to advise NATO's political authorities on the measures that are needed to ensure the common defence of NATO and to give advice on military policy and strategy.

The Military Committee is supported by the International Military Staff (IMS) and led by a General/Flag. The IMS comprises military personnel who work on behalf of NATO, rather than in a national capacity. The IMS is responsible for preparing policy on military issues, which is then considered by the Military Committee, and also for the implementation of committee policies and decisions.

NATO's Partners are represented by Heads of Diplomatic Missions or Liaison Offices. There are also forums for consultation and discussion of political and military issues with non-NATO members that participate in NATO's partnership and outreach programmes, such as the EAPC and the PfP.

military command structure

NATO's military command structure has been significantly reorganized and simplified since the agreement at the 2002 Prague Summit to transform NATO. Since June 2003, as a result of decisions taken by NATO Defence Ministers, there have been two commands: Allied Command Operations (ACO) and Allied Command Transformation (ACT). ACO is based at Supreme Headquarters Allied Powers Europe (SHAPE) in Mons, Belgium, and is responsible for the daily running of NATO's operations. It is commanded by the Supreme Allied Commander Europe (SACEUR), who is also Commander, US European Command. ACT is based in Norfolk, Virginia and is responsible for the transformation of NATO's military capabilities. It is commanded by the Supreme Allied Commander Transformation (SACT), who is also Commander, US Joint Forces Command.

nato in a new strategic context

NATO's multifaceted process of reform can only be fully understood in the context of the changes that have occurred in the strategic environment since the end of the Cold War. This chapter provides an overview of the most significant events that took place in the 1990s and early 2000s, which had a direct impact on NATO and eventually on the nature and scope of its adaptation processes. The first part discusses the impact on the Alliance of the end of bipolar confrontation and the eventual dissolution of the Soviet Union. It then examines NATO's roles in the 1991 Gulf War and the conflict, throughout the 1990s, in the Balkans, both of which had important implications. The chapter then discusses the terrorist attacks of 11 September 2001 on New York and Washington, DC, which heralded the arrival of the post-9/11 era and the challenges posed by the 2003 Iraq War. The chapter continues by discussing how two different sets of conclusions can be drawn from these events: the first with respect to the relationship between them and NATO's post-Cold War survival and continued vitality; the second concerning the characteristics of the post-Cold War security environment, which is crucial for any understanding of post-Cold War NATO reform. It concludes by presenting the factors that have caused NATO to embark on reform. This chapter therefore puts into context the five following thematic chapters on different aspects of NATO reform.

1989 and the end of the cold war

The series of events that occurred between the fall of the Berlin Wall on 9 November 1989 and the official break-up of the Soviet Union on 25 December 1991 transformed the international security environment and, in particular, the parameters of European security. In this two-year transitional period, a wave of democratic revolutions spread across Central and Eastern Europe, German reunification took place, the Warsaw Pact disbanded and the Soviet Union broke up. It was in this context that President Bush anticipated a 'New World Order' in which compromise and negotiation would provide the means through which states would settle their differences.

These profound changes in the strategic environment had immediate implications for NATO. The first was that the end of bipolar confrontation meant that Western Europe was less threatened than it had been for the whole of the post-Second World War period. The European Allies therefore faced a significantly reduced threat either of military invasion or the possibility of the use of other forms of organized force against them. The second was that the dissolution of the Soviet Union meant that NATO's *raison d'être* disappeared. For forty years, NATO's primary function had been clear: the defence of Western Europe against the threat of the seemingly expansionist, or at least intimidating, totalitarian Soviet Union. With the conventional military threat to Western Europe significantly reduced and the Soviet Union no more, NATO's role and even its survival in the post-Cold War world was far from certain.

In spite of these profound changes, the prevailing opinion within NATO was that it should not be immediately disbanded and a consensus quickly emerged that it should remain, at least in the short term. The most important reason for this was that although Russia was undergoing a process of internal reform, it still retained substantial military forces. Whilst the collapse of the Soviet Union appeared to have reduced the prospect of a major war in Europe, many privately considered that it did not remove the possibility entirely and a residual threat remained. This resulted in the widespread consensus that NATO was still needed as an insurance policy and that the Article 5 collective defence provision was likely to remain relevant in the short to medium-term.

Although there was consensus that NATO should be retained, there was still considerable debate about the ways in which it could and should reform. Competing visions of the parameters of NATO's future roles characterized the discussions that took place in the immediate post-Cold War period. Some Allies, most notably the French, perceived a need to retain NATO as a defensive organization but also saw a chance to develop other institutions that would gradually assume increasing responsibility for European security. The end of bipolar confrontation seemed to provide an opportunity to develop the EU's nascent Common Foreign and Security Policy (CFSP) and to bolster the role of the WEU as the EU's potential security and defence arm. As it was increasingly improbable that Article 5 would be necessary, this view essentially sought to confine NATO to a defensive role that seemed likely to become less and less important. Another view, articulated by the then Secretary General of NATO, Manfred Wörner, was that NATO from its very beginning had not simply been a military organization, but had been multi-faceted. Wörner sought to counter claims that NATO was no longer of use by pointing out that 'the Treaty of Washington of 1949 nowhere mentions the Soviet Union'.[1] Former NATO officials also proposed radically different missions that had little widespread support, ranging from managing student exchanges, to fighting drug trafficking, to promoting the transfer of environmental-control and energy-conservation technology to Eastern Europe.[2]

Despite these competing perspectives, the debate about NATO's future was overtaken by international events, initially Iraq's August 1990 invasion of Kuwait and the subsequent Gulf War from January to February 1991 and later the beginning of the break-up of the former Yugoslavia in late 1991. Both conflicts had direct implications for NATO and consequently added impetus to the debates surrounding the parameters of its post-Cold War role.

the 1991 gulf war

On 2 August 1990, following a dispute between the two countries over exploitation of oil rights in the Gulf, Iraq invaded Kuwait. Within twelve hours of the start of the invasion Iraq had defeated the Kuwaiti forces and annexed the country. The invasion was the first major international crisis of the post-Cold War era, which shifted the focus of media attention and public policy from events in Europe to developments in the Middle East.

The Gulf crisis presented a number of challenges to the international community. The primary concern was Saddam Hussein's potential to disrupt the flow of vital resources by wielding the 'petro-weapon'.[3] The likelihood of oil market instability, which could have caused chaos in the global economy, ensured that for most members of NATO, as well as for the wider community, the crisis in the Gulf involved a vital interest. The second concern was Iraq's violation of internationally recognized borders by its invasion and annexation of Kuwait, which provided further grounds for the international community to act. As a result, a series of United Nations Security Council (UNSC) Resolutions, condemning the Iraqi actions, swiftly followed. The UNSC initially imposed mandatory sanctions on Iraq,[4] declared the Iraqi announcement that Kuwait was the 19th province of Iraq to be null and void,[5] and eventually authorized 'all necessary means' to ensure Iraq's withdrawal from Kuwait.[6] After Iraq's failure to respond to these UN Resolutions, military action against Iraq began during the night of 16–17 January 1991.

the unique implications of the gulf crisis for nato

The interests of the international community, the need for Arab acquiescence to the execution of any military operation and the fact that the conflict was between the international community as a whole and Iraq, not between NATO and Iraq, meant that the response to Iraq's invasion of Kuwait was never going to be a NATO operation. The unique challenge to NATO was the threat that Iraq potentially posed to Turkey. Of all the Allies, Turkey was the most vulnerable and the knowledge that Iraq possessed a range of air and missile capabilities, in conjunction with its willingness to use chemical weapons, as demonstrated during the Iran–Iraq War, highlighted the risk to its security. Iraq's invasion of Kuwait in August 1990 therefore raised the possibility of NATO being called upon to activate Article 5. This represented an unprecedented situation and provoked a rapid response.

On 10 August 1990, the NAC was convened in emergency session to decide NATO's response to the invasion of Kuwait. Foreign ministers of NATO member states consulted and exchanged information on developments in the Gulf. On the same day, NATO decided formally to raise the level of intelligence reporting in the Southern Region which was conducted by Allied Forces South's (AFSOUTH) Intelligence Division and the Southern Region Joint Operational Intelligence Council (JOIC).[7] NATO's response to Iraqi aggression was Southern Guard, whose mission was 'to be ready to counter any threat that may develop in the Southern Region of Allied Command Europe as a result of the Middle East crisis'. Three concerns dominated NATO's agenda: the risk of terrorism, which could occur in any part of the region, SCUD missiles and long-range air and chemical attacks, which were likely to be confined to south-eastern Turkey and the potential threats to air and sea communications through the Mediterranean to southern bases.[8] Less than a week after Iraq's invasion of Kuwait, NATO Airborne Early Warning (NAEW) aircraft, operated by personnel from thirteen countries, were moved to locations in eastern Turkey. NAEW flew missions over southern Turkey throughout the Gulf crisis and monitored activity occurring several hundred miles into Iraq.[9]

On 14 September, the Naval On-Call Force Mediterranean (NAVOCFORMED) was activated and began operations in the eastern Mediterranean: the first time in its history that it had played a crisis response role. On 17 December, Turkey requested that NATO deploy aircraft of the ACE Mobile Force-Air (AMF-A) (which consisted of Belgian, German and Italian strike and reconnaissance aircraft), to south-east Turkey by 15 January 1991, the UN deadline for Iraq to pull out of Kuwait. After fractious discussions among NATO members, DPC approved this request on 2 January 1991.[10] The AMF's operational role began on 13 January 1991. As Operation Desert Storm progressed and the risk to Turkey increased, due to the launch of SCUD missiles intended to hit Israel but which could theoretically reach the south-east of Turkey, Operation Southern Guard was divided into two sections. The first, Operation Dawn Set, was designed to enhance defence and early warning for south-eastern Turkey. The second, Operation MedNet, began in January 1991 and was a series of measures designed to monitor air and sea routes in the Mediterranean. By February 1991, Operation MedNet ensured that all shipping from the Strait of Gibraltar to the Suez Canal was monitored.[11]

an informal nato role in operation desert storm

As well as NATO's formal defensive role, NATO forces played an important role in the Gulf War. NATO Allies were active in the US-led coalition, which comprised forces from 36 countries. The agreement within NATO was that members of the Alliance should each contribute to the coalition in the Gulf in their own way and that NATO would provide a forum for close consultation. Twelve of

NATO's (then sixteen) members committed forces to the US-led coalition, with the largest contributions coming from the United States and the United Kingdom.[12]

As well as the participation of forces from its member states, NATO also played an important 'virtual' role in Operation Desert Storm. The most obvious contribution in this respect was the use of NATO basing, infrastructure and pre-positioned equipment during the crisis. As General George Joulwan, Commander-in-Chief of the US European Command (USEUCOM) commented, the existence of NATO: 'gives [the United States] access to basing and infrastructure necessary for force projection both [in Europe] and in [the Persian Gulf]. This proved critical during Desert Shield and Desert Storm, where 95 per cent of the strategic airlift, 90 per cent of the combat aircraft and 85 per cent of the naval vessels were staged from or through USEUCOM's [area of responsibility]. This would have been practically impossible without USEUCOM basing and infrastructure, to include equipment pre-positioned in theater to supply reinforcing forces'.[13]

The NATO Allies also responded to a request from William Taft, the US Ambassador to NATO, that they should supply air- and sealifts to facilitate the arrival of US troops in the Gulf.[14] Moreover, American air operations against northern Iraq originated from NATO bases in Turkey, Spain and the United Kingdom. For example, Operation Proven Force, which involved over 300 aircraft that flew over 5,000 sorties, was based in southern Turkey and, significantly, prevented Iraq from using northern bases as safe havens. Aerial tankers operating from France, Greece, Italy and Spain supported these operations.

A further NATO influence in the crisis in the Gulf was the use of common NATO training, structures and procedures to co-ordinate the coalition forces. Badsey comments, in this respect: 'in theory, NATO doctrine applies only in the context of the NATO Alliance and area; in practice none of those NATO members involved in the Gulf War could easily dispense with the doctrine within which they had planned and trained for decades, or wished to do so'.[15] Ships belonging to NATO members, for example, had common procedures and tactical publications, some of which could be passed to non-NATO members, such as Australia.[16] These coalition forces subsequently adopted standard NATO operating procedures and secure signalling systems. Other members of the coalition had to rely on normal ship-to-ship radio, which demonstrated the comparative effectiveness of these common NATO procedures.[17]

The withdrawal of Iraqi forces from Kuwait on 28 February 1991 signalled the end of hostilities in the Persian Gulf and ensured that Operation Desert Storm was a brief conflict. However, despite its short duration and even though some had seen NATO as redundant in the face of Iraqi aggression,[18] NATO and its member nations had performed a variety of roles during Operation Desert Storm: a successful formal defensive role within the Southern Command region, assistance to the coalition's offensive operations in Iraq through the use of NATO infrastructure in Europe, facilitation of coalition operations through the use of NATO procedures, the contribution of forces from NATO member states to the US-led coalition and consultations and the exchange of information in the NAC. NATO's diverse informal and formal contributions proved to be an important component of the first major military conflict of the post-Cold War world.

conflict in the balkans

Soon after the victory of the coalition forces in the Persian Gulf, international attention refocused on Europe. In contrast to the issues in the Gulf, the outbreak of conflict in the Balkans did not initially appear directly to threaten either NATO or the vital interests of the Allies (and of the United States in particular). Moreover, even though the breakup of Yugoslavia occurred close to NATO territory, the lack of a direct threat meant it was officially outside NATO's defensive mandate. After the announcement by the Yugoslav Defence Minister, on 7 May 1991, that Yugoslavia was in a state of civil war, many perceived the conflict in the former Yugoslavia as 'the hour of Europe',[19] a view that was shared by the Bush Administration, which encouraged the EU to deal with the crisis. NATO's initial response, in November 1991, simply urged 'all parties to co-operate fully with the European Community in its efforts under the mandate given to it by the CSCE, both in the implementation of cease-fire monitoring agreements and in the negotiating process within the Conference on Yugoslavia'.[20] From the outset, managing the conflicts in the former Yugoslavia was seen not as NATO's responsibility but rather as that of the EU. The EU chose to address the crisis through diplomacy, in the form of a series of peace missions representing the presidency, followed by civilian monitors. These diplomatic measures were complemented by agreement to contribute to an intervention force to be employed in operations for which the UN had overall responsibility. The United Nations Protection Force (UNPROFOR) was set up in February 1992.

Despite European attempts to manage hostilities, the magnitude of the Yugoslav crises very quickly revealed that the EU was far from being the capable security actor that the proclamation of 'the hour of Europe' suggested. The Balkans represented one of the most intractable set of problems in Europe: the CFSP was still embryonic, the EU, unlike the United States, had little international standing beyond its members' territories, its decision-making processes were incoherent, as shown by the initial failure to formulate a common policy over the recognition of Croatia and Slovenia, it lacked diplomatic experience and, once a common position had been reached and a diplomatic approach initiated, the WEU did not have adequate military capability to conduct operations without the support of the United States. This last issue was very serious, as it quickly became clear that, unless diplomacy was backed by force, it would fail. A general lack of appreciation of the scale of the unfolding crisis contributed to the difficulties the EU faced. In conjunction with the weaknesses of the EU's approach to the crisis, it became apparent that the Conference on Security and Co-operation in Europe (CSCE) and the UN were also incapable of resolving the conflict. The failings of EU decision-making processes, the inadequacies of alternative institutions and the necessity of a diplomatic and military contribution from the United States meant NATO emerged as the most effective vehicle to address the conflict. Even though France initially blocked NATO's involvement in the former Yugoslavia, because it perceived its role as encroaching on the sort of contingency envisioned for a potential European military capability, it eventually conceded that only NATO, with its capacity for facilitating joint planning and inter-operability, could manage the crisis.

nato's roles in the balkans

In contrast to the rapid response to the Gulf crisis, these influences ensured that NATO's involvement in the Balkans was gradual, a regrettable characteristic of the crisis.[21] NATO's involvement in the former Yugoslavia began in 1992, with NATO performing limited supporting roles to the UN. The NAC, meeting in Helsinki in July 1992, implemented Operation Maritime Monitor to monitor the UN arms embargo and economic sanctions in the Adriatic. NATO's Standing Naval Force Mediterranean (STANAVFORMED) was subsequently mobilized. Operation Maritime Monitor became

Operation Maritime Guard in November 1992, which indicated a shift from observation to implementation. Thus, for the first time, NATO was ready to use force to implement a UNSC Resolution. One month earlier, in October 1992, NATO air operations had begun. Operation Sky Monitor observed the no-fly zone over Bosnia and in April 1993, NATO activated Operation Deny Flight, which enforced it. Operation Deny Flight eventually resulted in NATO's first-ever combat action, when two American F-16s shot down four Bosnian Serb Galeb aircraft. NATO's role in the air increased in Operation Deliberate Force of August 1995, a three-week graduated campaign of air strikes against Bosnian Serb military targets.

the implementation force

NATO's involvement in the former Yugoslavia deepened after the US-brokered General Framework Agreement for Peace, also known as the Dayton Peace Accord, was signed on 14 December 1995. A NATO-led multinational Implementation Force (IFOR) was subsequently created. Following UNSC Resolution 1031 of 15 December 1995, which authorized IFOR's mission, IFOR began deploying to Bosnia Herzogovina on 16 December 1995 to implement the military provisions of the Accord. UNPROFOR handed over command of military operations in Bosnia to IFOR on 20 December 1995. IFOR's military mission was three-fold: to secure an end to fighting, to separate the forces of Bosnia Herzogovina's two newly created entities and to demobilize their heavy weapons and forces and to transfer territory between these two entities. These three tasks were completed by 27 June 1996.

IFOR also contributed to the civilian aspects of the Dayton Peace Accord. Without a secure environment, political and civil reconstruction would have been seriously hindered, so IFOR's implementation of the military aspects of the Dayton Peace Accord was a crucial first step. IFOR also co-operated closely with governmental and non-governmental organizations and offered support services to these bodies, including transport assistance, emergency accommodation, medical treatment and evacuation, as well as restoring telecommunications and electricity, gas and water supplies.

Although all NATO nations contributed to the IFOR, it was more than simply a NATO operation. From the outset, non-NATO forces were integrated into the unified command structure to work alongside those from NATO. By the end of the 60,000-strong IFOR mission, 18 non-NATO countries were participating, of which 14 were part of the PfP programme.[22]

the stabilization force

The deployment of the IFOR and achievement of its objectives resulted in a far more stable environment. However, there was wide-spread recognition that the situation would continue to be unstable and there was an ongoing need for support, once IFOR's mission had been completed. This resulted in the creation of a smaller Stabilization Force (SFOR), which replaced the IFOR in December 1996.

The SFOR's mission, which continues but will be taken over by the EU at the end of 2004, following NATO's decision in June 2004 to conclude it,[23] is to 'deter hostilities and stabilize the peace, con-tribute to a secure environment by providing a continued military presence in the Area Of Responsibility (AOR), target and co-ordinate SFOR support to key areas including primary civil implementation organizations, and progress toward a lasting consolidation of peace, without further need for NATO-led forces in Bosnia and Herzogovina'. The mission has evolved and today the SFOR is also responsible for tasks as diverse as contributing to the reform of the Bosnian military, seeking out war crimes suspects in order to bring them to justice and helping refugees and other displaced people return to their homes.

Like IFOR, the SFOR has great diversity in its composition. Although NATO has provided the majority of the forces, the number of non-NATO countries that have participated is greater than the total number of NATO countries. Participating non-NATO coun-tries have included those that are part of NATO's partnership and outreach programmes, as well as countries that are far removed from NATO's territory and have no link with them, such as Argentina, New Zealand and Australia.

the kosovo force

Throughout the 1990s, the UN had mandated NATO's interventions in the Balkans. By the late 1990s, however, a lack of consensus in the UNSC caused the most controversial phase of NATO's involvement in the former Yugoslavia. Violence in Kosovo, a Yugoslav province predominantly populated by ethnic Albanians, erupted in 1998, as a result of the Serbian government's policy of ethnic cleansing and the expulsion of over 300,000 ethnic Albanians from Kosovo. During 1998 the violence escalated and threatened to spread throughout the Balkans.[24] The Serbian government refused to comply with demands from the international community to withdraw its troops from

Kosovo, end its repression of ethnic Albanians and allow refugees to return to their homes and it seemed that the ethnic cleansing campaigns that had occurred in Bosnia and Croatia would be repeated in Kosovo. The moral imperatives of intervention, springing from an awareness of the consequences of inaction, resulted in Operation Allied Force. This operation, which ran from 24 March to 10 June 1999, was an air war against Serbian targets. Its most controversial aspect was that, unlike other NATO interventions, it was self-authorized rather than UN-mandated, resulting from the failure of the UNSC to agree on the intervention, primarily due to Russian and Chinese opposition. After 78 days, the Serbian government finally backed down, resulting in the eventual withdrawal of Serbian military and paramilitary forces and the return of ethnic Albanians to Kosovo.

Following the end of Operation Allied Force, a Kosovo Force (KFOR) arrived on 12 June 1999, to enforce and keep the peace. Unlike Operation Allied Force, the KFOR operated, and continues to operate, under a UN mandate and from a military-technical agreement signed by NATO and Yugoslav commanders. The KFOR's objectives are to establish and maintain a secure environment in Kosovo, including public safety and order, monitoring, verifying and when necessary, enforcing compliance with the agreements that ended the conflict and to assist the UN Mission in Kosovo (UNMIK), including core civil functions until these are transferred to UNMIK.

In the early part of 2004, violence once again erupted in Kosovo. NATO responded by deploying additional troops from its operational and strategic reserves, to ensure that KFOR had the resources necessary to continue to stabilize the region. At present, KFOR's mission is of indefinite duration, a feature that was reflected by the statement issued by NATO leaders at their meeting in Istanbul in June 2004, confirming that KFOR's presence is still essential to enhance security and promote the political process in Kosovo.[25]

nato missions in the former yugoslav republic of macedonia

In addition to IFOR, SFOR and KFOR, NATO has also conducted a series of missions in the Former Yugoslav Republic of Macedonia (FYROM). NATO's missions began on 22 August 2001, with Operation Essential Harvest, which, at the request of the Macedonian government, saw 3500 troops sent to the FYROM to disarm ethnic Albanian groups and destroy their weapons. Following this month-long operation, which ended on 26 September 2001, NATO began Operation Amber Fox. This operation had the specific mandate to contribute to the protection of the international monitors overseeing the implementation of a peace plan. The requirement for a continuing military presence in the FYROM, in order to minimize the risks of destabilization, resulted in Operation Allied Harmony, which was agreed on 16 December 2002. Operation Allied Harmony was taken over by the EU on 31 March 2003.

the evolution of nato's roles in the balkans

NATO's involvement in the Balkans began in 1992 with sea, air and ground operations carried out under the authority of the UNSC and peaked with the use of air power against Serbia in March 1999 without a UN mandate. In managing the conflicts in the former Yugoslavia through non-Article 5 missions of crisis management, peacemaking and peacekeeping, NATO 'shifted from the role of a "subcontractor" responding to UN requirements to a more active participant in seeking to stop the fighting and in defining its own mission and mandates'.[26] In 2004, thirteen years after the outbreak of conflict in the Balkans, NATO retains a presence, albeit a scaled-down one, which continues to affirm the importance of its role in the region.

the terrorist attacks of 9/11

Until 2001, managing the conflict in the Balkans had absorbed the vast majority of NATO's attention. In September 2001, however, a new challenge emerged, which has since dominated the agenda. On the morning of 11 September 2001, nineteen terrorists, who were later identified as members of the al-Qaida network, hijacked, almost simultaneously, four commercial aircraft from Dulles, Newark and Boston airports. Two of the planes were flown into the World Trade Center in New York, causing its Twin Towers later to collapse, the third ploughed into the Pentagon in Washington, DC, and the fourth, which is now believed to have been heading for either the US Capitol or the White House, crashed in a field in western Pennsylvania, after resistance by its passengers. Despite conflicting reports of the number of casualties in the immediate aftermath, the sheer scale of these co-ordinated actions made it clear that they were by far the most devastating terrorist attacks in American history and the most dramatic since the bombing of Pearl Harbor.

In the following hours and days, countries around the world rallied around the United States and gave an unprecedented demonstration of support and solidarity. NATO's response was particularly striking. On the evening of 11 September, the NAC met to discuss the terrorist attacks and released a statement expressing its solidarity with the United States. Most significantly, on 12 September, NATO invoked the principle of Article 5 for the first time in its history, which was an extremely rapid response, given that NATO works by consensus.[27] The unprecedented invocation of the principle of Article 5 was not suggested by the United States, but originated from a telephone conversation between the NATO Secretary General Lord Robertson and the British Prime Minister Tony Blair. The irony of NATO's response to 9/11 was profound on three levels: Article 5 was invoked as a response to an attack on the continental United States rather than on the territory of a European Ally, the impetus for the invocation of Article 5 came from a NATO Ally on behalf of the United States, not from the United States in defence of a NATO Ally, as had been expected throughout the Cold War and the invocation was a response to a terrorist attack by a non-state actor, rather than to a conventional military attack by a state. This was a defining moment for NATO. The only condition that was stipulated when NATO invoked the principle of Article 5 was that it would only be confirmed if and when it were proven that the terrorist attacks against the United States had been directed from abroad. The Allies agreed that this provision should be present to avoid the potentially disastrous situation of having invoked Article 5 in response to attacks that could have been carried out by nationals of a NATO member state, or even of the United States itself.

On 2 October 2001, in a statement to the press following a series of briefings by US officials, the NATO Secretary General Lord Robertson announced that investigations had revealed compelling evidence that the al-Qaida terrorist network, headed by Osama bin Laden and protected by the Taleban regime in Afghanistan, was responsible for the terrorist attacks against the United States and that as such, the attacks had clearly been directed from abroad. The invocation of NATO's Article 5 provision of collective defence was confirmed on 2 October, for the first time in NATO's history.

operation active endeavour

In the days following the terrorist attacks on New York and Washington, DC and the invocation of the principle of Article 5 there were reports that NATO had begun planning a retaliatory military response;[28] claims that were quickly denied by NATO officials.[29] Once the invocation had been confirmed, however, NATO took a number of unprecedented steps. On 4 October, at the request of the United States, Lord Robertson announced that eight measures both of individual and collective nature would be taken by NATO, to expand the options available in the campaign against terrorism. The eight measures were: to enhance intelligence sharing and co-operation, both bilaterally and in the appropriate NATO bodies, relating to the threats posed by terrorism and the actions to be taken against it; to provide, individually or collectively, as appropriate and according to their capabilities, assistance to the Allies and other states which are or may be subject to increased terrorist threats as a result of their support for the campaign against terrorism; to take necessary measures to provide increased security for facilities of the United States and other Allies on their territory; to back-fill selected Allied assets in NATO's area of responsibility that are required to directly support operations against terrorism; to provide blanket over-flight clearances for the United States and other Allies' aircraft, in accordance with the necessary air traffic arrangements and national procedures, for military flights related to operations against terrorism and to provide access for the United States and other Allies to ports and airfields on the territory of NATO nations for operations against terrorism, including for refuelling, in accordance with national procedures. In addition, the NAC agreed that the Alliance was ready to deploy elements of its Standing Naval Forces to the Eastern Mediterranean to provide a NATO presence and demonstrate resolve, and that the Alliance was similarly ready to deploy elements of the NAEW force to support operations against terrorism.[30]

In what came to be a significant remark, Lord Robertson said that it should not be assumed that these measures meant that NATO would automatically be involved in collective military action but that it was 'open to the United States to act on its own, or to do so in association with any group of states'.[31] On 8 October, NATO's response to 9/11 deepened, when Lord Robertson confirmed the United States' request for five AWACS and their crews to deploy to the United States to patrol the skies of New York and Washington, DC, a move that was widely assumed to enable the specialized

American surveillance aircraft that had been performing this mission to be deployed elsewhere. On 9 October, two AWACS aircraft deployed to the continental United States from Geilenkirchen in Germany and three more flew to the US in the following days. This response was entitled Operation Eagle Assist. In addition to these unprecedented steps, elements of NATO naval assets that had been on exercise off the coast of Spain were re-assigned to the Eastern Mediterranean. The Standing Naval Force Mediterranean (STANAVFORMED), which consisted of nine ships, from eight NATO countries, bolstered NATO's presence in the Eastern Mediterranean through Operation Active Endeavour.[32] From this time onward, NATO began to perform its first operational role in an Article 5 context in and around Europe, and also in the United States.

a central role for nato after 9/11?

In the weeks following 9/11 there was neither resistance to the measures NATO took nor great concern about the way in which the United States initially dealt with the crisis. NATO's bold steps seemed to indicate that it was more robust than ever and that the Allies had perhaps found the unity of purpose and vision that had arguably been weakened since the loss of its *raison d'être*.[33] As the war against terrorism progressed, however, this positive reading of NATO's role was revealed to be misleading.

The United States responded to the attacks by launching Operation Enduring Freedom on 7 October 2001. Operation Enduring Freedom was a series of military strikes against the Taleban leadership and al-Qaida forces in Afghanistan, conducted with support from the United Kingdom. It was expected that the United States would take the lead in responding to the terrorist attacks because it was they who had been attacked and few were surprised that only the United Kingdom operated in a supporting role from the outset. This was not simply due to the 'special relationship' between the UK and the US but also because the UK was the only country with military assets that the US could use and because of its comparatively rapid politico-military decision-making process. However, it soon became clear that, in spite of the virtually unconditional nature of the remaining Allies' offers of military assistance, the United States would initially pursue an essentially unilateral military campaign. The US concentrated its requests for help from the NATO Allies to information-sharing and intelligence. When the United States did request military assistance, it only asked some

NATO Allies for limited and very specific tasks and some for nothing at all. The US' reluctance to engage NATO as an institution in the first months of the war against terrorism was perceived by many as being highly problematic. One analyst suggested: 'in the elaborate dance being conducted over European participation in the US war in Afghanistan the steps are as follows: the Europeans pretend that they want to send troops to Afghanistan, the Americans pretend that they want them there and all participants have to pretend that the dance is taking place to the music of NATO [...] If NATO were revealed to be completely irrelevant to the greatest security crisis of the era, some wicked dissidents might really begin to wonder why it is still around'.[34] Colin Powell's comment that 'not every ally is fighting but every ally is in the fight'[35] was not sufficient to address the concerns that had been raised. By early November 2001, the NATO Allies were playing a more active role in the operation in Afghanistan, partly as a result of British lobbying of the United States, yet their contribution remained limited. Significantly, their participation did not adequately address some of the questions that had been raised about NATO's peripheral role, its apparent inability to respond to the security threats highlighted by 9/11 and the subsequent implications for its relevance and long-term vitality.

the international security assistance force

Some – but not all – of the questions raised after 9/11 about NATO's value in the war against terrorism were answered in 2003. NATO's role in this war, and in Afghanistan in particular, has gradually grown since its initial defensive actions in the Mediterranean and the continental United States. The most prominent of its present roles is its current leadership of the International Security Assistance Force (ISAF). Following the end of offensive operations in Afghanistan, the ISAF was established, in accordance with the Bonn Agreement of 6 December 2001, to maintain security in Kabul and its surrounding areas, which would enable the Transitional Authority and the UN to operate in a secure environment. ISAF I was led by the UK from December 2001 to June 2002, ISAF II by Turkey between June 2002 and January 2003 and ISAF III jointly by Germany and the Netherlands from February to August 2003. NATO's initial involvement in ISAF began after Germany and the Netherlands' request for support in the planning and execution of ISAF III. This was an obvious role for NATO, given that its operational planning staff are used to putting together operational plans on a multilateral basis. This initial NATO role grew when it took over the command, control and co-ordination of ISAF IV on 11 August 2003. Several factors combined to cause NATO's adoption of the command of the ISAF to emerge as desirable. Finding countries that were willing to lead the ISAF, and had the experience and capability to do so, had proved difficult. Moreover, the change in the leadership of the ISAF every six months meant there was a lack of continuity and stability; NATO command would ensure continuity and stability through a long-term commitment, as well as solving the problem of finding countries that were willing and able to lead it. Moreover, NATO command of the ISAF would demonstrate its value in the war against terrorism.

Since the initial adoption of ISAF command, NATO's role has increased. On 6 October 2003, NATO announced that the ISAF would expand its operations from Kabul to Kunduz, in accordance with UNSC Resolution 1510. In July 2004, there were 6,500 troops under NATO command and increases in the number of NATO forces have been agreed in order to ensure security for the September 2004 elections. Moreover, NATO leaders, meeting in Istanbul in June 2004, agreed to expand the ISAF's role by establishing four more Provincial Reconstruction Teams (PRT).[36] The ISAF subsequently took command of PRT in Mazar-el-Sharif and Maimana on 1 July 2004.

the evolution of nato's roles in the war against terrorism

To date, NATO's record of contribution to the war against terrorism has been mixed. The invocation of the principle of Article 5 on 12 September 2001 and its confirmation on 2 October 2001 seemed to promise much, yet, as the initial operations in Afghanistan showed, the 'central role for NATO' that some had anticipated did not materialize. However, NATO's role grew, initially as a result of Operation Active Endeavour and more recently as a result of its support for and eventual leadership of the ISAF. But, despite these developments, later chapters will show that, within the wider context of the war against terrorism, questions remain about NATO's ability to play a major role in the long-term.

the 2003 iraq war

The 2003 Iraq War raised additional questions about NATO's future vitality. This war was the 'perfect storm' for transatlantic relations, as it combined many of the issues that have divided the Allies, including the use of military force versus diplomacy, strategies to deal with 'rogue' states and the role and influence of the UN. Moreover, whilst after Operation Desert Storm there had been a consensus about how to deal with Iraq, gradual policy divergence among NATO Allies emerged during the 1990s. A transatlantic dispute over Iraq was inevitable.

Even before 9/11, the Bush Administration's more robust stance toward Iraq had been identifiable. Following 9/11, however, the challenge of dealing with Iraq became ever more pressing. The diplomatic build-up to the Iraq War, which lasted over a year, revealed serious differences in policy preferences and strategies between the Allies and members of the wider international community. The divisions among the NATO Allies were often portrayed as a breach between the United States and others, when in fact the real split was within the transatlantic community as a whole. The letters written by those countries in favour of the Iraq War illustrate this. The leaders of the Czech Republic, Denmark, Hungary, Italy, Poland, Portugal, Spain and the United Kingdom sent a letter to the *Wall Street Journal* in January 2003, expressing their support for the United States, without consulting other European countries such as France and Germany.[37] One week later, Albania, Bulgaria, Croatia, Estonia, Latvia, Lithuania, Macedonia, Romania, Slovakia and Slovenia did likewise.[38] This demonstrates not only the divisive nature of the Iraq War but also the fact that the divisions caused were not a simple split between the United States and other existing and some soon-to-be NATO members.

As in the 1991 Gulf War, NATO was not directly involved in the 2003 Iraq War. However, a parallel to the 1991 Iraq War was that NATO would have to respond to the prospect of war in Iraq because of the potential defence implications for Turkey. This issue provoked a crisis in the Alliance and paralysed NATO.

In February 2003, Turkey officially requested that NATO begin preparation for its defence in the event of a war with Iraq by providing AWACS, Patriot anti-missile batteries and anti-biological and anti-chemical warfare units. This request provoked a crisis in NATO, as France, Germany and Belgium refused to agree to Turkey's request. Their reason was that they held the view that beginning to provide support to Turkey before discussions in the UNSC had been concluded would pre-judge their outcome. Without consensus between the Allies, NATO was unable to begin taking defensive measures for Turkey. On 10 February 2003, Turkey requested the invocation of the Article 4 provision of consultation, in the hope that it would resolve the situation, yet there was still no agreement among the Allies. The disagreement about the appropriate response to Turkey's request for defence support and the failure of NATO to agree went right to the heart of its original function – collective defence. The credibility problem that resulted from this stalemate was crucial. The NATO Secretary General, Lord Robertson, eventually resolved the crisis by convening the DPC. This was a shrewd move, because France has not participated in the DPC ever since it left NATO's military command structure in 1966. In the DPC, Germany and Belgium backed down and consensus was finally reached. When, on 19 February 2003, the DPC authorized defensive measures to assist Turkey, Operation Display Deterrence began on 26 February 2003 and ended two months later on 30 April 2003.

In spite of the eventual resolution of Turkey's defence request, the war over Iraq, as well as the rifts before and after represented one of the most damaging incidents in transatlantic relations in recent years. Resolving the crisis by convening the DPC did not silence those who believed that NATO had been irreparably damaged by the Iraq War. Over a year after President Bush declared an end to major combat operations, serious questions remain about the damage done to NATO by the 2003 Iraq War and its ability to withstand future disputes among the Allies.

the significance of developments in the post-cold war environment

The 1991 Gulf War, the conflict in the Balkans, the consequences of 9/11 and the 2003 Iraq War were very different events in their nature, their duration, the demands they placed on NATO and their implications for NATO reform. None the less, a number of conclusions can be drawn about their significance for NATO and for defence planning in the post-Cold War environment.

the relationship between post-cold war developments and nato's initial survival and continued vitality

The first conclusion that can be drawn concerns the relationship between NATO's continuing value and its post-Cold War survival. In addition to continuing to institutionalize transatlantic relations, one of the main reasons NATO has endured since the end of the Cold War is the comparative advantage it retains as a military organization. Yost comments, in this respect, that 'because NATO continues to serve multiple security functions for its members (including policy coordination beyond collective defense matters), the disappearance of the specific threat that triggered the Alliance's formation – the Soviet Union – did not lead to its atrophy'.[39] Operation Desert Storm, for example, showed that NATO's traditional role of collective defence was still relevant, in spite of the end of bipolar confrontation and even though the circumstances in which NATO responded were very different to those that had been expected during the Cold War. More importantly, NATO's ability to transfer its diverse non-defensive competencies to a non-European context through helping in the co-ordination of a military operation in the Gulf added weight to the arguments of proponents of an ongoing role for NATO in the post-Cold War world. Fear of losing the benefits of NATO's formal and virtual roles was a key factor in ensuring its survival. More than a decade of conflict in the Balkans has re-emphasized this conclusion. Although NATO was not initially perceived as the obvious choice of military instrument, it eventually proved to be crucial for managing the conflicts and indeed to be the *only* institution that could stabilize the Balkans.

The second conclusion is directly related to the above: without conflict in the early post-Cold War period, it is uncertain whether NATO would have survived the end of the Cold War. The residual Soviet threat in the early post-Cold War years was an important influence in ensuring the initial continuation of NATO's place in European security but it is unlikely that this alone would have ensured its future role, particularly as the threat waned during the 1990s. For this reason, both the 1991 Gulf War, and, in particular, the outbreak and continuation of the conflict in the Balkans, were just as important for NATO's endurance as NATO was crucial for addressing them. General John Shalikashvili comments, in this respect that 'NATO remained relevant because of Bosnia. If we had not gone in, or the military performance had been poor, NATO would have been permanently crippled. But the Alliance ended any questions about its relevance by taking charge and demonstrating its military performance'.[40] A NATO official also candidly commented; 'in order to survive, an international organization can't just have a conceptual mission. Organizations seek out action. They need to do things. That's why NATO needs the Balkans as much as the Balkans need NATO. The Balkans is one security issue that NATO can actually do something about. We talked about dealing with drugs, terrorism, proliferation and the Mafia, but the truth is there is not much we can really do about them. The thing about the Balkans is that what NATO has to offer is exactly what they need. We have a product that they want – peacekeeping and providing security'.[41] As well as insurance against the possible resurgence of the Soviet threat and NATO's strengths both as a formal and virtual military alliance, its persistence and consolidation in the post-Cold War world can also be explained in terms of the *need* for sustained military engagement throughout the 1990s, particularly in the former Yugoslavia.

the weaknesses of nato's post-cold war interventions

Despite the strengths NATO demonstrated in the Gulf and the Balkans, the third conclusion is that the very conflicts that consolidated NATO's role revealed some of its internal weaknesses. This conclusion can be demonstrated in three areas: the difficulties of defining NATO's strategic priorities, the increasing complexity of the decision-making process and, once a consensus has been reached, the weaknesses of NATO's collective military capabilities.

The first internal weakness has been the impact of the progressive decline in the commonality of shared risks and, as a result, an increasing gap in the strategic priorities of the Allies. The conflict in the Balkans was particularly indicative in this respect. 'Yugoslavia', Schake comments, 'provides the first genuine example of a European crisis in which the Europeans wanted to take action and the United States did not'.[42] This not only showed that there was no longer a guarantee of American underwriting of and intervention in European security but also that the main reason for this was that, post-Cold War, European security problems no longer affected the North American Allies in the same way nor to the same extent as the remaining European Allies. There was obviously a difference in the vulnerability of the Allies to the Soviet threat during the Cold War, yet the removal of this threat, in conjunction with the outbreak of conflict in Europe, widened the existing gap. As the following chapter will show, this trend has had important implications for the debates surrounding the development of NATO's non-Article 5 missions.

The impact of 9/11 and the conclusions that have been drawn by the Allies are perhaps more encouraging, and it is possible that 9/11 reversed the trend of increasing strategic divergence by presenting a threat that will perhaps unite the Allies. The publication of the National Security Strategy (NSS) of the United States in 2002 and the EU's response in the European Security Strategy (ESS) in 2003 demonstrated that there is an increasingly common assessment of the threats facing the Allies. However, it is far from certain whether the NATO Allies see themselves as being affected in the same way and to the same extent as the United States, given the reality of a post-9/11 United States 'at war' as opposed to other Allies, who perceive themselves as less affected by international terrorism. Broadly convergent threat perception – even though it has never been total convergence – has traditionally been the foundation of NATO. If the threat perception becomes too wide, then NATO faces considerable potential problems.

Even if the threat of international terrorism represents a new unifying force for the Allies, there remains a lack of consensus about the precise role NATO could and should play in addressing this threat and indeed about the strategies that should be employed. The conclusions of the NSS and the ESS are revealing, as they appear to take different approaches. Moreover, as tackling international terrorism requires a multifaceted response, including accurate intelligence and vigilant law enforcement and immigration services, as well as other methods, such as border patrols, many argue that NATO's largely military competencies are ill-suited to a campaign in which military force is a component of a solution rather than a solution in itself.

Reaching a consensus about the nature and extent of the threats facing NATO and agreeing on the appropriate response, as well as minimizing the damage to NATO when such consensus is difficult to reach (as during the 2003 Iraq War), are important hurdles for NATO. Once agreement has been reached a further internal weakness that has been evident in NATO's post-Cold War operations is its military capabilities. As noted in the introduction, a military capabilities gap existed throughout the Cold War but its operational impact was minimal, because NATO was never called upon to act. However, the operational demands placed on NATO since the end of the Cold War have caused this issue to become one of its central challenges.

Military capabilities were the most important influence in NATO's limited response to 9/11. Much discussion of the United States' response to the invocation of Article 5 has focused either on how the US did not wish to conduct a 'war by committee' by having to reach a consensus of eighteen Allies before acting, or on how the necessity of avoiding adding substance to claims of a 'clash of civilisations' between the Islamic world and the West ruled out a NATO role. These two elements partly explain the United States' response. However, the most important influence on the US decision not to engage NATO, beyond defensive measures in and around Europe and in the continental United States, was the disinclination to be tied down in decision-making processes with eighteen Allies whose military capabilities were *simply not useful*, thereby running the risk of restricting the United States' room for manoeuvre and wasting valuable military planning time. Whilst they did not wish the invocation of Article 5 to be an empty gesture, American officials indicated that there was no great enthusiasm to conduct retaliatory military operations through the NATO integrated command structure when there were alternative – and more effective – ways to work.

Military capability has not only brought into question the role NATO can play in the future; it has also caused serious disputes among the Allies on the course and conduct of NATO operations. For example, the military inadequacies of the Allies during NATO's Balkan interventions caused the United States' contribution to be disproportionately large. One implication of this was that the US assumed that it would enjoy a degree of political authority matching its military commitment. As one American commander commented during the Kosovo campaign: 'It's my evaluation that NATO cannot go to war in the air against a competent enemy without the United States. If that's the case, and we're going to provide 70 per cent of the effort [...] then we need to have more than one of nineteen votes'.[43] The remaining Allies robustly disputed the United States' assumption of leadership, which provoked damaging disputes about the course and conduct of Operation Allied Force. This led to claims by the United States of a 'war by committee' and by the remaining Allies of American dominance. NATO's interventions in the Balkans raised significant questions about the sustainability of the military imbalance in NATO and the impact of this on the cohesion of the Alliance.

changes in the post-cold war security environment

In addition to the conclusions that can be drawn about the impact of the end of the Cold War on NATO, wider changes in the strategic environment have affected the security agenda. These changes are crucial for understanding the dilemmas they have caused and the rationale behind the adaptations that NATO has undergone.

the nature of post-cold war conflict

The nature of post-Cold War conflict is the first change affecting NATO. The threat of large-scale conventional military invasion of

Western Europe by Warsaw Pact forces was the scenario that had guided the Alliance's force planning throughout the Cold War, ensuring that NATO's force structure was geared to defence. Events in the early post-Cold War period indicated that this scenario was now highly unlikely. In place of massive conventional military invasion, new challenges, emanating from beyond NATO's traditional area, have become increasingly prominent. The elastic concept of 'non-traditional' security challenges includes the proliferation of WMD and their delivery systems, international terrorism, international crime, illegal trade in fissile materials and other dangerous substances and the consequences of political instability or ethnic or religious conflict, for example, forced migration.

the nature of post-cold war security threats

The consequences of regional conflict, particularly of instability in Europe resulting from political, religious or ethnic enmity, represent an important new characteristic of the post-Cold War security environment. Bipolar confrontation ensured that regional conflicts were kept in check, to reduce the risk of conflict escalation through superpower involvement, which meant that the bipolar world was largely stable and predictable. The end of the Cold War removed this restraint, making the multipolar world far less stable. Of crucial importance for NATO, one of the lessons of the regional conflict in the Balkans was that political instability or conflict on NATO's periphery could have a 'spillover' effect, resulting in migratory flows into or across NATO territory or could serve as a catalyst for conflict in other regions, thus directly affecting NATO security. Similar phenomena on the periphery of the North Atlantic area, whether in North Africa or Eastern Europe, would have the same effect.

WMD are an additional challenge the Allies have faced. The US-led coalition's overwhelming conventional military superiority during Operation Desert Storm quickly and efficiently defeated Iraqi forces, which was initially reassuring, but misleading as a gauge for the future pattern of military conflict. The main reason for this was that this superiority would make it increasingly unlikely that future opponents would seriously consider challenging the United States in particular, or other NATO states in general, but would instead seek alternative methods of warfare that would minimize conventional military and technological superiority. These asymmetric threats could take many different forms including terrorism, urban combat or the potential use of WMD, yet attention has focused on the implications of the proliferation of Nuclear, Biological or Chemical

(NBC) weapons, particularly when in the hands of nations hostile to the United States or US interests. As Chapter Six will show, the risk of the use of WMD in future conflicts involving the US and other NATO Allies might impede their ability to deploy forces, conduct combat operations or carry out peacekeeping and humanitarian missions. WMD could also potentially be used as direct threats against NATO territory, which would place NATO populations at risk. The extent of the threat of WMD is fiercely contested, as the discussions leading to the 2003 Iraq War showed, because, in addition to distinguishing between capabilities and intentions, there are a host of social and economic factors that could reduce the probability of the acquisition or use of WMD by states or non-state actors. Nevertheless, advances in and the spread of weapons technology have caused the theoretical – if not the actual – risk of the use of WMD to increase, which has made the European Allies in particular, and the NATO Allies as a whole, more vulnerable to this form of attack.

International terrorism gradually increased in prominence during the 1990s and dramatically surged after 9/11. Although some NATO members had experience of domestic terrorism, the nature of international terrorism has been very different in terms of the underlying reasons for it, the methods employed by terrorist groups, the scale of devastation it causes and the policy tools that can be employed to counter it.

Changes in the nature of the threats facing the NATO Allies have ensured that the Allies now face a wealth of diverse security challenges. The diversity of these threats is quite different to the dangers of large-scale conventional military conflict or nuclear war faced by the Allies during the Cold War.

the location of conflict

In addition to changes in the nature of the threat, the location of future conflict has also changed. During the Cold War, the battleground was Western Europe, yet post-Cold War, the challenges that are likely to threaten NATO's security are no longer principally found within its traditional borders but are spreading outwards.[44] The nature of the post-Cold War threats has caused the delineation of theatres of conflict to become increasingly blurred. As a result, developments beyond NATO territory, whether within Europe or beyond, are increasingly likely to affect its security. Geographic distance, as a means of security, is being eroded, a conclusion that applies as much to the implications of WMD as it does to the spill-over effects of conflict resulting from political, religious and ethnic enmity or international terrorism. The Allies' increasing vulnerability to threats originating from beyond its borders is one of the most significant lessons for NATO, in the light of the events examined in this chapter.

The diversity of the out-of-area concerns that have demanded NATO's attention in the post-Cold War world has presented a dilemma that did not exist during the Cold War. Because the *raison d'être* of NATO is no longer found in the shared perception of the monolithic threat of the Soviet Union to the Atlantic and specifically West European, area, prioritizing the threats to the Alliance's security has become problematic, particularly when the Allies are no longer all affected in the same way or to the same extent.

To summarize, there have been many changes in the security environment since the end of the Cold War: from stability to instability; from a limited number to a wealth of threats; from clearly defined to increasingly diverse threats; from a broad consensus about priorities to increased potential for transatlantic discord. As a result of these influences, the post-Cold War context has presented a far less straightforward environment for defence planning, in terms of shaping threat perception, defining strategic priorities and forging consensus about appropriate responses.

conclusion

The basic lesson of the post-Cold War period is that NATO's survival was not inevitable, but depended on its ability to respond to radically changed strategic circumstances and demonstrate its continuing relevance in a post-Cold War and post-9/11 world. In the light of the new security environment and the threats outlined above, and the weaknesses that have emerged during its interventions in the 1990s and beyond, NATO has had to embark on a multifaceted reform process in order to ensure its ongoing pre-eminence in the Western security architecture.

The change in the nature of the threats facing NATO in the post-Cold War context was an early indication that the best strategy that NATO could pursue was to project stability into neighbouring regions (a strategy eventually addressed through the initiation of an enlargement process and through outreach and partnership programmes) and to have the willingness and ability to project its military power beyond its members' territory if necessary, which was

addressed through the adoption of new missions. The redefinition of
NATO's roles and responsibilities during the post-Cold War period
has been profound. Addressing security issues, whether beyond or
within NATO territory, whether political or military, whether potential or actual, has become a prominent part of NATO's political and
operational activities. NATO's responses have taken many forms and
encompassed both measures designed to prevent conflict emerging
in the first place and those designed to respond more effectively
when prevention fails. The emergence of new missions to respond to
the effects of conflict or chaos beyond NATO's borders, a shift in its
capabilities away from a defensive posture toward smaller, more
mobile expeditionary forces, the initiation of programmes to
improve the capabilities of the NATO Allies, outreach to Central
and East European and Mediterranean states, a partnership
programme with Russia and Ukraine and, most recently, a focus
on combating WMD and international terrorism have all featured
on NATO's agenda. It is to these programmes of reform that we
now turn.

summary

- The transformation of the international security environment
  and, in particular, the parameters of European security following
  the end of the Cold War raised many questions about NATO's
  chance of survival without its *raison d'être*.
- The outbreak of war in Iraq and the conflict in the Balkans provided answers to some of these questions, by demonstrating the
  benefits of NATO's formal and informal military roles, which
  were a key influence on its post-Cold War survival. NATO subsequently played an irreplaceable role in the management of the
  conflict in the Balkans throughout the 1990s and since.
- As well as demonstrating its ongoing utility, NATO interventions
  in the 1990s also revealed internal weaknesses. These include a
  decline in the commonality of shared risks, the complexity of
  decision-making in a post-Cold War context and the problems of
  increasingly incompatible military capabilities.
- The United States' reluctance, following 9/11, to use NATO
  beyond defensive measures, caused a crisis of confidence in
  NATO, as did the Allies' initial inability to agree on defensive
  measures for Turkey before the 2003 Iraq War. The implications
  of the war on terrorism have also provoked much discussion of
  NATO's prospects in the post-9/11 context.

- Changes occurring in the strategic environment following the end of the Cold War and 9/11, including those related to the nature of conflict, its conduct, its location and its consequences, have been profound. NATO has had to adapt to attempt to meet these challenges.
- Projecting stability into neighbouring regions through enlargement and partnership initiatives to minimize the risks of instability, as well as projecting military force into neighbouring and more distant regions to ensure stability after conflict has occurred has been NATO's two-fold post-Cold War strategy. This strategy can be demonstrated by each of the areas of post-Cold War NATO reform.

missions redefined: nato's post-cold war operations

introduction

The redefinition of NATO's missions since the end of the Cold War has been profound. From being purely a collective defence alliance, NATO has performed the full spectrum of military missions in the post-Cold War context. The expansion of the functional scope of NATO's missions, from a focus on Article 5 collective defence missions to non-Article 5 missions of crisis management, peacemaking and peacekeeping is a key characteristic of its post-Cold War reform. In addition to this functional adaptation, NATO has undergone a process of geographic adaptation and has expanded the parameters of its missions. Rather than remaining focused on the North Atlantic area, and on Western Europe in particular, NATO has acted beyond its members' territory, initially in the Euro-Atlantic area but most recently well beyond this region, in Afghanistan. Due to pressures resulting from the end of the Cold War and, more recently, 9/11, NATO has become an Alliance that performs the full range of military operations and that has a global reach rather than a regional focus. The adoption of these new missions is the most significant reform that NATO has initiated since the end of the Cold War.

This chapter begins by presenting the historical context of the debate surrounding NATO's functional and geographic adaptation and the constraints that prevented it from undertaking out-of-area missions during the Cold War. It goes on to discuss the pressures that caused NATO to expand the parameters of its missions in the post-Cold War and post-9/11 environment and the main areas of controversy that accompanied these changes, with particular attention on the changes in the geographic scope of NATO's missions following 9/11 and the discussions that preceded them. The chapter then assesses the main challenges that functional and geographic adaptation pose for future NATO interventions and concludes by identifying the main ways in which NATO could respond to solve these problems.

historical context

Events occurring beyond NATO territory were traditionally termed 'out-of-area' issues and referred to developments beyond the area defined by Article 6 of the North Atlantic Treaty and, more generally, outside Europe, that were relevant to the interests of the Allies, either individually or collectively.[1] 'Out-of-area' originally referred to large-scale combat operations but in recent years the term has become more elastic, now covering the entire spectrum of military operations (including crisis management, peacekeeping and peace-making) conducted beyond NATO members' borders, in Europe, in nearby or distant areas.[2]

Chapter One demonstrated how NATO's management of crises in the Euro-Atlantic area and beyond was crucial in the post-Cold War and post-9/11 period, but the concept of NATO performing an out-of-area role also featured during the Cold War. In fact, an out-of-area dimension was present from NATO's inception, as, from very early on, the impact of the Cold War was not restricted solely to Western Europe, nor even to the North Atlantic area. The outbreak of war in Korea in June 1950, for instance, not only compelled the Allies to turn their attention from the European continent to events far beyond but also provided the impetus for the transformation of NATO into a permanent, integrated, military structure, set in motion the West European re-armament programme and caused American troops to return to Western Europe in large numbers. In spite of this early influence, there was disagreement from the outset among the Allies about the role NATO should play in addressing conflicts beyond its members' territory.[3]

One of the main reasons for Cold War disagreement were the formulations contained in the North Atlantic Treaty, which specified that the Article 6 geographic boundaries applied 'for the purpose of

Article 5'. Achilles comments, in this respect, 'the treaty area, as defined in Article 6, is simply that in which an armed attack would constitute a *casus belli: there was never the slightest thought in the mind of the drafters that it should prevent collective planning, manoeuvres or operations south of the Tropic of Cancer in the Atlantic Ocean, or in any other area important to the security of the Parties'.*[4] This conclusion echoes that of the then Secretary of State, Dean Acheson, who in a press conference in March 1949 stated that the North Atlantic Treaty contained 'no limiting clause' to prevent the allies from undertaking military action following 'an attack to security outside the treaty area'.[5] The terms of the North Atlantic Treaty did not preclude NATO engagement beyond the parameters stipulated in Article 6, but simply did not make it obligatory. Two interrelated dilemmas subsequently emerged: the extent to which NATO should accept that its security could be jeopardized by events taking place beyond the treaty area[6] and the extent to which members' national interests could reasonably be presented as NATO-wide concerns. The crux of the issue was the support that the Allies could expect from NATO and from each other in areas and circumstances not formally covered by the North Atlantic Treaty.

The flexibility contained in the North Atlantic Treaty provided ample opportunity for Cold War discussion of NATO's response to security issues beyond its members' territory. Discussion of security issues during the Cold War almost invariably resulted in disagreement about NATO's role, whether with respect to the Suez crisis, the Vietnam War or the Yom Kippur War. The out-of-area conundrum was gradually compounded during the Cold War by the realization that bipolar confrontation over Western Europe had effectively resulted in a stalemate, which was largely due to NATO's effectiveness in managing the Soviet threat in the European theatre.[7] As a result, the paradoxical conclusion increasingly drawn during the Cold War, and particularly in its latter stages, was that out-of-area issues represented the greatest threat to the interests and security of the NATO Allies, a conclusion that appeared to be substantiated by developments in regions beyond the North Atlantic Area.[8] However, in spite of these influences and even though attempts were made within NATO to consider contingency planning for out-of-area operations, the Allies were unable to agree on what constituted a threat to NATO as a whole rather than to individual members. As a result, internal opposition prevented NATO out-of-area interventions and the involvement of the Allies took the form of purely national responses to out-of-area issues or the formation of *ad hoc* coalitions of willing Allies.

Although Cold War discussions about NATO's response to out-of-area issues often proved to be highly contentious, the key factor that prevented them undermining the unity of the Allies was the gravity of the Soviet threat. The difficulties created by attempts to achieve a consensus about out-of-area issues, coupled with the imperatives of maintaining a united front during the Cold War, meant that a role for NATO in out-of-area issues was essentially out of the question.

toward an out-of-area role in the post-cold war context

Although the history of NATO during the Cold War was marked by the distinct lack of a consensus over how to deal with out-of-area issues, pressures resulting from the end of the Cold War caused it to respond very differently. This was not an inevitable development, particularly in the months following the fall of the Berlin Wall. Even though NATO demonstrated the utility of its formal and informal roles during the 1991 Gulf War there was, following the end of hostilities, little debate about whether a formal out-of-area role could or should be developed, even though the then Secretary General Manfred Wörner commented, in an address to the North Atlantic Assembly in 1990, that Alliance solidarity had been greater during the Gulf conflict 'than in any previous out-of-area conflict [...] there is a widespread feeling that some Allies and the Alliance as a whole can and should do more'.[9] One reason was the unique set of circumstances surrounding the Gulf War: Iraq's clear breach of international law, the common threat of a disruption to the flow of vital resources, Soviet and Chinese acquiescence, subsequent UN approval for intervention, five months of preparation before the conflict began and a swift victory with remarkably few coalition casualties meant that it was unlikely to be a model for future military interventions. The specificities of Operation Desert Storm ensured that it was a weak basis from which to draw any conclusions about NATO's potential for future military operations. This caused the Allies to exercise caution about how best to adapt NATO to the post-Cold War world. A further reason for the absence of a more vigorous debate about NATO's post-Cold War functional and geographic adaptation was the continued existence of the Soviet Union, which provoked concern that any adaptation of its missions could antagonize the Soviet Union and detract from its core role of collective defence in Western Europe.

In spite of these constraints, the recognition of a shift in the strategic context and in NATO's priorities was identifiable in the early post-Cold War period. NATO's first post-Cold War Strategic Concept, agreed in November 1991, reaffirmed the central function of collective defence but also recognized that 'the threat of simultaneous, full-scale attack on all of NATO's European fronts has effectively been removed and thus no longer provides the focus for Allied strategy'. The Strategic Concept now spoke of 'multifaceted' and 'multi-directional' risks that were likely to originate 'from the adverse consequences of instabilities that may arise from the serious economic, social and political difficulties, including ethnic rivalries and territorial disputes, which are faced by many countries in central and eastern Europe'. This could result in 'crises inimical to European stability and even to armed conflicts, which could involve outside powers or spill over into NATO countries, having a direct effect on the security of the Alliance'. The emphasis of the Strategic Concept subsequently shifted NATO's military posture, which had been focused on defence of its territory, to one that ensured greater operational flexibility. The reconfiguration of NATO military forces to make them smaller and more flexible and to equip them to carry out the potential new missions of crisis management and peacekeeping under the auspices of the UN or the Organisation for Security and Co-operation in Europe (OSCE) was agreed as an objective. However, the continued existence of the Soviet Union, the lack of agreement over which institution should have primary responsibility for crisis management operations in Europe and the difficulties posed by Germany's Basic Law, which prevented German troops operating outside NATO territory, were significant hindrances that impeded the 1991 Strategic Concept from formally addressing NATO's potential out-of-area role. As a result, it made no reference to NATO's out-of-area missions, even though its provisions clearly provided the basis for future out-of-area operations, should the strategic environment and the position of the Allies change.

The lack of reference to out-of-area operations in the 1991 Strategic Concept did not mean there had been any lack of critical debate about NATO's more general role in the post-Cold War context. Increasing NATO's role in co-managing the immediate post-Cold War European security environment, as well as initiating a dialogue with former adversaries, became a focus during this time. As Schake suggests, the Bush Administration's strategy for NATO reform hinged on expanding NATO's role beyond that of collective defence and enhancing other political and military functions.[10] From an American perspective, the emphasis on enlarging NATO's scope became a precondition for ensuring the Alliance's relevance. However, in spite of the out-of-area dimension that this shift in emphasis implied, promoting NATO's ability to act in operations beyond its traditional geographical boundaries, within or beyond Europe, was not then a priority.

an out-of-area role in the euro-atlantic area

The parameters of the out-of-area debate began to change, from late December 1991, as a result of two different influences. The dissolution of the Soviet Union in December 1991, which allowed NATO to be rethought in a way that had not been previously possible, laid the foundation for the more explicit discussion of NATO's role beyond its traditional functions and boundaries. The dissolution of the Soviet Union was crucially important because, without its traditional enemy, NATO's search for a role in the post-Cold War world became increasingly pressing. Although many continued to see NATO as a valuable insurance policy against the resurgence of what was, by now, the 'Russian' threat, the increasing improbability of this indicated that there was even more need for the Alliance to adapt beyond its traditional role of collective defence and beyond its traditional geographical remit, if it were to remain relevant and survive. Senator Richard Lugar succinctly articulated this perspective in a speech to the Overseas Writers' Club in Washington, DC in June 1993, in which he stated that NATO had to go 'out-of-area' or it would go 'out-of-business'.[11] Analysts reiterated the view that there was a clear link between an out-of-area role for the Alliance and its future vitality.[12]

The second influence was the increasing gravity of conflicts in the former Yugoslavia and the failure of the international community to deal with this crisis. When discussion of NATO's potential contribution began, it could thus focus on a tangible problem rather than an abstract scenario. This was of crucial importance for overcoming some of the Allies' initial concerns about a possible NATO intervention and for persuading reluctant members, such as France, that the development of an out-of-area role was both desirable and necessary. The pressure of events in the Balkans enabled NATO to build upon the foundations of the 1991 Strategic Concept and resulted in major changes in the nature and scope of its post-Cold War operational roles.

NATO formally addressed the question of out-of-area missions in June 1992, at the NAC meeting in Oslo. NATO members declared that they were prepared 'to support, on a case-by-case basis in accordance with our own procedures, peacekeeping activities under the responsibility of the CSCE, including by making available Alliance resources and expertise'.[13] In December 1992, Foreign Ministers of NATO member states also stated that NATO was prepared to support peacekeeping operations under the authority of the UNSC and signalled that NATO would respond positively to any further requests for its assistance in this area.[14] Chapter One demonstrated how NATO's missions grew, between 1992 and 1995, to encompass air, land and sea operations and how this initially secondary role was consolidated after the Dayton Peace Accords through the NATO-led IFOR, SFOR and KFOR. NATO redefined itself from a collective defence organization for Western Europe to an organization that was increasingly an instrument for crisis management, peacemaking and peacekeeping in Europe as a whole. NATO's missions in the former Yugoslavia were therefore crucial to the reshaping of its post-Cold War identity.

an out-of-area problem in the post-cold war environment

NATO's interventions in the Balkans answered some of the questions that had been raised about NATO's ongoing place in the European security architecture, by demonstrating its relevance to post-Cold War security. In spite of the benefits for the continuation of NATO's role and for the stabilization of the Balkans, the development of non-Article 5 missions also exposed internal weaknesses, particularly in terms of the value placed on these missions by the United States and the potential implications this had for US commitment.

One of the keys to understanding this phenomenon is the set of criteria that US policy-makers use to assess US military interventions. Yost comments, in this respect, 'partly as a result of the Vietnam trauma, US policy currently holds that foreign military engagements must be justified by their significance for core national security interests [...] or be manageable within finite constraints of duration, risk and cost'.[15] When these criteria are applied to the conflict in the Balkans the following conclusions can be drawn. In terms of core national interests, the United States did not seem to have any

at stake in the former Yugoslavia. In 1993, for example, the then
Secretary of State Warren Christopher dismissed the Bosnian crisis as
being 'a humanitarian crisis a long way from home, in the middle of
another continent'.[16] Moreover, the duration of NATO involvement
in the former Yugoslavia was open-ended, the nature of warfare there
meant that the risk of American casualties was high and the cost of
the Alliance's involvement was undefined. This last issue was particularly problematic, given the initially disproportionate contribution of
the United States to NATO's Balkan interventions.[17] Although NATO
continued to contribute to a key strategic priority of the United States
– the stability of Europe – questioning of the value, benefits and risks
of non-Article 5 missions in the former Yugoslavia by US analysts and
officials reflected a widespread sentiment that, although regional
conflict in Europe stemming from ethnic or religious enmity was a
threat to the security of the Alliance, such contingencies represented,
at best, third-rate US security concerns.[18] These characteristics of
NATO's missions reinvigorated the domestic debate about the extent
and nature of the United States' contributions and increased scrutiny
of the precise nature of the post-Cold War bargain that the US was
striking with the other Allies.

toward a 'global' nato

During the 1990s and the early 2000s, the main focus of the out-of-
area debate was on NATO's expanded role within the Euro-Atlantic
area rather than on its potential role beyond this region; a reflection
of the attention accorded to and imperatives of responding to
developments in the Balkans. None the less, there was an additional
dimension to the out-of-area debate during the 1990s: the potentially extra-European dimension of NATO's missions. This aspect
of the debate has assumed particular importance since 9/11 and
ensuring NATO is able to respond to European *and* global security
issues has progressively become its central political and military
dilemma.

The extra-European aspect of the out-of-area debate was initiated and sustained by a minority of analysts and officials in the
United States who, throughout the 1990s, advocated the expansion
of the geographic scope of NATO's missions from the Euro-Atlantic
area to regions well beyond. NATO's ability to project power beyond
Europe would see it become the vehicle for organizing the defence of
the West's vital strategic interests against post-Cold War threats.[19]
The dual aims would be for NATO to have a role in the management

of global security threats whilst maintaining its stabilizing function in Europe. NATO was seen as a desirable vehicle for this role, given the habits of co-operation shared by the Allies and its effectiveness in shaping a transatlantic consensus.[20]

The impetus behind these American proposals was the identification of a perceived structural flaw: a disjunction between NATO's most prominent missions – the management of collective defence and security in Europe – and the vital strategic interests of its members. Asmus *et al.* comment, in this respect,

> A primary cause of this deterioration of NATO's effectiveness is a growing divergence between US and European security priorities and apparently differing perceptions on the two sides of the Atlantic regarding vital national interests. This important shift is seen in Washington's reluctance to commit ground troops in Bosnia and the domestic U.S. debate regarding the enlargement of NATO to East Central Europe, both of which underscore American ambivalence about the degree to which, in the absence of a hegemonic threat to the Continent, the United States still wants to bear the burdens of being a European power. There is thus a disconnect between current NATO missions and top US concerns regarding serious threats to perceived American vital interests: proliferation, the Persian Gulf, and Northeast Asia.[21]

The main influence on this aspect of the out-of-area debate came from the conclusions that had been drawn, by some US analysts and officials, about the characteristics of NATO's Balkan interventions and their relationship to US strategic priorities. Proponents of these proposals argued that the longer NATO was seen to be failing to address vital American interests, the less support there would be for NATO in the United States. NATO's future vitality was seen to be increasingly dependent on its ability to meet the extra-European challenge. Asmus *et al.* suggested, for example, that 'the only penetrating justification for the continuation of NATO is its direct relevance to the commonly perceived security problems facing the United States and its European allies. If it does not pass that test, it should and eventually will go out of business'.[22] An Alliance that had a more expansive view of the geographic scope and focus of its missions, it was argued, would respond to the intra- *and* extra-European challenges of the new strategic environment, which would increasingly address US strategic priorities, revitalize an Alliance that had lost its central strategic purpose and ensure it remained the West's security organization of choice.

Until the autumn of 1997, extending NATO's missions was largely an academic debate that had limited support within sections of the US political community. However, although these proposals resonated well among members of Congress, they remained on the periphery of the out-of-area debate and did not generate much interest or any legislation. None the less, the extra-European aspect of the debate reappeared in the United States in a very specific way in the autumn of 1997, when extending the geographic scope of NATO's missions found support among senior officials in the Clinton Administration, particularly among the then Secretary of State Madeleine Albright and members of her inner circle.

Between 1997 and 1999, the Clinton Administration proposed that NATO should defend common interests *whatever* their origin. For example, in her statement to the NAC in December 1998, Albright commented:

> The new Strategic Concept must find the right balance between affirming the centrality of Article V collective defense missions and ensuring that the fundamental tasks of the Alliance are intimately related to the broader defense of our common interests [...] I know that there are those who try to suggest that by assuming these new missions, or by talking about common Euro-Atlantic interests beyond collective defense, we are somehow tinkering with the original intent of the North Atlantic Treaty. I've said it before; I will repeat it again today: this is hogwash [...] We are neither altering the North Atlantic Treaty, nor attempting to create some kind of a new 'global NATO'. What we are doing is using the flexibility the Treaty always offered to adapt this Alliance to the realities of a new strategic environment and the challenges we must face together in the twenty-first century.[23]

The vast majority of the remaining Allies rejected the Clinton Administration's proposals and preferred that NATO continue to act out-of-area but not out of the Euro-Atlantic region. The reasons for this reluctance to consider an extension of NATO's missions were four-fold. First, a preoccupation with NATO's existing roles in the Balkans and a concern that the adoption of missions beyond Europe could potentially over-extend it. Second was the conviction that security issues beyond Europe did not directly threaten NATO. Spanish Foreign Minister Abel Matutes commented, after one NATO meeting, that events occurring '8,000 kilometres 5,000 miles from us – in Korea, for example, that is to say in the Antipodes – cannot be considered a threat to our security'.[24] Third, even where there was a recognition of the existence of extra-European threats to NATO's security, most notably the threat of WMD, the NATO Allies did not perceive either the extent of the threat or its imminence in the same way as did many within the United States. The need to address these threats was perceived as less pressing than it was in the US. Finally came the crucial issue of NATO's relevance. The stress that was placed on maintaining NATO's focus on the Euro-Atlantic region demonstrated that the majority of the Allies did not share the perception that non-Article 5 missions in the former Yugoslavia were not addressing strategic priorities. As a result, reforming NATO to address extra-European concerns in order to ensure its relevance was simply unnecessary.

the 1999 strategic concept

The emergence of a more vigorous debate about the geographic parameters of NATO's out-of-area missions can be explained by the Allies' decision to meet in Washington, DC in April 1999 to agree a new Strategic Concept to guide the Alliance in the 21st century. This was a crucial event, because the 1991 Strategic Concept had been agreed before NATO had adopted out-of-area missions. Although NATO played a pivotal role throughout the 1990s in the Balkans, NATO's out-of-area role had not been officially recognized and the drafting of a Strategic Concept provided an opportunity to discuss and define the parameters of NATO's missions.

The new Strategic Concept eventually agreed by the Allies reaffirmed collective defence as NATO's principal mission, as well as the importance of other components of the Alliance, such as the commitment to preserving the transatlantic link and the maintenance of a stable security environment in Europe. Much of the document, however, addressed non-Article 5 missions, reflecting the importance of this aspect of NATO reform within the wider process.

By the time of the Washington Summit, there was little controversy about the functional and geographic scope of NATO's out-of-area roles in Europe, although the legal basis remained controversial, as the debates surrounding Operation Allied Force demonstrated.[25] The Strategic Concept confirmed that, in addition to the maintenance of its Article 5 role, NATO was prepared to perform the full range of non-Article 5 missions including conflict prevention, crisis management, peace support and humanitarian operations. The new

Strategic Concept also defined NATO's geographic area of competence as 'the Euro-Atlantic area', differing from that found in the
North Atlantic Treaty, which refers to the 'North Atlantic area'.[26] By
sanctioning non-Article 5 missions in the Euro-Atlantic area, the
1999 Strategic Concept established out-of-area operations as a key
component of NATO's post-Cold War reforms and confirmed
NATO's evolution from a defence institution for Western Europe to
one that, whilst retaining its defensive role, played a stabilizing role
in Europe as a whole.

The wording of the new Strategic Concept eventually agreed
upon appeared to end the debate about NATO's role beyond Europe
by referring to its area of competence as 'the Euro-Atlantic area'.
Although this area was not defined, an indication of the flexibility of
the Strategic Concept,[27] the general consensus among the NATO
Allies after the Washington Summit was that, for the time being at
least, out-of-area did not mean out of Europe.

In spite of the 'resolution' of the out-of-area debate, there
remained an inherent dilemma in the Strategic Concept, which
can be demonstrated by considering how it defines the nature and
origin of threats to the Alliance or those 'affecting the security of the
Euro-Atlantic area'. The Strategic Concept identified a very broad
range of risks and also acknowledged their implications for NATO's
security. Paragraph 20 states, for instance:

> Notwithstanding positive developments in the strategic environ-
> ment and the fact that large-scale conventional aggression against
> the Alliance is highly unlikely, the possibility of such a threat
> emerging over the longer term exists. The security of the Alliance
> remains subject to a wide variety of military and non-military risks
> which are multi-directional and often difficult to predict. These
> risks include uncertainty and instability in and around the Euro-
> Atlantic area and the possibility of regional crises at the periphery of
> the Alliance, which could evolve rapidly. Some countries in and
> around the Euro-Atlantic area face serious economic, social and
> political difficulties. Ethnic and religious rivalries, territorial dis-
> putes, inadequate or failed efforts at reform, the abuse of human
> rights, and the dissolution of states can lead to local and even
> regional instability. The resulting tensions could lead to crises
> affecting Euro-Atlantic stability, to human suffering, and to armed
> conflicts. Such conflicts could affect the security of the Alliance by
> spilling over into neighbouring countries, including NATO
> countries, or in other ways, and could also affect the security of
> other states.[28]

The Strategic Concept thus acknowledged that threats to the security of the Alliance and the stability of the Euro-Atlantic area could originate from outside but did not indicate how this could affect the geographic scope of the Alliance's missions. The ambiguity of the Strategic Concept is to be expected, not simply because of the nature of the pre-Washington debates and the need to bridge the gap between the different positions of the Allies, but also because ambiguity gives flexibility. Crucially, however, recognition of the potential implications of extra-European threats to NATO's security and the stability of the Euro-Atlantic area also meant that the debate about NATO's role beyond Europe was likely to re-emerge in the future.

changed perceptions of nato's out-of-area role post-9/11

Throughout the 1990s, the extra-European aspect of NATO's out-of-area debate was neither prominent nor excessively contentious, for three reasons. First, the conflict in the Balkans and NATO's multi-faceted reform process focused NATO's attention on events occurring in Europe and ensured that the agenda was full enough to minimize the impact of contentious debates about whether it should take the step beyond. Significantly, each of these activities gave NATO an irreplaceable role to play in European security and thus ensured its relevance in the post-Cold War security environment. Second, the debate over NATO's response to extra-European threats remained abstract and the necessity for this reform potential rather than actual. In contrast to the events-driven nature of NATO reform to address the conflict in the Balkans, many of the Allies simply did not perceive reform to enable NATO to act beyond Europe as either necessary or pressing. Finally, the extra-European out-of-area debate was muted because NATO's involvement in the former Yugoslavia during the 1990s, particularly in Kosovo, had seriously strained its political and military cohesion. This resulted in wariness about contemplating further NATO interventions, whether within Europe or beyond.

In spite of these influences, the inevitability of a security threat outside the Euro-Atlantic area affecting NATO's security was graphically demonstrated by 9/11. 9/11, and the subsequent war against terrorism, dramatically underscored the importance of the extra-European aspect of the debate and the necessity for NATO to undertake missions beyond the Euro-Atlantic area. These developments placed extra-European operations high on NATO's agenda and pro-voked a renewed discussion within NATO about potential interventions beyond Europe.

In the months following 9/11, officials and analysts urged the Bush Administration to commit the Allies to a reformed NATO that explicitly recognized it could operate globally.[29] NATO officials reached similar conclusions. General Klaus Naumann commented, for example:

> the United States and its allies must find ways to revitalize NATO. This must go beyond enlargement and new cooperative arrangements with Russia. NATO can no longer remain the regional defence alliance it used to be. It must become a global alliance, ready to defend its member countries' interests wherever they are at risk and able to act as the core of future *ad hoc* coalitions of the willing.[30]

The Bush Administration did not initially show great interest in this concept, primarily because of the attention being accorded to the early operations in Afghanistan. Nevertheless, members of the Bush Administration gradually came round to the idea of enhancing NATO's ability to act beyond Europe. There was no one single reason for this shift but important influences were the ongoing benevolent view of NATO in the United States, in conjunction with concerns about its relevance to the war against terrorism. The desire to 'make NATO work' gave impetus to the change in the Bush Administration's position. By the early part of 2002, many of the Allies who had previously resisted an extra-European role for NATO had also begun to appreciate that changes in the strategic environment would affect the geographic scope of the Alliance's missions. 9/11 subsequently proved to be a sufficient catalyst to overcome some of the obstacles that had featured in earlier discussions.

nato's post-9/11 definition of the geographic scope of its missions

There was no reference to the geographic scope of NATO's missions in the Communiqués issued at the December 2001 meetings of NATO Foreign and Defence Ministers. The Final Communiqués instead accorded attention to the NATO–Russia relationship, the enlargement process and the relationships with partner countries and reaffirmed the necessity for NATO to continue its efforts to defend against terrorism and the threat of WMD. But, by the May 2002 meeting of NATO Foreign Ministers, in Reykjavik, NATO gave the first indications of the way in which it would define the geographic scope of its missions, post-9/11. Heeding the advice of the early 1990s, that it had to go 'out-of-area' or face going 'out of business', NATO responded to the global nature of security threats by acknowledging that, in a post-9/11 environment, it would have to go global or go bust. Paragraph 5 of the Final Communiqué states:

> To carry out the full range of its missions, NATO must be able to field forces that can move quickly to wherever they are needed, sustain operations over distance and time, and achieve their objectives. This will require the development of new and balanced capabilities within the Alliance, including strategic lift and modern strike capabilities, so that NATO can more effectively respond collectively to any threat of aggression against a member state. We look forward to decisions by Defence Ministers on specific recommendations for the development of new capabilities, for approval by Heads of State and Government at the Prague Summit.[31]

The wording of the Communiqué released after the May 2002 NAC meeting, which has been repeated in NATO documents and by NATO officials ever since, marked a clear departure from the formulations contained in the new Strategic Concept agreed at the Washington Summit: no geographic limits to NATO's future missions were specified, which potentially sanctioned NATO forces to intervene 'wherever they are needed'.[32] As Chapter One showed, the agreement that NATO should be able to perform a full range of operations beyond the Euro-Atlantic area resulted in NATO's first ever mission outside that area, when it took over command and co-ordination of the ISAF in August 2003.

challenges for nato's future operations

Events since the end of the Cold War have initiated profound shifts in the functional and geographic scope of NATO operations. From being a collective defence organisation that was never called upon to act, NATO expanded the range of its missions to encompass non-Article 5 interventions, which have been a frequent occurrence, post-Cold War. Moreover, from the Cold War period, when out-of-area was out-of-the-question, to the post-Cold War period, when out-of-area did not mean out-of-Europe, NATO now finds itself in the post-9/11 context when global Alliance engagement has become a reality. For many, this dual adaptation has consolidated NATO's position and demonstrated its continuing value and relevance. Whilst it is difficult to argue that the continued adaptation of NATO to the changing strategic environment could somehow be detrimental, there remain some constraints on its ability to achieve the objectives it has set itself. These may prove to be serious obstacles, hindering the development of NATO's out-of-area missions, in spite of the political will to do so.

why nato?

The first challenge that NATO will face is agreeing which cases and circumstances can justify a NATO intervention. This is an important issue, because although there is no longer a doctrinal restriction on the functional or geographic scope of NATO's missions, the Allies are not obliged to engage NATO even if the provision is there. In order for intervention to occur, NATO will have to be perceived as the most advantageous option so will have to prove to the United States, and the Pentagon in particular, that there is a value-added benefit to its involvement, beyond political symbolism. This is the thrust of Donald Rumsfeld's comment that 'the mission must determine the coalition, the coalition must not determine the mission',[33] a concept that has been repeatedly emphasized by the United States since 9/11. This issue is problematic for NATO, as it is difficult to imagine a situation in which NATO as an institution, as opposed to a coalition of willing NATO and non-NATO Allies, will be most advantageous. The position of the US is clearly very important in this respect. As Binnendijk and Kugler comment,

> the United States has developed a distinctly utilitarian stance towards multi-lateralism. It is willing to cooperate with allies, but only when their presence enhances prospects for victory. When allied forces are too weak to matter, or are not interoperable with US forces, the United States is inclined to use only its own forces rather than fight a 'war by committee'.[34]

Clarke and Cornish echo this assessment by stating,

> the fact remains [...] the US is more inclined to view NATO as a useful basis for *ad hoc* military coalitions, that it values the political weight of the alliance over its military capabilities, and that when the US engages in any serious expeditionary operations it is likely to do so using forces and command structures from Central Command (CENTCOM) or Pacific Command (PACCOM), where there is very little commonality, or even familiarity, with NATO forces and procedures.[35]

The conclusion reached in the United States, that a NATO response to the events of 9/11 would have been a hindrance rather than a help, is something that will need to be addressed and resolved if NATO is to continue to play a key role in ensuring European and wider security.

decision-making dilemmas

The rapidity of NATO's decision-making processes is a second obstacle. The need for a consensus among the twenty-six Allies brings into question whether NATO will be able to respond quickly enough to the pressure of events and whether an initial consensus between the Allies will hold. The unpredictable evolution of crisis situations is a significant influence, as a consensus could quickly turn to conflict, particularly over strategy, which could only undermine the cohesion of the NATO Allies and potentially damage the long-term health of NATO. NATO has reformed its command structures in order to shift the focus away from regional commands to functional commands in order to give greater flexibility. Although this is a step in the right direction, it still does not address the basic question of the actual decision-making process. Significant questions therefore remain about the dynamics of NATO's present and future decision-making processes and the implications for its ability to respond effectively and coherently to crises.

military capabilities

Even if the Allies agree to engage NATO, ensuring that political agreement can be translated into military action is a further crucial influence on its ability to respond to crises. As the following chapter will show, the capabilities gap is certainly not a new issue on NATO's agenda but existing difficulties of interoperability have gained greater significance, post-9/11 and restricted the contribution that NATO and its members have been able to make to operations involving the United States, whether within or outside the NATO context. The failure to resolve this crucial issue will have serious implications for NATO's future vitality, because if it fails to sustain the interest and commitment of its members with respect to its military capabilities, the dynamism behind NATO as a military instrument will diminish. Restoring interest in NATO as an instrument capable of performing the full range of missions, wherever it is called upon to do so, is a key question to address but certainly not one that has any easy answers.

future policy options

The constraints outlined above show that, although the conceptual hurdles that the Allies have overcome with respect to NATO's functional and geographic adaptation are impressive, this appears, to date, to be the simplest part of their response. In spite of the serious obstacles outlined above, however, there remain clear benefits to NATO operations, which may influence the decision about whether to engage it in the future. There is already some flexibility within NATO's existing mechanisms with respect to decision-making and the configurations of military operations. Adaptation of existing processes could therefore provide a way forward.

A starting point for discussion of these problems is viewing them in context. Although the recent emphasis on coalition operations seems to be a key obstacle, it is important to recognize that the basic concept of coalition operations is not a new issue on NATO's agenda. NATO's operations in the former Yugoslavia and in Afghanistan were NATO-led, rather than NATO-only, and therefore resembled coalition operations, even if the command belonged to NATO. It is therefore difficult to argue that the recent emphasis placed on the flexibility provided by coalition operations involving NATO and non-NATO states somehow sets a precedent.

The benefits of the decision-making process within NATO and, in particular, the impact and strength of consensus decision-making in the Alliance is a further factor. Reaching a consensus in NATO always has been, and will remain, difficult. However, whilst it is difficult to reach a consensus, once one has been reached and a policy agreed, it is very difficult to change it. This ensures that NATO decisions are permanent and binding. The dynamics of coalition operations tend to be far less stable and the scope for a change in the positions of participating nations much greater. This was demonstrated in 2004 by Spain's decision to withdraw its troops from operations in Iraq, a policy change resulting primarily from a change in government. This move would have been far less likely had the force in Iraq been under NATO command. The greater degree of predictably that stems from NATO operations may therefore be a considerable influence on future decisions about potential interventions.

Consensus decision-making also has benefits, particularly, although not exclusively, for smaller NATO nations. Within a coalition, smaller and less strategically important nations can be effectively overlooked. Consensus decision-making is therefore particularly important for them, as it provides a guarantee that their views will be taken into consideration and that they will not simply be taken along with the policies and priorities of the larger states. That said, consensus is just as important to the United States as it is to a small NATO state such as Luxembourg. The confidence-building effect of Alliance decision-making is therefore an additional benefit of NATO operations.

Although it is counter-intuitive, NATO enlargement, rather than hindering the decision-making process, may in fact help it, as the arrival of seven new Allies in 2004 has caused NATO to reconsider its present decision-making process and initiate potential change. There is no prospect of NATO making a shift away from unanimous decision-making to QMV. However, there has been discussion about introducing a form of 'constructive abstention' that would allow the Allies to reach a consensus more quickly. The constructive abstention mechanism would enable any NATO ally that had concerns about a potential operation to signal their reservations, without vetoing the decision to act. Given its benefits, the introduction of some form of constructive abstention is almost inevitable.

In terms of the contributions of the Allies, the experience of the Iraq War has shown that the United States needs political and military support from other countries. This will remain the case in the future, not simply because of the legitimacy that can be gained from acting with others but also because of the present and likely future constraints on the US military. As Binnendijk and Kugler observe, 'US military superiority stems from the high quality of its armed forces, not their quantity: US forces are stretched thin. Allied contributions will be vital if US forces are called upon to deal with more than one major crisis at a time'.[36]

Given the pattern of past military operations involving the NATO Allies, it is likely that future operations will be NATO-led or comprise a coalition of willing NATO Allies. Meeting the challenge posed by coalition operations will be a preoccupation for NATO in the coming months and years. In terms of matching the flexibility that coalition operations provide, a desirable solution, that NATO may consider, is the further development of flexible coalitions within a permanent Alliance, in other words, coalitions that have NATO at their core. This concept would see different NATO members participating in different operations according to their policy priorities and military capabilities. This arrangement, whereby members participate in different operations, is increasingly likely to become a possibility if the number of NATO operations continues to grow, as not all members will be able to participate in every operation. There has already been an indication that this is a way forward, given that certain members are currently focusing their efforts on particular operations, for example, in Afghanistan. This configuration would mean that political endorsement by all NATO members of a given NATO operation would be necessary but their participation would not be obligatory. These NATO-led operations would, of course, be open to NATO Partners and non-NATO members, which would increase the flexibility needed to respond to crises.

These policy options show that there is already some flexibility in NATO's existing mechanisms. This is an important point, as it demonstrates that there are options to consider which have the potential to maximize the benefits of NATO operations but also provide an answer to critics who have argued that the impact of NATO's composition and internal dynamics on operations make it a relic in the post-9/11 world.

conclusion

The issue that featured in both the intra- and extra-European aspects of the out-of-area debate was the realization that security concerns occurring in, or emanating from, areas beyond NATO territory could affect the security of the Allies and that, to respond effectively, NATO would have to adapt its original mission of collective defence. This realization has resulted in NATO devoting considerable attention, in its policy statements and actions, to non-traditional missions and non-traditional security threats beyond its borders, both near and far. This broadening of the Alliance's agenda has safeguarded its position as Europe's pre-eminent security institution by ensuring that, in the absence of a threat that justifies a collective defence posture in Western Europe, its main operational activities relate to challenges that occur in or emanate from beyond its borders.

The emphasis that has inevitably been placed on force projection has caused a dilemma, however, as it has placed great strains on NATO's collective military capabilities. Agreeing that NATO should have a global reach is one thing; quite another to ensure that it has the capability to do so. This is crucial given the main impetus behind recent changes: the realization that NATO had to remain relevant in the fight against 'new' global security threats. As the following chapter will show, ensuring that Allies are able to operate together has been one of the key political and military dilemmas confronting NATO and may hold the key to ensuring its future vitality.

summary

- The adoption of new out-of-area missions was not an inevitable development in the early post-Cold War context. Although pressures resulting from the end of the Cold War eventually provided a key role for NATO, its post-Cold War missions in the Balkans also exposed internal weaknesses, particularly with respect to the value placed on these missions by the United States and the degree of US commitment they demanded. This resulted in a questioning of the precise bargain the US was striking with other NATO Allies.

- Discussion of extending its missions beyond the Euro-Atlantic area emerged in the United States in the latter part of the 1990s, in part to address what some perceived as the structural flaw that had emerged in NATO. This eventually resulted in the Clinton Administration attempting to gain the Allies' approval for NATO to defend common interests whatever their origin, a proposal that did not gain great support.

- The 1999 Strategic Concept fudged the position by referring to NATO's area of responsibility as 'the Euro-Atlantic area' and acknowledging that threats to the security of the Allies and the stability of the Euro-Atlantic area could emanate from beyond this region. The extra-European aspect of the out-of-area debate therefore resulted in a stalemate.

- 9/11 changed perceptions of the nature and origin of threats to NATO and resulted in some significant shifts in the positions of the Allies regarding the geographic scope of its missions. NATO subsequently removed the geographic 'limits' by stating that it could field forces that could move quickly to wherever they were needed.

- The change in the functional and geographic scope of NATO's missions since the end of the Cold War has been profound. NATO now performs a full range of military operations, from its long-standing collective defence role to new non-Article 5 missions of crisis management, peacemaking and peacekeeping in members' territory, both in the Euro-Atlantic area and now globally.

- In spite of the changes to NATO's missions, challenges remain. These include demonstrating the value of NATO operations, solving decision-making dilemmas and improving capabilities. However, there is some flexibility in NATO's existing mechanisms that may provide solutions to these problems and demonstrate its value. The problem of military capabilities remains, however.

the alliance rebalanced? equipping nato for its missions

introduction

The issue of burden sharing between the Allies has grown in importance from the early 1990s onwards, since NATO began to play an active operational role in the management of European and wider security. Such discussions are not a product of the post-Cold War period, however. Debates, particularly about the financial burden assumed by the United States, characterized the Cold War and there were frequent accusations that the European Allies were free-riding on the US security guarantee. In the post-Cold War context the thrust of the debate changed to discussion of the relative roles and responsibilities of the Allies in the management of European and wider security. This new feature of an old debate emerged for two reasons. First, the end of the Cold War provided an opportunity for the European Allies to develop the 'European pillar' within NATO, meaning that their role and influence both within NATO, and in European security more generally, could grow. Correcting this Cold War imbalance, through the adoption of a more active role, would therefore fulfil an objective that had been prevented by the constraints of bipolarity. Second, once the parameters of NATO's post-Cold War missions had been decided upon, the next step was to make certain that its members were suitably equipped to perform these tasks. This would ensure that the European Allies were able to contribute to security in their own backyard, thus enhancing their role in the management of European security, and thereby meeting post-Cold War calls for increased burden-sharing from the US.

In spite of these changes, the most basic lesson of this period is that NATO's post-Cold War operations have exposed serious weaknesses in its collective military capabilities, and in particular the incapabilities of the European Allies. These weaknesses have caused interoperability with the United States to be increasingly difficult, which has in turn compromised the efficiency of NATO's oper-ations, placed a disproportionate share of the costs of missions onto the United States and caused serious disputes between the Allies about the course and conduct of operations. Rather than heralding the beginning of a greater European role in European security, NATO's post-Cold War operations have shown just how dependent on the political and military might of the United States the Allies are. The debate about capabilities and burden sharing has therefore increased in intensity, complexity and gravity as NATO's functional and geographic adaptations have developed. The severity of the political and military strains that have emerged as a result of the military capabilities gap has showed that the *status quo* is not sus-tainable. Bridging the gap and ensuring that the Allies are equipped to perform the full range of NATO's missions together, which would decrease the likelihood of damaging debates about burden-sharing and enhance the effectiveness of operations, in Europe and beyond, is the central political and military dilemma facing NATO.

This chapter examines how NATO has attempted to manage the capabilities gap that first opened in the early 1990s and to establish a greater balance between the roles of the United States and other NATO Allies.

The chapter is divided into two parts. Part One places the issue in context, by defining the capabilities gap, discussing the impact it has had on NATO's post-Cold War operations and explaining why it exists. Having laid this foundation, Part Two addresses the evolution of the debate about how to improve the capabilities of the European Allies and enhance their contribution to European security, which would rebalance the Alliance. It begins by explaining why and how the EU was initially meant to provide the framework through which a greater European contribution to European security would be achieved and summarizes why the focus shifted to NATO. It then discusses the main capabilities initiatives that were launched within NATO and highlights the problems and pitfalls associated with them. The chapter continues by showing how and why the debate about improving capabilities shifted, in the latter part of the 1990s, from a

NATO- back to an EU-based debate. The final part of the chapter assesses the capabilities initiatives that NATO has launched since 9/11 and considers whether they are likely to address some of the long-standing problems that have emerged since the end of the Cold War.

the capabilities gap

The capabilities gap between the United States and the other NATO Allies can be defined as 'the aggregate of multiple gaps relating to the organisation and conduct of large-scale expeditionary operations'.[1] These multiple gaps include gaps in technology, procurement, spending, research and development and between force structure policies and strategic cultures. Their combined impact has led to US superiority in planning operations, deploying forces and conducting and sustaining operations. Its military superiority is especially striking in areas that are essential for force projection, including air- and sea-lift, as well as in other areas necessary for the smooth conduct of military operations, such as command, control, communications and intelligence (C^3I). It is important to note, however, that the capabilities gap is not merely a question of insufficient force levels, because the total number of European and Canadian forces is greater than that of the United States. Critically, however, the total number of deployable forces that can operate efficiently and effectively with their American counterparts is far smaller, because of the various gaps outlined above.[2] The former Secretary General Lord Robertson pointed this out in November 2003 by stating, 'I put it bluntly, the overwhelming part of the [Europe and Canada's] 1.4 million soldiers are useless for the kind of missions we are mounting today. In other words, the non-US NATO countries have lots of soldiers, but far too few of them can be deployed'.[3] These weaknesses have resulted in European and Canadian over-dependency on US military assets in all of NATO's post-Cold War operations.

the impact of the capabilities gap on nato's post-cold war operations

During the Cold War the capabilities gap was 'virtual', because NATO was never put to the test. This virtual gap became actual post-Cold War, as NATO interventions began and grew in functional and

geographic scope during the 1990s and afterwards. NATO's interventions in the Balkans, and, more recently, its response to 9/11 have
provided evidence of the shortcomings of the Allies' capabilities and
raised serious questions about the declining level of interoperability
between US forces and those of other members. Although all NATO
interventions in the early 1990s demonstrated these characteristics,
the most commonly cited example of the impact of the capabilities
gap is Operation Allied Force. It is important, however, to exercise a
degree of caution about the lessons that can be drawn from this
operation, as the United States, due to domestic constraints and the
legacy of previous military interventions, chose a strategy that
played to its strengths and not to those of other Allies. Arguably, the
decision to prosecute an air war artificially enhanced the capabilities
gap, particularly in terms of air power and precision-strike weapons.
None the less, the operation reinforced some existing lessons of
NATO's post-Cold War operations and revealed some additional,
significant, problems.

Operation Allied Force was NATO's toughest political and military challenge in the 1990s. Once the decision to act against
Milosevic had been taken, which itself was highly controversial and
divisive, fourteen of NATO's (then nineteen) members contributed
aircraft. The Czech Republic, Iceland, Luxembourg and Poland did
not have appropriate capabilities and Greece did not participate for
political reasons. During the 78-day air war, NATO aircraft conducted over 38,000 sorties, of which over 14,000 were strike missions. Of those 38,000 sorties, the United States flew slightly more
than 60 per cent. 70 per cent of the 14,000 strike missions and 90 per
cent of attacks with precision-guided munitions were performed by
the United States, because only 10 per cent of European and
Canadian aircraft could deliver these munitions. The level of the
Allies' contributions increased as the conflict progressed, though
this was primarily due to an improvement in the weather, because
many of the Allies did not possess capabilities that allowed them to
operate in the poor weather conditions which characterized the early
days of the conflict. Operation Allied Force therefore demonstrated
weaknesses in European and Canadian air capabilities and the
difficulties that they experienced when attempting to operate with
US air forces.

On 10 June 1999, Operation Allied Force ended. Although NATO
had prevailed, the post-conflict analysis provided a number of wor-
rying lessons about the capabilities gap that brought into question
its inclination and ability to conduct future operations. The course
and conduct of the operation had revealed a serious deficit in many

diverse aspects of European capabilities, including an ongoing shortage of strategic lift capabilities, inadequate capabilities for the suppression of enemy air defences, problems of weapons compatibilities, weaknesses in target identification, insecure communications and incompatible information systems. The UK Defence Select Committee concluded, for example, 'Overall, Operation Allied Force demonstrated just how far the European NATO nations are from having a capability to act without massive US support'.[4] This conclusion was echoed by the former NATO Secretary General Lord Robertson, who commented:

> The Kosovo air campaign demonstrated just how dependent the European Allies had become on US military capabilities. From precision-guided weapons and all-weather aircraft to ground troops that can get to the crisis quickly and then stay there with adequate logistical support, the European Allies did not have enough of the right stuff. On paper, Europe has two million men and women under arms – more than the United States. But despite those two million soldiers, it was a struggle to come up with 40,000 troops to deploy as peacekeepers in the Balkans. Something is wrong, and Europe knows it.[5]

In addition to the specific weaknesses revealed by Operation Allied Force, a number of wider conclusions can be drawn about the impact of the capabilities gap on future NATO operations. First, the gap matters for the conduct of military operations, because increasing problems of interoperability between the Allies compromise their effectiveness and efficiency. This not only has military implications but would also have serious political implications, particularly in the United States, if US servicemen died as a result of the deficiencies of NATO's collective capabilities.

Second, the capabilities gap transfers a disproportionate share of the burden and responsibility of conducting military operations onto the United States. The then Deputy Secretary of State Strobe Talbott told the Royal Institute for International Affairs on 7 October 1999, 'many Americans are saying: never again should the United States have to fly the lion's share of the risky missions in a NATO operation and foot by far the biggest bill. Many in my country – notably including members of Congress – are concerned that, in some future European crisis, a similar predominance of U.S. manpower, firepower, equipment and resources will be neither politically nor militarily sustainable, given the competing commitments our nation has in the Gulf, on the Korean Peninsula and elsewhere

around the world'.[6] The implications of deficiencies in NATO's collective capabilities will not only cause domestic controversy within
the United States about the nature of the contemporary transatlantic
bargain, but is also likely to continue to provoke serious intra-
NATO disputes, because as long as the United States supplies the
bulk of the military hardware, the Allies' influence on strategy will
be minimal, which, if Operation Allied Force is a guide, will cause
divisive disputes between the Allies and damage NATO cohesion.
Moreover, there are implications for transatlantic relations more
generally, for, as long as the European and Canadian Allies remain
allied to the United States because of military weakness, they will
be of limited value, a situation which is not sustainable in the
long term.

Third, although the capabilities gap was evident during NATO's
Balkans interventions, it will be of even greater significance for its
future operations beyond Europe. Weaknesses in the Allies' force
projection capabilities made problematic the deployment of forces
to a region as close as the Balkans, so its ability to deploy forces to
regions far beyond this is likely to be even more challenged. If this is
not addressed and resolved, the result could conceivably be the
United States conducting high-intensity war-fighting and performing specialized tasks, due to its superior capabilities, whilst the
other Allies are only able to conduct low-intensity but high-risk
peacemaking and peacekeeping operations, due to their generally
less advanced capabilities. What has been termed the 'US makes the
dinner, the Europeans do the dishes' scenario is neither politically
sustainable nor desirable, as such a division of labour could endanger
the long-term health of NATO by progressively undermining the
unity of strategic vision and purpose that has traditionally been one
of its core components. None the less, without significant changes,
this may be inevitable.

Last, the growing disparity in military capabilities will further
compromise operations involving coalitions of willing NATO Allies
in non-NATO operations, given NATO's informal co-ordinating
mechanisms. Failing to bridge the capabilities gap therefore has serious implications both for NATO and for transatlantic security relations in general.

explaining the capabilities gap

There are numerous reasons for the existence of a capabilities gap.
The first explanation for the capabilities imbalance that emerged

over the post-Cold War period concerns levels of defence spending: in particular, inadequate defence spending by Allies other than the United States. There is a long-standing and significant discrepancy between the defence spending of the United States and the remaining Allies, something that has long been a source of contention within NATO. Despite the periodic re-emergence of the burden-sharing debate during the Cold War and post-Cold War periods, the spending gap has continued to grow. That the European and Canadian Allies spend less on defence than the United States is not a new phenomenon; what has changed is the gap between the two sides of the Atlantic, which has widened over the course of the post-Cold War period and in particular since 9/11. Defence spending generally decreased following the end of the Cold War, as many states sought to profit from the 'peace dividend' and then stagnated, as other pressing issues, such as the challenges posed by ageing populations, began to compete for resources. Defence spending in most NATO states did not rise after 9/11, apart from small increases in the United Kingdom and France. If current trends continue, levels of defence spending in the majority of NATO states will therefore be maintained rather than increased. The situation in the US is very different. As in many NATO member states, US defence spending fell after the end of the Cold War but then increased slightly just before 9/11. US spending also dramatically increased following 9/11 and is set to continue rising for at least the next decade both as a response to post-9/11 conditions and to meet the additional costs of the war on terrorism. The US defence budget is projected to rise from $329 billion in 2001 to $405 billion in 2004 to $470 billion in 2007.[7] As a result of 9/11, the already long-standing spending gap between the Allies has widened.

A second, related, explanation is the composition of NATO and the impact this has had on the efficiency of defence spending. The capabilities debate is often reduced to a comparison of the levels of US and 'European' defence spending as if they were the only two entities within NATO. Analysts often point out, for example, that whilst NATO Allies other than the United States spend almost 60 per cent of what the US spends on defence, they only achieve approximately 10 per cent of the capability. Although the sum of European defence spending may well equal 60 per cent of the United States', these analyses fail to take into account that, rather than there being only one collective budget, each NATO Ally has its own defence budget and its own spending priorities, which ultimately are decided by national governments. This is a critical aspect of the capabilities debate, because much of the problem can be explained by the fact that most of the Allies have, until recently, attempted to fulfil all military tasks nationally and improve capabilities individually, rather than pooling their assets and resources. This partly explains why the members of NATO other than the United States may spend 60 per cent of the US defence budget but only get 10 per cent of the capability. Pooling of resources and efforts would enable NATO's European and Canadian members to benefit from economies of scale, which would lead to more efficient spending and therefore better capabilities than any member could achieve alone. Until recently, however, this has not occurred, primarily because of the important political dilemmas that such pooling would cause, which have exacerbated the capabilities imbalance.

The Allies also differ from the United States in how they allocate available defence resources. In recent years, the United States has accorded much attention and allocated increasing resources to applying new forms of advanced technology warfare. The so-called 'Revolution in Military Affairs' – the major change in the nature of warfare brought about by the innovative application of new technologies – will result in a fundamental change in the character and conduct of military operations, as this gradual shift from platform-centric to network-centric warfare is designed to achieve greatly increased operational effectiveness. The United States is progressively taking to the technological battlefield. Instead of exploiting the advantages offered by new technology, many of the Allies remain on the conventional battlefield, show little or no intention of enhancing their capabil-ities in this area and instead continue to spend too much money on personnel compared to equipment. Their technological base is therefore not only inferior to that of the United States but also unlikely to improve in the near future. The gap between the technological capabilities of the United States and other Allies has raised additional concerns about the future compatibility between most NATO forces and US forces.

In addition to inadequate defence spending and the inefficient use of the spending there is, the capabilities gap can also be seen as a legacy of the Cold War and, in particular, the organization of NATO's forces. During the Cold War, NATO's defence planners worked on the assumption that the main threat to its security was massive, conventional invasion by Warsaw Pact forces. NATO forces were expected to fight in place, ensuring that most were configured for defence. The only exceptions were France, the United Kingdom and the United States. France and the United Kingdom retained an expeditionary capability, a legacy of their former world power status, their colonial pasts and the continuation of extra-European

Table 1 Comparisons of defence expenditure by NATO member states, 1985, 2001 and 2002. (Source, The Military Balance 2003–4.[8])

	Defence expenditure								
	US$m			US$ per capita			% of GDP		
	1985	2001	2002	1985	2001	2002	1985	2001	2002
NATO North America									
Canada	11,164	8,326	7,771	440	269	247	2.2	1.2	1.1
United States	380,899	299,917	329,616	1,592	1,049	1,138	6.1	3.1	3.3
NATO Europe									
Belgium	3,583	2,953	3,435	363	287	332	2.9	1.3	1.3
Bulgaria	1,424	362	378	159	46	48	2.9	2.8	2.5
Czech Republic	n/a	1,158	1,401	n/a	112	136	n/a	2.1	2.1
Denmark	1,858	2,456	2,564	363	463	483	2.1	1.6	1.6
Estonia	n/a	65	93	n/a	47	68	n/a	1.2	1.6
France	30,659	32,438	38,005	556	545	636	3.9	2.5	2.5
Germany	29,393	26,729	31,465	387	326	383	3.2	1.5	1.5

Greece	3,439	5,245	6,154	346	495	579	7.0	4.6	4.4
Hungary	2,060	902	1,083	193	91	110	6.8	1.7	1.8
Iceland	n/a	n/a	n/a	n/a	n/a	n/a	n/a	n/a	n/a
Italy	13,729	21,528	24,210	240	374	421	2.2	2.0	1.9
Latvia	n/a	84	141	n/a	35	60	n/a	1.2	1.8
Lithuania	n/a	209	233	n/a	56	63	n/a	1.8	1.8
Luxembourg	74	156	193	203	358	438	1.0	0.8	0.9
Netherlands	5,731	6,083	7,330	396	383	459	2.9	1.6	1.6
Norway	2,651	2,884	3,434	638	641	759	2.8	1.8	1.9
Poland	21,644	3,436	3,400	582	89	88	20.5	2.0	1.9
Portugal	964	2,277	2,945	94	228	294	3.2	2.1	2.3
Romania	1,204	962	999	53	43	45	1.7	2.5	2.3
Slovakia	n/a	383	439	n/a	71	81	n/a	2.0	2.0
Slovenia	n/a	275	311	n/a	138	156	n/a	1.5	1.5
Spain	5,856	7,007	8,253	152	176	206	2.4	1.2	1.2
Turkey	3,489	7,018	8,727	69	104	127	3.1	4.9	5.1
United Kingdom	35,003	33,967	35,249	619	571	590	5.2	2.5	2.4

interventions and are exceptions to the general rule. However, the United States' expeditionary capabilities make it unique among the NATO Allies. The US has not fought a war on its own soil since the War of Independence, instead fighting its wars far from home. This crucial factor, in conjunction with the United States' geographic position and the minimal conventional military threat that has been posed to the US homeland, has ensured that US forces have, from the outset, been configured almost exclusively for force projection, which has inevitably resulted in highly developed expeditionary capabilities.

Differences in the strategic priorities of the Allies are also important as they influenced the military capabilities acquired by NATO members, thus exacerbating an existing force projection gap. The United States' preparation for operations in distant theatres is a reflection of its status as a global power, with global interests, which has needed to intervene globally in order to protect those interests. The remaining NATO Allies (with the exceptions of the United Kingdom and France) are regional powers with regional interests. As a result, in the post-Cold War context, they have anticipated the need to prepare for operations in or around the European theatre rather than in areas well beyond. NATO members have therefore developed their militaries according to divergent models and requirements. It is only since 9/11 that there has been recognition of the need to reconfigure forces for deployment to distant theatres.

The impact of these differences in the Allies' force postures and expeditionary capabilities was not particularly significant during the Cold War, due primarily to the failure to agree on NATO's extra-European role and the focus on the collective defence of Western Europe. However, the post-Cold War shift in emphasis from collective defence to force projection, which resulted from the decrease in the risk of conventional military invasion of Western Europe and the emergence of conflict beyond NATO's borders, caused their significance to grow. As it became clear that, rather than waiting for crises to come to them, NATO forces would have to be able to go to crises, the development of force projection capabilities became an essential part of NATO's post-Cold War reform process. However, because of the Cold War legacy, the starting points of the Allies were very different; from the outset, the United States and, to a lesser extent, the United Kingdom and France were much better placed than the remaining Allies to meet this requirement. Due to the very slow reform processes of many of the Allies, as a whole they have been – and remain – highly dependent on the United States in several areas essential for force projection, including air- and sea-lift capabilities and the mobility and sustainability of forces.

A final influence is the force structure of NATO members and, in particular, the impact of conscription. Many of the Allies have retained conscription, which has had an effect on military effectiveness, first, because training is shorter and less specialized than for professional forces and second, the use of conscripts in overseas operations is often prohibited. France, Italy, Portugal and Spain are in the process of eliminating conscription, yet Bulgaria, Denmark, Germany, Greece, Poland, Romania and Turkey retain it, even though some are reducing the number of conscripts taken in each year. Until all NATO forces are fully professional there will inevitably be efficiency differences, which will affect the overall capabilities gap.

addressing the gap and redressing the balance

A number of different issues have caused the capabilities gap to grow in importance since the Cold War period: the beginning and subsequent growth of NATO's operational role following the end of the Cold War, the decline in the resources available for reforming and equipping forces to adequately and effectively conduct such missions and the growing problems of interoperability among the Allies. The gravity of the implications of the capabilities gap for NATO's past, present and future operations has made improving capabilities one of the most pressing items on the agenda. Alongside these trends, an additional dimension to the capabilities debate emerged in the post-Cold War period in the form of US calls for increased burden-sharing and European calls for an enhanced role within NATO and in the management of European security more generally. The combined impact of these trends has made finding innovative solutions to the capabilities gap essential. It is to these initiatives that we now turn.

the origins of the european security conundrum

In order to understand fully the evolution of the post-Cold War debate over how to enhance the military capabilities of the European and Canadian Allies and to rebalance their roles, it is necessary briefly to consider the foundations of the European security architecture. Much of the post-Cold War security conundrum can be explained by post-Second World War developments, which saw the formation of two security institutions: the WEU in 1948 and NATO in 1949. Even though the WEU was formed before NATO it was effectively redundant as soon as NATO came into being, due to NATO's greater credibility via the link to the United States. None the less, the existence of the WEU provided the basis for European military capability, which would enhance the role of the European Allies. Throughout the Cold War there were a number of different plans to increase the European role, for example the Fouchet Plans of 1961. All these initiatives floundered, primarily because of disagreement about the nature of the US role in Europe and the impact of a European military capability on NATO. Although all the European states agreed that the United States should be involved in European security, the area of contention was the relative degree of United States/European influence. Two groups emerged: the 'Europeanists', led by France, argued for more say and influence for the Europeans in their relationship with the US and for a strengthened European military capability – the WEU – which would in turn strengthen and encourage US engagement in Europe; the 'Atlanticists', led by the UK, argued that the *status quo* should be maintained and that a European military capability would weaken the Alliance and encourage US disengagement. This meant a lack of common vision and contrary views about the impact of an enhanced European role on NATO. The want of agreement between Europeans and the constraints and imperatives of bipolar confrontation ensured that the *status quo* remained and that the Cold War solution to the European security dilemma was based entirely on NATO and the United States.

post-cold war moves toward an enhanced european role in european security

In the early post-Cold War period, when questions about NATO's role in European security without its *raison d'être* had yet to be answered, an opportunity to rethink European security architecture seemed to present itself. The end of bipolar confrontation removed the constraints that had prevented the European Allies from playing a more active role in European security and members of the EU could also now consider how to continue the process of integration in the areas of security and defence policy. The Maastricht Treaty, signed in November 1991, saw the emergence of a new policy – the CFSP – which embraced all the means by which the EU sought to exercise influence in foreign affairs. The Maastricht Treaty also anticipated a revival of the WEU, which would play an essential role as the EU's defence arm, by implementing CFSP decisions. Alongside these developments in European integration, additional factors gave impetus to the discussion of a greater European role in European security. Calls for increased burden-sharing were emanating from across the Atlantic and the nature of the United States' future commitment to European security was uncertain, given its lack of enthusiasm for dealing with the outbreak of conflict in the Balkans. Under these influences, the conflict in the former Yugoslavia seemed to herald 'the hour of Europe' and an opportunity for the EU to put into practice the policies it had recently agreed. As Chapter One demonstrated, this European approach to the challenges of the post-Cold War security environment was fundamentally flawed. The main weaknesses of the EU's approach to the former Yugoslavia – divided diplomacy and military feebleness – resulted in political and military dependence on the United States and the subsequent emergence of NATO as the only credible solution to the Balkan crises.

The deployment of the IFOR in 1995 seemed to end the debate about the EU's role in European security.[9] This was a crucial development for proponents of a greater European role, because it seemed to confirm that, for the moment, a European military capability was out of reach. As a result the EU's plans for a security and defence capability were abandoned. This is a significant conclusion to draw, particularly with respect to the position of France. France initially blocked NATO involvement in the former Yugoslavia, because it perceived that this was encroaching on the sorts of missions envisaged for a European military capability. The realities of European security in the 1990s undermined this approach and, in December 1995, the French Foreign Minister, Hervé de Charette, announced France's intention to pursue a different approach to strengthening Europe's contribution to European security. This move heralded the beginning of a *rapprochement* between France and NATO, which was both an acknowledgement of the lack of European support for a European military capability constructed outside NATO and a recognition that only NATO was able to cope with the realities of European security.

the european security and defence identity

Although the deployment of the IFOR answered the question of which institution would manage European security, the question of how a greater European contribution to European security could be facilitated remained. Due to the consolidated role of NATO, the answer to this question was: from *within* NATO rather than outside. A key development was the initiation of a process of internal adaptation, in particular the European Security and Defence Identity (ESDI), which became the framework through which a more substantial European contribution to NATO could be achieved. At the January 1994 Brussels Summit the creation of an ESDI within NATO was first proposed.[10] The ESDI had two main goals: first, it would provide an arrangement whereby Europeans could assume a larger share of the burden for security missions through access to those NATO assets and capabilities that were essential, such as logistical support and C^3I; second, it would reinforce the transatlantic link, because the provision of a mechanism that enabled the European Allies to conduct military operations using NATO assets would meet the need for transatlantic burden-sharing and reduce the likelihood of American frustration with the Europeans' inability to act.

the combined joint task force concept

An essential part of the ESDI process was the Combined Joint Task Force (CJTF) concept; 'combined' referring to the co-operation of two or more countries and 'joint' referring to two or more services. The CJTF was an important development, because it was the military expression of the ESDI and therefore built on it. The CJTF concept offered two advantages for NATO's post-Cold War missions. Its primary objective and benefit was the versatility and flexibility it presented in creating coalitions of the willing which could perform a wide range of tasks beyond Alliance territory. These coalitions would not be restricted to NATO members but could also incorporate non-NATO members, particularly those participating in NATO's outreach and partnership programmes. Second, because the CJTF concept was a device designed to enable the formation of coalitions within the NATO context, there was also scope for these coalitions to be *all-European* if the United States or Canada chose not to intervene. For proponents of a strengthened European role in European security the emergence of ESDI and the CJTF concept were highly significant: the CJTF mechanism would provide the framework for potentially all-European coalitions, European command of the CJTF was ensured through the involvement of the WEU and the ESDI would provide access to the assets that the WEU-led CJTF would need to conduct military operations. These mechanisms would therefore reinforce the European pillar within

NATO through the provision of forces that were 'separable but not separate'.

NATO added substance to this conceptual framework at its 1996 Berlin Summit, where the structures for an effective European pillar and the means through which ESDI could be conducted – the CJTF concept – were officially set in place. This event was significant, because agreement on these mechanisms could only be reached when France came to accept that a European capability could not be built separately from NATO. France's acceptance of the weaknesses of a separate European military capability and its *rapprochement* with NATO made these developments possible. The WEU was designated as the institution with which NATO would work to improve European capabilities. Moreover, intricate 'Berlin Plus' arrangements were established: a set of post-Berlin discusions designed to tighten the nuts and bolts on the ESDI and CJTF mechanisms and assure the Allies' access to NATO assets. The Berlin Plus process was crucial, as although the Berlin Summit had agreed the general framework there was still a need to sort out the details. Berlin Plus sought to answer a number of questions vital to the successful realization of the ESDI concept, for example, the circumstances in which NATO assets could be used, the procedures that would be followed if NATO were already using its assets, and so on.

Although much conceptual progress had been made in Berlin, subsequent discussions highlighted one of the key weaknesses of the ESDI concept: the nature of 'NATO' assets. NATO has very few collective assets – those that belong to NATO rather than to individual members – and most of those it does have are not particularly useful for force projection. The 'NATO' assets on which a WEU-led CJTF would be dependent for its operations – air-lift, sea-lift, airborne refuelling capabilities and satellite intelligence – were, and remain, primarily US-owned. This was an important stumbling block, as it meant that the United States could exercise a major degree of control over WEU-led operations by refusing or restricting access to its assets or simply being unable to provide access to them if they were already being used. This state of affairs had obvious implications for the development of a strengthened 'European pillar' within NATO.

In spite of these outstanding practical issues, the conceptual progress made in Berlin meant there was a real possibility of an ESDI satisfactory to both the United States and the European NATO Allies: NATO was recognized as the primary European security organization and through the ESDI the European Allies' contribution to European security would be enhanced and acknowledged. As a result, Europeans and Americans alike welcomed the Berlin decisions as allowing the European Allies to take on more responsibility for their own security, thus addressing the issues of burden-sharing and military capabilities and strengthening the Alliance.[11]

toward an eu 'solution'

Despite the changes that had been initiated and the progress that had been made to enhance the European pillar within NATO, a number of set-backs emerged. The first stumbling block was the weaknesses of 'Berlin Plus'. The complexity of the issues on the agenda meant that progress was very slow. In particular, the United States showed a reluctance to allow the Europeans access to assets essential to any WEU-led operation. Although understandable, the United States' objections to allowing Europeans access to sensitive but crucial US assets highlighted the limits of the ESDI process and brought into question how useful it would be in facilitating potentially all-European coalition operations.

The second set-back was the Franco-American dispute over AFSOUTH, NATO's Southern Command. A potential change to the command of AFSOUTH emerged in 1997 and France saw an opportunity to put the ESDI concept to the test. Its perception of the ESDI process was that it meant real European influence as it was, after all, meant to strengthen the European pillar within NATO. France, as a Mediterranean European power, asked to take over command of AFSOUTH; a request denied by the United States, which kept the command role. In many respects, this dispute was avoidable, as there never was a prospect of French command of AFSOUTH: even if the United States had supported it, the other Mediterranean NATO partners would have objected. In any case, for France, the AFSOUTH dispute was highly indicative of what ESDI was really about: an *identity* that brought little real European influence within NATO, rather than a *capability*. As a result, *rapprochement* between France and NATO stalled and the ESDI process became blocked.

The final set-back was the legacy of NATO's problematic Balkan interventions and, in particular, the 'Kosovo effect' – the sense of impotence experienced by the Allies during Operation Allied Force. Chapter Two showed how the nature of the United States' role in the former Yugoslavia – missions that were low on its list of priorities and its disproportionately large contribution, because of the inadequacies of the other Allies – led to a questioning of the precise nature of the bargain the US was striking with its NATO Allies. The remaining Allies, for their part, concluded that the United States was not fully committed to NATO's out-of-area roles and that it would only get involved and define strategy on its own terms, which meant a reduction of European influence in spite of the ESDI. Moreover, even if the Europeans led an all-European coalition, the US would not necessarily allow it to use the assets it needed. This had major implications, particularly for the EU, as it reflected the fact that, whilst the EU was an economic giant, it remained a military dwarf, unable to intervene even in conflicts in its own backyard. The conclusions drawn throughout the 1990s increasingly indicated the need for a European solution, in spite of ESDI. Moreover, as a result of the stalling of France's *rapprochement* with NATO, European members increasingly came to the conclusion that any European military capability would have to be constructed outside NATO and, in fact, using the EU.

the saint malo defence initiative and the emergence of esdp

As a consequence of these difficulties, the European Security and Defence Policy (ESDP), an EU political project, emerged in the late 1990s. The British Prime Minister, Tony Blair, launched the ESDP process in Pörtschach, Austria in October 1998 where he stated that he was in favour of a European security and defence capability that would enable EU member states to act together without the United States.[12] Blair's declaration lifted a fifty-year British veto on the development of such a European capability outside NATO. Two months later, in December 1998, during the annual Franco-British summit in Saint Malo, the French President, Jacques Chirac, and Mr Blair added substance to this initial concept and announced a bold and creative Franco-British defence initiative. The Saint Malo declaration affirmed that NATO remained 'the foundation of the collective defence of its members'.[13] However, it also stated that the EU should have 'the capacity for *autonomous* action, backed up by credible military forces, the means to decide to use them and a readiness to do so, in order to respond to international crises'.[14] The declaration therefore left open the possibility that the EU could act outside NATO, thus potentially providing an additional EU military capability for Europe.

1999 saw the emergence of key EU initiatives building upon the Saint Malo Declaration. The Cologne European Council, in June

1999, reached agreement to transfer the functions of the WEU to the EU, with the exception of the WEU's Article V collective defence clause. This provided the basis for a shift from WEU–NATO relations to EU–NATO relations. Moreover, a Headline Goal (HG) was announced at the December 1999 European Council meeting in Helsinki, which outlined the EU's intention to create a Rapid Reaction Force (RRF) comprising 50,000–60,000 troops, available at 60 days notice, attended by appropriate air and maritime assets and sustainable in theatre for up to one year. The RRF would conduct the so-called 'Petersberg' tasks – humanitarian and rescue missions, peacekeeping and tasks of combat forces in crisis management, including peacemaking – when NATO as a whole chose not to intervene in a conflict, and would rely on forces and assets normally assigned to NATO. The reliance of the EU on NATO assets therefore built upon the foundations of the Berlin Plus procedures. EU members committed themselves to meet the HG by 2003.

The emergence of the Franco-British defence initiative and the delineation of the HG were significant in several ways for the burden-sharing and capabilities debates taking place within NATO but in one way in particular. Developing a European military capability would clearly serve the purpose of continuing European integration in defence, a process that had stalled in the 1990s but this development was also perceived by many as increasing the likelihood of tangible improvements in European capabilities. This was because many saw increasing defence spending as being easier to sell politically in the name of the EU, rather than NATO. The EU might therefore be more effective in bringing about changes in the budgets and spending priorities of its members than NATO had been. These potential improvements would of course have a knock-on effect for NATO, because the improvement of European capabilities would make the European Allies attractive partners, rather than problems, which would also address the burden-sharing debate. By using the EU to construct a European military capability, the transatlantic link would be safeguarded, a reversal of the traditional logic of the 'Atlanticist' position represented by the United Kingdom and others.[15]

the defence capabilities initiative

The stalling of the ESDI process and the emergence of EU initiatives did not mean that NATO's own capabilities initiatives stopped. Alongside developments in EU security and defence policy, NATO launched its first major response to the inadequacies of many of the

NATO Allies' capabilities in the Defence Capabilities Initiative DCI). Improving capabilities was clearly an essential aspect of the ESDI, so the DCI was seen as a logical component of this process. The DCI emerged as a result of proposals from the Pentagon in 1998 and was unveiled at the Washington Summit in April 1999. The DCI was a set of 58 goals, which established several overlapping priority areas: deployability and mobility of Alliance forces, sustainability, surviv-ability, effective engagement and interoperable command, control and information systems.[16] Enhanced mobility and deploy-ability would ensure that forces would be able to deploy quickly beyond NATO territory. Improvements in sustainability would enable the Allies better to maintain forces at a distance from their home bases and ensure that there were sufficient numbers for force rotation. Focusing on survivability would ensure that forces and infrastruc-ture were better protected against threats. Advances in effective engagement would ensure that the Allies would have the ability suc-cessfully to engage an enemy in all types of operation. Last, interop-erable communications would ensure that command, control and information systems were compatible, enabling forces from different NATO countries to work together efficiently. Through improve-ments in all these areas, NATO's future operations would become more effective and members agreed to channel their efforts into improving capabilities within the DCI framework.

The DCI did not emerge because of the ESDI debate but was complementary to it, because improvements in European capabil-ities would automatically result in an enhanced role, strengthening the European pillar as the European Allies would be less reliant on the United States. It was also expected that the DCI would have some success, as, rather than being based on theoretical situations, the goals identified in the DCI were based on the experience of NATO operations in the Balkans. As a result of the DCI in April 1999 and the HG in December 1999, an attempt to reach capability goals was pursued both within NATO and the EU.

the impact of 9/11: toward real improvements in capabilities?

Following 9/11, ensuring improvements in capabilities gained new importance. The significance of the capabilities gap was reinforced in the initial response to 9/11, because although the United States' decision to act alone in Afghanistan was greeted with almost universal disapproval, many of the Allies were aware that they were unable to contribute in any meaningful way. This conclusion was clearly important for the immediate response to 9/11 but it also had implications for future military interventions, as lack of military capability would limit political options, thus making US military unilateralism inevitable rather than avoidable. The former Secretary General Lord Robertson's long-standing emphasis on 'capabilities, capabilities, capabilities' increased post-9/11, due to the realization that NATO's future vitality and relevance to the war against terrorism was on the line, as was the future of transatlantic security relations more generally.

In preparation for the June 2002 meeting of Defence Ministers, NATO carried out an assessment of the progress that had been made by members since the launch of the DCI. The review concluded that if spending trends continued, the Allies would only implement 50 per cent of the goals. Although some improvements had occurred, only 26 of the 58 specific goals had been fully realized, 16 had been partially realized and little progress had been made on the remaining 16. There were particular weaknesses in areas such as suppression of enemy air defence and jamming, combat identification and levels of deployable forces. In spite of US-led attempts to bridge the capabilities gap within NATO by means of the DCI, the gap between the Allies remained, due in large part to the failure of the Allies to take the DCI seriously but also because the DCI was too ambitious and too unfocused. The experience of NATO's post-Cold War interventions, together with the lack of progress of the DCI, brought into question whether NATO would – or could – intervene as an Alliance again. The EU's stated aim of reaching the HG by 2003 was also looking unlikely and without new impetus to these initiatives, the prospects for improving capabilities – whether within the EU or NATO – seemed very bleak.

In spite of the conclusions that can be drawn about the lack of progress made, the impact of 9/11 has resulted in some potentially far-reaching changes in NATO's capabilities initiatives. At the June 2002 meeting of Defence Ministers, NATO Allies quickly acknowledged that their future contribution to the war against terrorism would be limited by their capabilities. Paragraph 1 of the Statement on Capabilities issued after the June 2002 meetings of Defence Ministers states: 'The range of actions which NATO will be able to take in the future in response to terrorism and other challenges will depend on the success of our efforts to modernize the Alliance's military capabilities'. Paragraph 4 reiterates this essential need:

We recognise that the ability of the Alliance to fulfil the full range of its missions in the changing strategic environment will depend largely upon our ability to increase substantially the proportion of our combat forces and support forces that are available for deployment on operations beyond home territory or where there is no substantial host nation support. This is a significant challenge, on which work has already begun in the light of the force structure review. We are committed to meet it.[17]

As a result, there was recognition that a greater effort to improve capabilities was required, which would focus on capabilities essential to the full range of NATO operations. This resulted in the unveiling of a new initiative at the Prague Summit – the Prague Capabilities Commitment (PCC) – to replace the DCI.

prague capabilities commitment

The PCC is different from the DCI, as it is based on NATO member states making national commitments and agreeing to specific deadlines, rather than simply setting general goals without securing national commitments. This ensures that there is more pressure on NATO members to deliver the goods, as they will be 'named and shamed' if they fail. It is also far more focused than the DCI and prioritizes four key operational capability areas: ensuring secure command, communications and information superiority, improving interoperability of deployed forces and key aspects of combat effectiveness, ensuring rapidly deployable, sustainable forces and defending against chemical, biological, radiological and nuclear (CBRN) attacks. If the objectives of the PCC are fulfilled, the number of large troop-carrying aircraft in Europe will quadruple, a fleet of air-to-air refuelling aircraft will be established, the number of precision-guided munitions will increase by approximately 40 per cent and most of NATO's deployable forces will be equipped to defend against CBRN attacks. The PCC is therefore designed to encourage interoperability and close widening gaps in the capabilities of the Allies.

The PCC also addresses one of the critical influences on the capabilities debate identified earlier in this chapter, namely, spending limited resources more efficiently. Two important solutions it encourages are role specialization and the pooling of resources and assets. Specialization is an important component of any capabilities drive, as it can focus attention on areas where there are critical deficiencies and also ensures that smaller NATO members are able to contribute to the overall effort by filling niche capabilities. In this respect, the challenges of 9/11 have perhaps shifted the balance in the smaller NATO members' favour, as they can increasingly play on the same level as the larger forces. If the need is for special forces, for example, Norway, potentially, has just as much capability as the United Kingdom. Encouraging more efficient use of resources, through joint procurement and asset sharing also meets the need for existing budgets to be spent more wisely and effectively. This in turn increases the possibility of improving capabilities without large increases in defence spending.

There are, of course, drawbacks to some of the aspects of the PCC, in particular the implications of specialization. This new emphasis makes it unlikely that any country will attempt to fulfil the full range of military tasks. Of the Allies other than the United States, only the United Kingdom and France are likely to retain anything near the full range, although in comparison to the United States their capabilities will be far less advanced and much smaller in size. Specialization may create political dilemmas for other NATO members, as they will have to be reliant on fellow members for tasks that have traditionally been performed by their own armed forces. There is also a danger that smaller NATO members may attempt to free-ride, by providing capabilities that, whilst necessary, are relatively inexpensive to produce, for example medical or decontamination units. Ensuring all members spend appropriate sums on defence will be a key challenge. In spite of these potential risks, the PCC is the most innovative solution that NATO has put forward to address the capabilities gap and the one that holds the best chance of tangible improvements in its collective capabilities.

the nato response force

In addition to the PCC, NATO announced the creation of a NATO Response Force (NRF). This is not separate, but is designed to work with the PCC as a catalyst to quicken the push toward improved capabilities. The proposal originated at an informal meeting of NATO Defence Ministers in Warsaw on 24–25 September 2002 who were briefed by the US Secretary of Defense, Donald Rumsfeld, about the creation of a permanent NATO response force of 5,000 to 20,000 troops. The Defence Ministers approved the concept of a rapid response force and sent it for NATO and SHAPE consideration before it was presented to Heads of State and Government at the Prague Summit in November 2002. American calls for a NATO strike force resulted in the formal decision to form an NRF at the Prague Summit.

The NRF will comprise small and highly mobile units, able to deploy within seven to 30 days to regions beyond Europe, where NATO interests are threatened, and could fulfil a range of missions, from evacuations to humanitarian interventions to all-out war. At the top level is a small, rapid response capability of mostly special forces, supported by units that can deploy once the initial group is in place. Due to reach full operational capability by October 2006, the NRF will provide NATO with a self-contained and self-sufficient combined joint expeditionary force, able to respond at short notice to international crisis situations whether in the Euro-Atlantic area or well beyond. Unlike other interventions, where NATO has assembled a force in response to a specific situation, the NRF will be a standing force available for immediate use. The exact composition of the NRF would of course be determined by the nature and scope of the operation in question.

The NRF is a highly important development, for a number of reasons. First, it is a response to the recognition that the growing capabilities gap between the United States and the remaining Allies would sideline NATO in future conflicts. In September 2002, when the NRF had yet to be formalized, the US Defense Secretary Donald Rumsfeld commented, 'If NATO does not have a force that is quick and agile, which can deploy in days or weeks instead of months or years, then it will not have much to offer the world in the 21st century'.[18]

Second, the NRF was US-proposed and can be seen as an attempt to restore the military dynamism behind NATO. This is a very important consideration, because it arguably demonstrates continued US interest in using NATO as a military instrument.[19]

Third, the NRF does not hinge on significant increases in defence spending by the NATO Allies. Richard Kugler, who was one of the main architects of the plan, estimated that the NATO force would absorb only 2 to 3 per cent of total European defence spending, which could potentially overcome one of the obstacles that plagued NATO's attempts to bring into line and enhance its collective military capabilities.

Fourth, the NRF is significant because of the progress that has been made to date. In October 2003, eleven months after it had been approved and one year before the initial NRF was due to be activated, the NRF was launched at a ceremony in the Netherlands as the centre-piece of a new global strategy to fight WMD and international terrorism.

Last, the NRF reflects transatlantic consensus on the need for a high-readiness force, which would also serve as a mechanism for the improvement of NATO's collective military capabilities. Agreement to work toward the NRF reflects a consensus within NATO about the threats faced by the Allies, the kinds of operations that will need to be performed and the kinds of forces that will be required. The willingness to work together, as reflected by the NRF, represents a major step forward. For all of these reasons, it is considered to be 'one of the most important changes in the NATO Alliance since the signing of the Washington Treaty over 50 years ago'.[20]

A third and final strategy that NATO has developed since 9/11 is the transformation of its command structures, in particular the ACT, which is responsible for the transformation of NATO's military capabilities and designed to underpin the PCC, the NRF and any future capabilities initiatives that NATO may undertake.

future prospects

Throughout the 1990s there was a series of initiatives, initially within NATO but later also in the EU, designed to enhance the capabilities of the Allies with the aim of rebalancing the transatlantic relationship. This resulted in a complex debate that absorbed a significant amount of time and attention with respect to the formulation of institutional developments and intricate agreements, without producing any real improvements. Although NATO's record has been poor, it could be argued that the prospects of real progress in these areas have improved greatly since 9/11: the arrangements of the Berlin Plus process, guaranteeing EU access to NATO assets, were finally agreed in March 2003, the EU met its HG in 2003, NATO has launched two major, innovative, capabilities initiatives, one of which – the NRF – is progressing faster than expected and it has also transformed its command structure in order to underpin these changes. However, whilst these developments are encouraging, it would be premature to consider that the main obstacles in the capabilities debate have been overcome and that the Alliance is consequently well on the way to being 're-balanced'.

First, since the capabilities debate began, the onus has been on the European and Canadian Allies to improve their capabilities rather than on the United States to facilitate the process, even though criticisms can be made regarding the United States' reluctance to allow its assets to be used by all-European coalitions in NATO or EU-led operations. There may now be an agreement about access to NATO assets, but it remains to be seen whether this agreement will always work in practice. Operation Allied Harmony, which was handed over to the EU and renamed Operation Concordia in March 2003, provided the first example of the 'Berlin Plus' arrangements being employed. The EU will assume responsibility for the SFOR operation in 2004, a move that will also rely on the Berlin Plus mechanisms. Many have interpreted the success of Operation Concordia and the first-ever use of the Berlin Plus procedures as proof that it works. As noted previously, however, access to NATO assets can only be termed 'assured' if there are guarantees that the United States is willing to allow its assets to be used in the short-, medium- or long-term *and* is able to provide access, that is it is not already itself using those assets. This is a very questionable assumption to make, particularly given the current demands on the US military. Schake comments, in this respect, 'a real assurance of availability would mean that the EU's crisis-management priorities would take precedence over other global responsibilities and interests of the US'.[21] The strains on the US military resulting from continuing commitments and requirements around the world were apparent even before 9/11, which further exacerbated the situation. Given these constraints, it is difficult to imagine a situation in which the EU could have *guarantees* – which is what 'assured access' implies – that US assets would be available or able to be redirected for use by an EU-led force. The 'agreement' about assured access to NATO assets must therefore be seen as a theoretical rather than an actual result.

Second, the prospect of 'assured access' to NATO assets has done little to encourage members to spend more on defence and, equally importantly, to spend more wisely. It is perhaps indicative that, although some predicted that improvements would be easier to accomplish in the name of the EU rather than NATO, the evidence thus far indicates that the EU's record in this area has not been substantially better than NATO's. The experience of the 1990s and the political and military problems that emerged as a result of the capabilities gap do not appear to have been sufficiently troubling to change the *status quo*. This brings into question how serious the Allies are about enhancing the EU's role in security and defence and how seriously they take safeguarding the transatlantic relationship institutionalized within NATO.

Third, although the EU 'met' the HG in 2003 – a point which is debatable, given its elasticity and numerous contradictory analyses – the RRF has been developed primarily to enable the EU to perform

Petersberg tasks, rather than to tackle the capabilities gaps among the NATO Allies and in particular between the United States and other Allies.[22] Even though some of the assets that are required for Petersberg tasks, for example, airlift, are often the same ones needed for high-intensity operations, it appears that EU members have prioritized European integration over the demands of transatlantic relations, which may have serious implications for interoperability among the Allies. In this sense, the development of the RRF may have hindered rather than helped efforts to improve NATO's collective military capabilities. Moreover, the emergence of the RRF and the NRF increases the likelihood that the efficiency of the EU and NATO's operations will be compromised. The RRF and the NRF are, of course, two different forces, designed for different threats and different types of conflict. However, they will draw on the same forces and because resources are finite, the conduct of an EU operation may affect the availability of forces for a NATO operation and vice versa.

Fourth, recent developments have indicated that the EU's ESDP poses a potential challenge to NATO. Although a thorough discussion of this challenge is beyond the scope of this chapter, it stems from the spectrum of opinion about the parameters and eventual outcome of ESDP that has characterized the intra-EU debate from the outset. Although the United Kingdom and others pursued ESDP primarily, if not exclusively, as a means to improve capabilities, some EU members, notably France, have a far more ambitious view of its long-term nature. In the context of the EU's discussion of a Draft Constitution in 2003, some of the EU members that share France's view of ESDP advocated the inclusion of a mutual assistance clause, similar to NATO's Article 5 collective defence provision, as well as structured co-operation that would allow those EU members wanting to deepen their involvement in ESDP to do so. The Italian presidency of the EU eventually put forward a compromise position on mutual defence, to be incorporated into the Draft Constitutional Treaty, with the important caveat that any such commitment would remain 'consistent with commitments under NATO' for those states which are NATO members.[23] This appears to end the debate for the moment. However, the fact that such proposals have emerged so early in the development of ESDP raises questions about the future scope and direction of ESDP and how this might affect NATO.

Fifth, 9/11 led to a renewed commitment by the Allies to improve collective capabilities within NATO; clearly a worthwhile exercise. However, there is a degree of *déjà vu*, as NATO has been attempting to address this problematic issue for the whole of the post-Cold War period, with little success. The PCC and the NRF may successfully address NATO's capabilities imbalance, but they remain potential rather than actual capabilities. It remains to be seen whether 9/11 proves to be a sufficient catalyst for change and whether post-9/11 commitments, particularly those designed to equip the NRF, will translate into tangible improvements.

Even if the PCC targets are met, which is far from certain given the ambiguous statement by NATO leaders in June 2004 that the implementation of current capabilities targets was 'progressing',[24] there are potential dangers associated with the NRF. Some have perceived the NRF as making NATO a 'tool box' that will enable the United States to select the Allies and capabilities it needs for specific missions. This 'pick 'n' mix' approach, which has resulted from the recent emphasis placed on the 'mission determines the coalition' concept may progressively undermine NATO's traditional unity. Regardless of this possible outcome, without initiatives such as the NRF interoperability between the United States and other Allies will almost certainly be a lost cause. The potential benefits of the NRF far outweigh these potential costs, because the NRF is probably the last hope for NATO to maintain the United States' interest in its function as a military instrument, which has crucial implications, both for NATO and also for general transatlantic security relations.

conclusion

NATO's capabilities problem since the end of the Cold War has been due not to a lack of innovation but to a lack of implementation. The European and Canadian Allies must take the greatest responsibility for this lack of progress because most have wanted influence and authority without committing the necessary resources. 9/11 has increased the urgency of resolving some of the problems that have been prominent in this aspect of the relationships among the Allies since the beginning of the 1990s. In spite of much institution-building in the EU and much policy-framing in NATO there appears to have been little real progress. The challenges of rationalizing defence spending and investing substantial amounts of money remain, but neither of these is likely to be met. The most positive assessment that can be made of the capability initiatives launched by NATO is that they remain 'work in progress'. As a result, NATO remains asymmetric, in terms of the capabilities and commitments of its members. Capabilities, which have traditionally been NATO's weakest link, remain a crucial influence on NATO's future vitality, but not one in which there is much more certainty post- than pre-9/11.

Transforming NATO forces and improving NATO's military capabilities, which will result in the military credibility that NATO arguably currently lacks, will be one area that will guarentee NATO's ongoing relevance and utility both to the Allies as a whole and to the United States in particular. Ensuring that NATO is also equipped to deal with the 'new' security threats of WMD and international terrorism that now dominate the US' agenda is the other. It is to NATO's role in addressing these threats that we now turn.

summary

- A burden-sharing debate characterized Cold War discussions between the Allies and has become a far more serious issue post-Cold War. The desire of the European Allies to play a greater role in NATO, and in European security more generally, has largely been frustrated, because of a capabilities gap between the United States and other NATO Allies. The political and military implications of this gap for NATO's past, present and future operations have caused improving capabilities to become a central challenge for NATO.

- Although Allies other than the United States initially attempted to enhance their role in European security using the WEU, the weakness of existing mechanisms ensured that NATO eventually became the means through which this role would be enhanced. NATO subsequently developed the ESDI and CJTF concepts and initiated Berlin Plus procedures that were designed to allow the Allies access to vital NATO – or rather US – assets.

- The limitations of NATO's mechanisms caused an EU solution to re-emerge in the latter part of the 1990s. Although the subsequent outlining of a HG to equip a RRF was an EU project, potential improvements in capabilities also had benefits for NATO.

- In order to address the capabilities gap, NATO launched the DCI in 1999 but little progress was made. A new, more focused initiative was launched post-9/11, as was the NRF; both were designed to be catalysts for change. These changes were underpinned by the transformation in NATO's command structure.

- Despite conceptual progress, there remain a number of obstacles to overcome and key issues to resolve in order for NATO to be 're-balanced' and for tangible improvements in capabilities to occur. NATO's capabilities initiatives remain 'works in progress' and their eventual outcomes hold the key to NATO's future as a military instrument.

an alliance challenged: nato and 'new' security threats

Enhancing its ability to fight the 'new' security threats of WMD and international terrorism has become a key focus of NATO reform since the terrorist attacks on New York and Washington, DC on 11 September 2001. However, discussion about NATO's role in addressing these security threats is not new. Throughout the 1990s, debates took place among the Allies about the extent to which combating WMD and international terrorism should be a part of NATO's post-Cold War missions but they failed to resolve the issue. 9/11 provoked a major shift in the attention accorded by NATO to combating WMD and international terrorism and initiated some significant changes to its role in these areas. Combating WMD and international terrorism is now perceived as essential to preserving NATO's relevance in a changed strategic context, which has strengthened the long-standing American position that if NATO fails adequately to address the most pressing security concerns of the time, it will gradually fade into irrelevance. The current debate about its role in combating WMD and international terrorism is, therefore, not simply about what NATO can add to the existing efforts of other international organizations, but goes right to the heart of its future significance. None the less, although NATO's role is now more defined, significant obstacles remain, which brings into question whether the new focus on combating WMD and international terrorism will be sufficient to ensure its long-term vitality.

This chapter maps the efforts that NATO has made, since the end of the Cold War, to address the problem of WMD and, more recently, to address what is widely perceived to be a growing nexus between WMD and international terrorism. The chapter begins by demonstrating how the 1990–1991 Gulf War shaped NATO's view of the threats posed by WMD, which provoked increasing calls for the Alliance to deal with this threat. The differences among the Allies, the compromises that were necessary when the policy was formulated and the factors that influenced the different conclusions reached are identified. The impact of 9/11 is then addressed, demonstrating why it increased the importance accorded by NATO to WMD and, in particular, to international terrorism. The changes that were initiated and the progress that was made are discussed. The chapter concludes by identifying some of the obstacles remaining for NATO to overcome as it strives to redefine its approach to WMD and international terrorism.

Before beginning an analysis of NATO's response to WMD and international terrorism it is important to recognize a crucial change in the nature of the debate, which has occurred since 9/11. Until then, the debates about how to respond to WMD and international terrorism were, largely, separate. The WMD debate focused on states that were seeking to acquire or already possessed WMD materials or expertise rather than on non-state actors, such as terrorist groups, even though NATO acknowledged early in the post-Cold War period that non-state actors might attempt to acquire WMD.[1] The debate about terrorism, which was minimal within NATO, focused on domestic rather than international terrorism. This chapter reflects the characteristics of the debates that took place within NATO about its appropriate response to WMD and international terrorism initially by focusing on how NATO attempted to address the WMD, rather than the terrorist, threat. However, since 9/11, there has been a change in the parameters of the debates. WMD and international terrorism are now increasingly linked and much attention focuses on the possibility of non-state actors seeking to acquire WMD materials or expertise or on the use of WMD by non-state actors.[2] The contemporary WMD threat is increasingly two-dimensional, as it encompasses the threats posed both by states and non-state actors and added to this is the debate about international terrorism, regardless of the weapons that might be employed.

It is important to recognize the changed nature of the debate about WMD and international terrorism not simply because it explains the shift in focus by NATO since 9/11 but also because it has added complexity to the discussion of how it can respond. Of particular significance is the emergence of non-state actors as a key feature. As this chapter will show, the threat posed by non-state actors is even more difficult for NATO to address than the threat posed by states. This feature of the contemporary debate may be an important influence on NATO's ability to respond to the challenges posed by WMD and international terrorism.

historical context

The debate over WMD was an established part of the Cold War and WMD were an important concern for NATO. Certain features of the Cold War debate differentiate it from the contemporary debate, however. First, bipolarity was a defining feature of the Cold War context and the nation state was central. In this respect, the main players were the Soviet Union and the United States, given their possession of large quantities of WMD.

Second, the threat posed by WMD was Euro-centric, as the battleground was most likely to be Western Europe rather than regions beyond. Apart from the Cuban missile crisis, there was never an instance where either of the North American Allies were threatened by WMD.

Third, of all the different types of WMD, strategic nuclear weapons featured far more prominently than biological, chemical or radiological weapons. This was not simply because it was anticipated that any conflict between the superpowers would involve nuclear, rather than biological or chemical weapons; it was also because of the importance of the US strategic nuclear commitment to Western Europe, which was designed to deter the Soviet Union from acting aggressively or attempting to coerce the Allies.

Fourth, there was a high risk of conflict escalation involving nuclear weapons during the Cold War, because a first strike by the United States would result in an equivalent or greater response by the Soviet Union and so on.

Fifth, whilst there was a high risk of conflict escalation, 'balance' was a stabilizing force. The concept of Mutual Assured Destruction (MAD) was stabilizing and a deterrent, as it underscored the risk of annihilation. In the event of a first strike by the United States on the Soviet Union, the Soviet Union would automatically retaliate using equal or even greater force, which would continue until both superpowers were destroyed. This realization ensured that the risk of the use of WMD by the Soviet Union or the United States was slight. Moreover, a series of mechanisms sought to encourage 'balance'. Arms control agreements and arms reduction agreements in the 1980s, such as the Strategic Arms Limitation Talks (SALT) and the Strategic Arms Reduction Treaties (START) I and II were significant in this respect.

Last, arms control agreements ensured that countries possessing WMD were known and their number relatively small. As a result of these features and mechanisms, the Cold War environment was dangerous but stable. Although events, such as the 1980s Iran-Iraq war, demonstrated that certain states would use WMD in conflict, these incidents were not seen as a direct threat to NATO. Following the end of the Cold War, however, perceptions of the risks posed by WMD changed.

the 1991 persian gulf war

The key event that provoked a shift in the attention accorded to WMD by NATO was the 1991 Gulf War, which highlighted a new set of challenges and changed the context of the WMD debate. The possession of WMD by Saddam Hussein, who was volatile, unpredictable and did not seem to respect traditional rules of engagement, showed that the stability and predictability of the Cold War was over. Iraq's use of chemical and biological weapons during the Iran–Iraq war and the possible use of these weapons during Operation Desert Storm, was a further problem, as it demonstrated that Cold War concepts such as deterrence now seemed to be redundant. The conclusion reached in NATO capitals was that it was increasingly likely that WMD would be used in future conflicts.

The third issue was the implications of these changes for future conflicts. Although the United States' conventional military superiority ensured defeat for any nation that fought it, its forces were ill-equipped for conflicts involving WMD. It became increasingly likely that states and non-state actors would either use WMD in the future, as a form of asymmetric warfare, to counter Western military strength or would threaten the use of WMD as a means to dissuade forces from intervening in regional conflicts.

The discoveries made by UN inspectors, following the victory of the international coalition, which revealed that Iraq's weapons programmes were far more advanced than previously thought, was a fourth challenge. This realization heightened concern about WMD proliferation around the world, as it confirmed the spread of the technology and the acquisition of longer-range and more advanced means of delivery by states. Of equal importance, the progress made by Iraq in developing WMD capabilities also showed that traditional non-proliferation efforts were failing.

The geographic location of states acquiring WMD, which had direct significance for NATO, was a final issue. Many of these states were situated in regions on NATO's periphery, such as the Mediterranean or the Middle East, which raised the prospect of WMD posing a direct threat to NATO territory and populations, particularly those in Europe.

In addition to these five challenges highlighted by the Gulf War, the transfer of expertise, materials and technology from the former Soviet Union into the hands of states wanting to acquire new or to improve existing capabilities added to the increasing visibility of WMD in the early 1990s. The increasing prominence of so-called 'flat-pack proliferation' demonstrated the growing problem of the WMD black market. Stemming the flow of expertise and 'loose nukes', particularly, although not exclusively, from the former Soviet Union, posed an additional challenge in the post-Cold War era.

Rather than posing a single type of threat, events in the early post-Cold War era demonstrated instead that a number of existing WMD threats to NATO had been exacerbated and new threats had emerged. One direct threat was the threatened or actual use of WMD against NATO populations and territory, a scenario that, during the Cold War, concerned the European far more than the North American members, given their closeness to the Soviet Union. Although the Soviet threat diminished after the end of the Cold War, the European Allies, and Turkey in particular, remained the most vulnerable to WMD because of their proximity to the Middle East, one of the main areas of proliferation. However, this direct threat was, and remains, theoretical and potential rather than actual as the assessment is based on geographic proximity alone and does not take into consideration the intentions of states possessing WMD. Moreover, the risks facing the European Allies are variable, given Libya's decision to terminate its WMD programmes in 2004. A second direct threat was the possibility of an opponent using or threatening to use WMD against NATO forces operating in theatre, whether in Europe or beyond, which could either cause a conflict to escalate or deter them from intervening in the first place.

In addition to these direct threats, there were a number of indirect threats posed by WMD. The danger of accidents involving WMD, the unauthorized use of WMD and regional instabilities caused by the proliferation of WMD resulting in changes in regional power balances in areas of vital interest to NATO were all significant. Potentially, the most serious indirect threat was the transfer of WMD expertise, materials and technology from regions far from NATO territory and populations to regions within their reach. This last indirect threat was particularly significant as such transfers could result in the emergence of a direct threat to NATO.

Events in the post-Cold War period showed that the parameters of the Cold War WMD debate had changed, hence the 'new' threats to NATO. First, while the nation-state was still central, 'rogue' states, such as Iraq, were attracting more attention. Second, from NATO's perspective, the threat posed by WMD was still Euro-centric because its European members remained most vulnerable, however, proliferation was increasingly occurring in the Middle East, South Asia and East Asia. Third, in place of strategic nuclear weapons, biological and chemical weapons, and, to a lesser extent, radiological weapons were becoming more prominent. Although NATO's nuclear strategy remained important, it appeared to be less central as a deterrent than it had been during the Cold War. Fourth, arms control and non-proliferation agreements seemed to be less and less relevant, given the discovery of illicit WMD programmes. The post-Cold War context was very different from the Cold War context and certainly far more unstable and unpredictable.

the evolution of nato's wmd initiatives

In the months following the end of the Gulf War, the United States began a concerted effort to raise the profile of WMD within NATO and to channel thinking about how it could address this threat. Thus began a pattern of American promotion of WMD initiatives throughout the 1990s, reflecting the fact that, of all the Allies, it was the US that was most concerned by the implications of the growing threat of WMD.

The first real indication of a shift in the attention given by NATO to WMD was the 1991 Strategic Concept. Rather than focusing solely on threats to the European theatre, as the Alliance had done throughout the Cold War, the Strategic Concept underlined the need for the Alliance to take account of the more 'global context' of security by recognizing that 'Alliance security interests can be affected by [other] risks of a wider nature, including proliferation of weapons of mass destruction, disruption of the flow of vital resources and actions of terrorism and sabotage'.[3] The Strategic Concept also acknowledged the 'problem' of 'the proliferation of ballistic missiles and weapons of mass destruction'; proliferation was subsequently elevated to a subject requiring 'special consideration'.[4] This was partly a response to the existence of 'loose nukes' in the former Soviet Union, but also a reflection of heightened concern regarding the proliferation and potential use of WMD in future conflicts, which had been provoked by the 1991 Gulf War. Soon afterwards, NATO's relevant intelligence groups began devoting more attention to the threat of proliferation, and conceptual work started on extended air-defence and theatre-missile-defence (TMD) requirements. The Strategic Concept also reaffirmed the importance of arrangements for 'consultation among the Allies under Article 4 of the Washington Treaty and, where appropriate, co-ordination of their efforts including their responses to such risks'.[5] This provision was not very significant, however, as the Allies have had the ability to consult each other and co-ordinate their positions ever since the signing of the North Atlantic Treaty: acts that are informal and therefore not binding. The Strategic Concept did not therefore signal a great change in Alliance strategy.

It was not until January 1994 that NATO leaders, meeting in Brussels, made more progress toward developing its strategy. The renewed discussion was primarily a result of a strong push by the United States, which believed that existing efforts were insufficient and a more concerted approach was required. The leaders affirmed that the proliferation of WMD and their means of delivery constituted 'a threat to international security' and was 'a matter of concern to NATO'.[6] They also decided to 'intensify and expand NATO's political and defence efforts against proliferation, taking into account the work already underway in other international fora and institutions',[7] which showed that they wished to avoid duplicating existing efforts. As a result of the Brussels Summit, two working groups were established, to ensure that NATO's approach to proliferation issues would have both political and defence dimensions. The first is the Senior Politico-Military Group on Proliferation, which deals with the political and preventative aspects of the Alliance's approach to proliferation. The second, the Senior Defence Group on Proliferation, is set up to ensure that NATO's defence posture can support non-proliferation efforts and also provide protection in case of the failure of these efforts. NATO also set an objective for the development of an 'overall policy framework' on proliferation to stimulate thinking about how to consolidate ongoing prevention efforts, how to reduce the proliferation threat and how to protect against it.[8] In its 'Policy Framework on Proliferation of Weapons of Mass Destruction', issued at the Ministerial Meeting of the NAC in Istanbul in June 1994 NATO raised the profile of the risk of the proliferation of WMD.[9] The Policy

Framework was a very broad document that outlined the parameters of NATO's interest in dealing with WMD proliferation but did not provide much detail on the specifics of this other than that its principal goals were to prevent the proliferation of WMD or to reverse it through diplomatic means.

The Berlin summit in 1996 further consolidated the changes that the Alliance had already initiated. The Foreign Ministers declared that the proliferation of NBC weapons and their means of delivery was 'a matter of serious concern to NATO as it can pose a direct threat to international security'. NATO remained 'committed to [its] aim to prevent proliferation in the first place, or, if it occurs, to reverse it through diplomatic means. NATO as a defensive alliance must bear the responsibility to ensure means to protect its members against the risks resulting from proliferation'.[10] Of particular concern were the growing risks on NATO's periphery and the role of suppliers of related technology, as well as the continuing risks of illicit transfers of WMD and related materials. This reflected an increasing concern about the transfer of WMD knowledge, materials and expertise, which had already been highlighted in the Policy Framework.

toward a more vigorous debate about wmd in the late 1990s

Until the latter part of the 1990s, the debate about NATO's response to WMD was not particularly prominent, as it was only one item on a much wider agenda of reform. However, a more vigorous debate emerged within NATO because of the planned Washington Summit, where the Allies would approve a new Strategic Concept to update the Alliance's purpose, relevance and capabilities as it moved into the 21st century. The summit therefore presented an opportunity to formalize the Alliance's response to WMD. In the run-up, the then US Secretary of State Madeleine Albright repeatedly raised the issue of WMD by stating that they posed the greatest threat to Western security. For example, in December 1997, in a speech to the NAC she stated:

> Many people believe that we no longer face [such] a unifying threat, but I believe we do, and NATO has recognized it before. It is to stop the proliferation of nuclear, chemical and biological weapons. It is to douse the combustible combination of technology and terror, the possibility, as unthinkable as it may seem, that weapons of mass destruction will fall into the hands of people who have no compunctions about using them. The threat emanates

largely from the Middle East and Eurasia, so Europe is especially at risk. It is the *overriding* security interest of our time, in the sense that it simply cannot be balanced against competing political or commercial concerns. We need to think more deeply about how to deal with this threat both through the alliance and outside it. A larger NATO in and of itself does not address it. We should keep these considerations in mind as we update NATO's strategic concept.[11]

In spite of the importance accorded by the United States to the WMD threat, the response of the remaining Allies was hesitant and two main problems emerged during the discussions: how NATO would be used and whether its efforts would add to the existing efforts of other international organizations. The precise nature of NATO's response to the threat of WMD was highly problematic for many of the Allies, as they felt that the United States had not adequately articulated how it intended to use the Alliance to counter the proliferation of WMD. In the absence of a clearer presentation of the United States' intentions and because it was known that it increasingly believed non-proliferation efforts were failing and alternative approaches were needed, many of the Allies were concerned that NATO's role in countering WMD might militarize the fight by involving pre-emptive strikes against 'rogue' states. The second question posed by Allies – whether NATO would add to or simply duplicate existing efforts – was also difficult, as most members felt that it would make more sense either to address the global problem of the proliferation of WMD in forums that were global in scope, such as the UN or to consolidate existing institutions which addressed this threat, thereby strengthening those institutions and the treaties and norms upon which they were founded.

In response, the United States insisted that the thrust of the WMD initiative was simply to facilitate the exchange of intelligence evidence and to heighten awareness within the Alliance. However, the Allies pointed out that the United States already possessed a considerable amount of the available intelligence, that it was generally reluctant to share it and that when it did, it tended to do so selectively. In spite of the apparent focus of the WMD initiative on sharing intelligence and heightening awareness, many of the Allies presumed that greater access to US intelligence would not be forthcoming. This led them to conclude that, if the thrust of the initiative were to harmonize perceptions of the threat posed by 'rogue' states or non-state actors, its existence would not radically change the *status quo*.

discussion of the terrorist threat in the 1990s

Between the threats posed by WMD and terrorism, discussion of NATO's response to WMD was by far the most vigorous. However, the threat of terrorism also featured in the debates among the Allies in the 1990s. The Ally that most strongly insisted terrorism be placed on the agenda and promoted it as a threat for NATO to combat was Turkey. Although the United States supported Turkey's efforts it did not initiate the discussions about how and why NATO should address this threat but did seek to link it to the WMD threat, as Albright's December 1997 speech showed. However, the general consensus among other Allies was that terrorism was primarily an internal threat and a domestic security concern, rather than an international security priority for the Alliance. As such, they saw NATO as an inappropriate forum for dealing with terrorism.

the 1999 strategic concept

The Strategic Concept resulting from the meeting of the Allies in Washington, DC in April 1999 reaffirmed that WMD posed a direct threat to NATO. Paragraph 22 states, for example:

> The proliferation of NBC weapons and their means of delivery remains a matter of serious concern. In spite of welcome progress in strengthening international non-proliferation regimes, major challenges with respect to proliferation remain. The Alliance recognises that proliferation can occur despite efforts to prevent it and can pose a direct military threat to the Allies' populations, territory, and forces. Some states, including on NATO's periphery and in other regions, sell or acquire or try to acquire NBC weapons and delivery means. Commodities and technology that could be used to build these weapons of mass destruction and their delivery means are becoming more common, while detection and prevention of illicit trade in these materials and know-how continues to be difficult. Non-state actors have shown the potential to create and use some of these weapons.[12]

This acknowledgement of the threat posed by WMD repeated earlier statements made by NATO.

NATO also addressed the issue of missile defences and stated,

The Alliance's defence posture against the risks and potential threats of the proliferation of NBC weapons and their means of delivery must continue to be improved, including through work on missile defences. As NATO forces may be called upon to operate beyond NATO's borders, capabilities for dealing with proliferation risks must be flexible, mobile, rapidly deployable and sustainable. Doctrines, planning, and training and exercise policies must also prepare the Alliance to deter and defend against the use of NBC weapons. The aim in doing so will be to further reduce operational vulnerabilities of NATO military forces while maintaining their flexibility and effectiveness despite the presence, threat or use of NBC weapons.[13]

NATO's missile defence initiatives were therefore restricted to the protection of NATO military forces, and not the protection of populations or territories.

The discussions leading to the Washington Summit also resulted in approval of the creation of a WMD Centre in the NATO International Staff in Brussels. The WMD Centre, established in May 2000, has several aims including: to maintain the Matrix of Bilateral WMD Destruction and Management Assistance Programmes, a database designed to expand information-sharing between member states on national contributions to WMD withdrawal and dismantling in the former Soviet Union; to serve as a repository for information on WMD-related civil response programmes in Allied nations; to support the Alliance Groups dealing with WMD proliferation and through them, the North Atlantic Council and to develop briefings, fact sheets and other information documents on WMD issues for a wider public audience.[14] To summarize, the WMD Centre's three main aims are: improving intelligence and information-sharing, enhancing military capabilities and supporting wider non-proliferation efforts.

Rather than signifying a new approach to WMD (the offensive strategy that some members feared in the run-up to the Washington Summit), the agreement to establish a new NATO centre to monitor the threat of WMD and help plan NATO responses, as well as the proposals to continue work on missile defences, continued the strategy of dealing with WMD by focusing on political and defensive measures. In spite of the more vigorous nature of NATO discussions, the differences among the Allies ensured that the end result at Washington was no greater progress, beyond the preventative and defensive measures that NATO had agreed during the 1990s.

the framing of nato's response to terrorism

The Strategic Concept also addressed the threat of terrorism, although it was a far less significant part of the document, reflecting its status during the 1990s. Paragraph 24 stated:

> Any armed attack on the territory of the Allies, from whatever direction, would be covered by Articles 5 and 6 of the Washington Treaty. However, Alliance security must also take account of the global context. Alliance security interests can be affected by other risks of a wider nature, including acts of terrorism, sabotage and organised crime, and by the disruption of the flow of vital resources ...[15]

The precise wording of Paragraph 24 caused long debates among the Allies. Although terrorism, sabotage, organized crime and the disruption of the flow of vital resources were identified as risks to Alliance security, the issue of terrorism was the most contentious aspect. Turkey wanted to include a whole paragraph devoted to NATO's role in countering terrorism in the Strategic Concept, a proposal supported by the United States. However, due to the lack of support from other Allies that characterized discussions leading to the Washington Summit, there was no consensus about NATO's role in combating terrorism. Due to these internal difficulties, terrorism was defined only as a 'risk' that could affect Alliance interests, a definition which was very vague. The Strategic Concept re-emphasized the consultative mechanisms that existed within NATO for discussion of terrorism and other 'risks' but no agreement for measures beyond consultation was forthcoming.

explaining nato's response to wmd and terrorism

From the early 1990s the Allies acknowledged that traditional measures to counter the threat of WMD were obsolete or failing and that a purely preventive approach was insufficient. Moreover, NATO recognized that WMD could pose a direct threat to its security and that terrorism was a risk. None the less, an overview of the WMD initiatives that NATO undertook during the 1990s shows that although the Allies agreed to strengthen defensive and preventive measures, their progress was far from straightforward. Instead of the threat of WMD forging a consensus, the remaining Allies met US attempts to enhance NATO's role with reluctance or concern, which ensured that any progress had to be based on a 'lowest common denominator' approach. As Joanna Spear has commented, 'European acceptance [of the importance of counterproliferation] is grudging, and this should be seen as auguring a war of bureaucratic attrition over its implementation'.[16] Progress to tackle the threat of WMD was slow and discussions about how to combat terrorism even less productive. Given the agreement among the Allies about the threat of WMD proliferation and the risk of terrorism, it seems paradoxical that so little progress was made. None the less, the WMD debate highlighted differences between the Allies in three areas – threat perception, NATO strategy and strategic priorities. These three issues underpin the WMD debate and explain why it was not more productive.

differences in threat perception

Differences in threat perception characterized discussions not only within NATO but also in other forums. The issue of the possession of WMD versus the intent to use them was the first area of disagreement. Threat is a factor of capability, intention and vulnerability so an assessment of the extent of a WMD threat depends on knowledge that a state has a WMD capability, the intention to use it and is able to exploit any of its target's weaknesses. In this respect, proximity to the Middle East, for example, does not necessarily make the European Allies more vulnerable to WMD than the North American Allies. Moreover, because biological and chemical weapons, in particular, can be produced in secret, assessing a state's capability can be very difficult, as discussions leading to the 2003 Iraq War showed. Given that the threat posed by WMD is not clear-cut, there was, and remains, a potential for the Allies to reach different conclusions about its nature and extent. In NATO discussions, the United States tended to highlight the capability itself, many of the remaining Allies placed emphasis on the intention of states possessing WMD or seeking to acquire a WMD capability and Turkey emphasized its vulnerability. Forging a common threat assessment within NATO was as problematic as forging a consensus in other forums.

A second, related, problem was the divergent perceptions of the immediacy of the WMD threat. Even though the Allies agreed that WMD could constitute a threat to NATO's security and were indeed the most pressing threat to Western security, they did not share the United States' perception of its imminence. This remained true even for some of the Mediterranean Allies whose location caused them to be the most exposed to any potential threat from proliferant states around NATO's periphery. Turkey was again the exception, in this respect. Although NATO leaders agreed that the threat of WMD needed attention, the lack of the sense of an imminent threat meant that arguments to enhance NATO's response to WMD, beyond preventive and defensive measures, were simply not compelling enough.

A third problem was the reluctance of many of the European Allies to raise the profile of the potential threat of WMD to Europe or the United States, because in comparison to the US, the debate over the threat of WMD in NATO member states was not nearly as developed or prominent. Prioritizing NATO initiatives in this area could have given the impression that national governments had not taken adequate measures to protect their populations against the WMD threat.

the problems posed by strategy

Agreeing on an appropriate NATO response to WMD was a second area of difficulty. There are several different policy options that can be used to combat the threat of WMD, including diplomacy, the adoption of international agreements and treaties, deterrence, containment and enforcement. Deciding which of these options provides the best strategy exposes many differences among NATO member states, as the 2003 war with Iraq showed. Discussion of NATO's role, however, raised issues that are specific to it. In general, members other than the United States were cautious about pursuing WMD initiatives in the NATO context. The doubts previously expressed about NATO's suitability for addressing the WMD threat, given the international nature of the problem, were one aspect of this debate. However, a second consideration was that NATO's primarily military competences could potentially militarize the fight against WMD. Here, the geographic scope of NATO's missions was significant. Chapter Two showed how the 1990s saw a debate between the NATO Allies about whether it should remain an alliance with regional responsibilities or be transformed into one with a global reach. The WMD discussions had clear implications for the geographic debate, because as long as NATO confined itself to Europe, the threat of WMD to its troops was small. This was because, apart from Turkey (which remained vulnerable), intelligence had shown that existing technology did not allow potential adversaries in the Middle East, for example, to target NATO territory populations or forces operating in Europe. By promoting initiatives to counter WMD, some Allies suspected that attempts to enhance

NATO's ability to deal with this threat was a smokescreen to hide potential interventions beyond Europe.

the relationship between strategic priorities and nato's relevance

In addition to differences in threat perception and strategy, the caution expressed by many Allies was also due to the fact that the issue underpinning the United States' efforts to enhance NATO's roles in countering WMD and, to a lesser extent, terrorism, was the concern that NATO should remain relevant to the most pressing security threats of the time. In contrast to the United States, which viewed WMD initiatives as the key measure in ensuring NATO's relevance, many Allies did not view tackling WMD as NATO's strategic priority even though they agreed that they were a threat.

Due to these disagreements, neither fighting the threat posed by WMD nor combating that posed by terrorism became a key component of post-Cold War NATO reform. Whilst of crucial importance, NATO's response to WMD and terrorism remained a largely abstract debate and the necessity for reform potential rather than actual. In contrast to the US, NATO's role in addressing the proliferation of WMD and terrorism was simply not high on the agenda of most of the Allies. This changed in September 2001.

the impact of 9/11 on the wmd and international terrorism debates

The terrorist attacks of 9/11 caused the prominence of WMD and of international rather than domestic terrorism to quickly rise to the top of NATO's agenda. The increased prominence of WMD and international terrorism debates was not simply a result of changed threat perception, but was also part of a wider debate about the relevance of NATO in a post-9/11 context. The realization that after 9/11 WMD and international terrorism would be the threats domin-ating the United States' agenda posed a problem for NATO, given the minimal role that it had played in addressing these threats. Unless it revisited the debate about its role and its response, NATO would be irrelevant to the most pressing security threats of the post-9/11 world.

In the weeks and months following, the prospect of becoming a casualty of 9/11 and the ensuing war on terrorism caused WMD, and international terrorism in particular, to rise to the top of NATO's agenda. Until 9/11, much of NATO's planning was based on the expectation that, of WMD and terrorism, the most serious threat was the possibility of a WMD attack on NATO populations, territories or forces. 9/11, however, highlighted a different threat: the nexus between WMD and international terrorism and the possibility of terrorists using WMD to inflict mass casualties. The emergence of a new type of terrorist threat, international rather than domestic in nature, and the need to demonstrate NATO's relevance, provided the impetus to revisit the WMD debate and, for the first time, to prioritize the threat of international terrorism in a way that the Allies had not done in the 1990s.

Despite the incentive to re-examine NATO's response to WMD and international terrorism, opinion was initially divided as to whether 9/11 would provoke significant shifts in NATO's response as, 9/11 notwithstanding, many issues central to this debate had not changed. None the less, some significant shifts happened and 9/11 proved to be a catalyst sufficient to overcome some of the obstacles that had featured in earlier discussions of NATO's response.

the post-9/11 shift in nato's role in combating terrorism

The emphasis that NATO has given to combating the threat of international terrorism has profoundly shifted since 9/11. In contrast to earlier debates, where NATO acknowledged terrorism but only defined it as a 'risk', due to the lack of a consensus about the degree of attention that it should be accorded and NATO's role in combating it, NATO has defined counter-terrorism as one of its core missions. This was, in many respects, inevitable because the debate about the relative importance of terrorism and, specifically, about whether NATO should adopt a counter-terrorism role was essentially ended by the invocation of the principle of Article 5 on 12 September 2001.

Consolidating NATO's response to the threat of international terrorism came under scrutiny very soon after 9/11. The US Deputy Secretary of Defense, Paul Wolfowitz, used his 26 September trip to NATO HQ for an informal meeting with Defence Ministers to reiterate that the Allies should raise counter-terrorism to the top of their agenda and concluded after the meeting 'we all agree now that counter-terrorism has to be a major alliance priority'.[17] Wolfowitz's conclusion appears to have been hasty, as there were indications of resistance within NATO to elevating international terrorism to a core concept. In the wake of 9/11 and as a response to the prospect of NATO enhancing its focus on countering international terrorism, France very quickly protested and took the position that NATO should not develop its role in countering the threat of terrorism any more than it already had done. There was a degree of ideological reflex to France's response, although a significant influence appears to have been that France simply did not perceive NATO to be the most effective instrument to address this threat.

In spite of some resistance, particularly from France, statements released after the December 2001 meetings provided the first official evidence of the attention NATO was now according to international terrorism. In addition to the communiqués that are normally issued following Ministerial meetings, NATO issued a separate statement entitled 'NATO's Response to Terrorism'.[18] The elaboration and publication of a text focusing on NATO's role in countering terrorism is illustrative of the shift in priorities that had taken place. Paragraph 5 states, for instance:

> We reiterate our determination to combat the threat of terrorism for as long as necessary. In keeping with our obligations under the Washington Treaty we will continue to strengthen our national and collective capacities to protect our populations, territory and forces from any armed attack, including terrorist attack, directed from abroad. We recognised this challenge in the Strategic Concept adopted at the Washington Summit, where we made clear that any armed attack on the territory of the Allies, from whatever direction, would be covered by Article 5 of the Washington Treaty and where we singled out terrorism as a risk to the security interests of the Alliance. Meeting this challenge is fundamental to our security'.[19]

The most striking feature of 'NATO's Response to Terrorism' is the recognition that the threat of terrorism is 'fundamental' to the security of the Allies. However, whilst this is a strong statement, France opposed US proposals for counter-terrorism to be a 'fundamental security task' hence the watered-down reference to 'fundamental to our security'.[20] This response reflects continuing French ambivalence about the desirability and feasiblity of NATO becoming increasingly involved in combating international terrorism.

The enhanced focus on international terrorism and WMD continued at meetings of NATO Foreign and Defence Ministers in May and June 2002. NATO also launched a comprehensive review of its existing military capabilities and those it would need to counter the threat of WMD and terrorism. Precision-guided weapons, transport aircraft, air-to-air refuelling, logistics to enable rapid deployment of NATO forces and defence against chemical, biological and radiological attacks were identified as being particularly important. This consensus was taken a step further at the 2002 Prague Summit, where a number of initiatives emerged as NATO priorities.

terrorism initiatives resulting from the prague summit

The communiqué issued following the meeting of NATO Heads of State and Government in Prague in November 2002 resulted in a definite answer being given to the question of how NATO should respond to international terrorism. Paragraph 4 stated:

> We underscore that our efforts to transform and adapt NATO should not be perceived as a threat by any country or organisation, but rather as a demonstration of our determination to protect our populations, territory and forces from any armed attack, including terrorist attack, directed from abroad. We are determined to deter, disrupt, defend and protect against any attacks on us, in accordance with the Washington Treaty and the Charter of the United Nations.[21]

In order to 'deter, disrupt, defend and protect', NATO announced a new Military Concept for Defence against Terrorism. The Concept was a result of work that had been commissioned at the December 2001 meeting of NATO Defence Ministers. SACEUR and SACLANT were charged with assessing the options for defending NATO against terrorism and the Concept produced set out four possible military roles: anti-terrorism, consequence management, counter-terrorism and military co-operation.

Anti-terrorism refers to the implementation of defensive measures to reduce vulnerability to terrorist attacks. Primary responsibility remains with member states but NATO can supplement their efforts if requested to do so. Actions that could take place within the anti-terrorism area might be intelligence-sharing, air and maritime protection or support for a member state seeking to evacuate citizens or forces from an area where there was an increased threat of terrorism. Second, the agreement by NATO to enhance its consequence management capabilities is designed to enable it to respond quickly and effectively in the aftermath of a terrorist attack. Third, the new counter-terrorism role prepares for NATO's use of offensive measures or for its support of national capabilities that would reduce the capabilities of terrorist groups. NATO-led or NATO-supported counter-terrorist operations would encompass a wide range of activities, from providing specialized anti-terrorist forces, to enabling coalition formation and enhancing interoperability, to back-filling national requirements. Fourth, military co-operation, the last measure taken by NATO, envisages greater collaboration with NATO Partners, Russia, Ukraine, members of the Mediterranean Dialogue and other organizations such as the European Union, as well as enhanced co-operation with civil authorities such as immigration, intelligence and security services.

wmd initiatives resulting from the prague summit

In addition to enhancing NATO's response to terrorism, the leaders also endorsed a range of WMD initiatives. Progress with respect to WMD initiatives encompassed three areas:

First, the Prague Summit saw agreement about the need to examine more closely NATO's options for defending against the threat posed by WMD. The Allies agreed to launch a Missile Defence feasibility study, to examine how NATO can best protect its territory, forces and populations against missile threats. The study should be completed by mid-2005. Although the concept of missile defences is not a new development, either in NATO or in member states, this new initiative goes beyond previous ones, in that it not only examines how NATO forces can be protected, but also considers the protection of territory and populations.

Second, the implementation of CBRN weapons defence initiatives was endorsed. These initiatives include a Prototype NBC Event Response Team, which could counter NBC threats; a Deployable NBC Analytical Laboratory, which could analyse the agents that might be being encountered; a NATO Biological and Chemical Defence Stockpile, which would ensure a supply of pharmaceutical and other medical counter-measures; a Disease Surveillance System and a Virtual Centre of Excellence for NBC Weapons Defence, which would improve training in all areas related to CBRN weapons.

Third, NATO took the decision to implement a Civil Emergency Planning (CEP) Action Plan, which would enhance both civil preparedness for potential CBR attacks against populations and NATO's ability to provide assistance to national authorities following terrorist attacks, including those involving CBRN weapons.

initiatives from the 2004 istanbul summit

The June 2004 meeting of Heads of State and Government in Istanbul built on the Prague Summit initiatives. Seven measures to enhance NATO's existing response to WMD and international terrorism were presented: improving intelligence sharing, through NATO's Terrorist Threat Intelligence Unit and the review of current intelligence structures at HQ; improving NATO's ability to respond quickly to national requests for assistance in protecting against and dealing with the consequences of terrorist attacks, including those involving CBRN weapons; providing assistance to protect major events including use of AWACS; enhancing Operation Active Endeavour's contribution to the fight against terrorism; continuing, through existing missions in the Balkans and Afghanistan, to help create conditions in which terrorism cannot flourish; ensuring enhanced capabilities to defend against terrorist attacks and increasing co-operation with Partners.[22]

As a result of 9/11, NATO elevated terrorism from a 'risk' to a core concept and began to address the need to improve its individual and collective capabilities. It also accelerated existing efforts to deal with the threat posed by WMD and provide a far more focused set of initiatives. The Prague and Istanbul initiatives demonstrated a stronger transatlantic consensus about the need to deal with these challenges than there had been in the past. However, alongside these changes there is much evidence of important continuities. The most significant is that NATO's policy on WMD and international terrorism remains a defensive strategy, focused on protecting NATO populations, territories and forces rather than an offensive strategy targeting specific countries and groups.

key influences on post-9/11 discussions of nato's response to wmd and international terrorism

The consensus forged in the aftermath of 9/11 about NATO's response to WMD and international terrorism stands in marked contrast to the debates that characterized discussions during the 1990s. This consensus is not a result of a single factor, but a combination of a series of influences.

The most significant explanation for the change in tone of the discussions is the impact of 9/11 on the security perceptions of the

Allies. In previous debates, divergent perceptions of the threats posed by WMD and international terrorism prevented a consensus about the immediacy of these threats and the importance that NATO should accord them, when it had other pressing issues on its agenda. In contrast, the reality of 9/11 meant that NATO had a specific case in front of it, rather than an abstract scenario, enabling the Allies to avoid a theoretical debate. As a result of 9/11, the Allies as a whole perceived countering international terrorism and WMD as an urgent priority. The terrorist attacks on New York and Washington, DC seemed to vindicate the position that the United States had taken over the nature and origin of future security threats to NATO, which it had attempted to place high on the agenda before, during and after the Washington Summit.

A second contribution to the rapid conceptual progress that NATO has made on its response to international terrorism and WMD was the already existing foundation for the post-9/11 changes. Although NATO's response to 9/11 continues the largely reactive, rather than pro-active, nature of post-Cold War reform, it is remarkable that there has been little need to place wholly new items on the agenda. In many respects, there has been a shift in emphasis and an increase in existing momentum rather than real changes in policy. The only exception is NATO's area of activity. The resolution of the 'out-of-area' debate in May 2002, when the leaders agreed that NATO could field forces 'to wherever they are needed', rather than being confined to Europe, removed obstacles present in earlier discussions about its response to WMD and international terrorism. With the acceptance that the potential risks to NATO would increase, due to extra-European operations, and that combating WMD and international terrorism might necessitate interventions beyond Europe, it became far more likely that the Allies would be able to agree on enhancing NATO's response to WMD.

The last impetus that has driven post-9/11 discussions was the importance of the link between NATO's vitality and its response to international terrorism and WMD. This is an area in which there was a profound shift. The debates about NATO's relevance to the threats of international terrorism and WMD and to the changed strategic context in general were indicative in this respect. Without a renewed debate about its response to WMD and international terrorism and subsequent agreement to prioritize these areas of activity, NATO's days were numbered. Regardless of 9/11, NATO would in all likelihood have faced questions about its relevance, but 9/11 focused the discussion in a way that was not expected.

future challenges

The events of 9/11 resulted in a greater resolve and forged a broader consensus about the need to focus on NATO's role in addressing the threat of WMD and international terrorism than there ever was. During the following months, NATO accelerated existing policy processes to deal more effectively with what many perceive as these two increasingly interrelated security threats. However, despite agreement on the seriousness of the threats posed by WMD and international terrorism and the need for NATO to enhance its efforts to counter them, significant obstacles remain. The 2003 war with Iraq highlighted a number of serious challenges that NATO will have to overcome if it is to consolidate its role in combating WMD and international terrorism. Overcoming these obstacles – or failing to – will determine whether the renewed focus on WMD and international terrorism will be sufficient to ensure NATO's ongoing vitality in the post-9/11 strategic context.

the doctrine of pre-emption

Defining the nature and extent of a future WMD or terrorist threat to NATO is a key area. Although there is a general perception that they pose a serious threat, agreeing which states pose the greatest threat will prove difficult. There may be cases where the threat will be obvious and the evidence compelling. In these scenarios, NATO is equipping itself with the improved capabilities to be able to respond quickly and effectively. However, unambiguous threats will always be the exception rather than the rule, given the difficulties associated with identifying those states that possess WMD and assessing their intentions. This is even more the case with non-state actors, which are difficult to detect in the first place. Deciding what action could and should be taken if a threat to NATO is anticipated rather than realized is a key problem.

Pre-empting a threat has long been permitted under Article 51 of the UN Charter, but in order for a state or alliance to act, an attack must be imminent and unambiguous. However, two particular trends have caused a new debate about pre-emption. First, advances in technology mean that the amount of time between the knowledge of an attack and the ability to respond is rapidly decreasing. Second, traditional tools, such as deterrence, appear to be of decreasing value against some states and non-state actors. To address these changes, the Bush Administration has made pre-emptive action an option in the United States' post-9/11 strategy. The doctrine of pre-emption, as outlined in the NSS, reflects a broader view of current law by asserting that force may be used even without evidence of an imminent attack to ensure that a threat to the United States does not grow over time. Anticipatory action is therefore permitted even when there is uncertainty about an enemy's capabilities, intentions, timetable or even target.[23] This is a significant change to the traditional understanding of pre-emption and to the rules governing pre-emptive action. Given the importance of this to US strategy, pre-emption is an issue that NATO will be unable to avoid.

Pre-emption will apply to any situation in which one or more of the Allies perceives a threat to be imminent. In spite of the controversy provoked by the Iraq War future pre-emptive action is inevitable. Pre-emption poses, however, many serious dilemmas for NATO. First is intelligence, given the central role this plays in assessing capabilities and intentions. Intelligence capabilities separate the Allies, because some are clearly in a better position to assess the nature and extent of a potential WMD or terrorist threat than others. The United States has the most intelligence, which it shares selectively, but is unlikely to want to share fully, as NATO is a large and porous organization, not particularly well-suited to intelligence sharing. This is highly problematic, as all the Allies would want to act on compelling evidence, which may not always be available. Moreover, in the light of the conclusions that have been drawn, to date, from the 2003 Iraq War, some NATO members are likely to be even more suspicious that available intelligence may be flawed, which will exacerbate an already difficult set of issues.

In addition to defining the grounds for NATO pre-emption of a threat, pre-emption also raises the contentious issue of the legal basis for NATO interventions. The need for, and desirability of, a UN mandate was a key feature of the run-up to Operation Allied Force in 1999, as well as of the Allies' discussions during the rewriting of the 1999 Strategic Concept. However, in the light of 'new' security threats, action is time-critical and time constraints render legal approval for pre-emptive action difficult, if not impossible.

Time constraints are also likely to pose problems for decision-making within NATO. This is because whilst some NATO members, such as the United Kingdom, have rapid politico-military decision-making processes, other members require prior parliamentary approval before intervention can be sanctioned. Although some Allies are seeking to modify existing processes, these constraints on the speed of decision-making bring into question how quickly NATO could act if presented with an imminent threat.

The nature of pre-emption – whether it is a defensive or offensive strategy – is also problematic. This poses a dilemma for NATO, given the strong emphasis that it has been placed on defensive measures as responses to WMD and international terrorism. Donald Rumsfeld addressed the debate about the nature of pre-emption by commenting in 2002:

> If a terrorist can attack at any time, in any place, and using any technique, and it's physically impossible to defend in every place, at every time against every technique, then one needs to calibrate the definition of "defensive". Because literally, the only way to defend against individuals or groups or organizations or countries that have weapons of mass destruction and are bent on using them against you, for example […] then the only defence is to take the effort to find those global networks and to deal with them as the United States did in Afghanistan. Now is that defensive or offensive? I personally think of it as defensive.[24]

It is far from certain, however, that many of the NATO Allies share this assessment. Former NATO Secretary General Lord Robertson ambiguously observed:

> We are a defence Alliance, we remain a defence Alliance, we do not go out looking for problems to solve […] But what we have to do now is soberly and sensibly look at the kind of threats that exist now, that might exist into the future […] threats in the future will not be the kind of threats we had in the past, the idea of large scale tank invasions of European countries is something firmly in the past, but the idea of chemical and biological attacks by states or by terrorists is certainly there and the threat of their use can also be a threat to our security and we must work out what we and others would do in circumstances where the threat exists.[25]

Deciding upon the nature of pre-emption – if the Allies are able to reach a consensus – may raise even more difficult dilemmas about how to respond. The doctrine of pre-emption presents a set of serious problems for NATO.

In short, the concept of NATO pre-empting attacks as part of its defensive function raises more questions about than it provides answers to NATO's post-9/11 role.[26] This is clearly not a short-term problem linked only to the question of Iraq but one that is likely to represent a long-term dilemma for NATO.

strategy

The question of strategy is the second difficulty. It is inevitable that there will be instances where NATO members will be unable to agree on the best strategy and tactics to employ in order to deter, defend, disrupt and protect against WMD or terrorist attacks. The discussions leading to the 2003 Iraq war were indicative of this.

Even if the Allies reach agreement over strategy, the multi-dimensional approach needed to counter WMD and international terrorism poses an additional problem. In order to counter these threats effectively, an approach that encompasses diplomatic, military, intelligence, law enforcement and financial facets is necessary. NATO is therefore not particularly well suited to a multi-dimensional campaign in which the military aspect is a component and not a solution in itself.

a low-profile role for nato in combating wmd and international terrorism?

NATO's contribution to combating international terrorism and WMD is likely to be constrained, due to the influences outlined above. However, this does not mean that it will be prevented from playing a role. In addition to the preparatory measures that NATO is taking with respect to, for example, consequence management, its most valuable contributions to combating international terrorism and WMD are likely to be in three areas: consultation and consensus-building, deterring terrorist groups through operations such as Operation Active Endeavour and stabilizing states or regions that may provide a safe haven for terrorist groups.

First, NATO's ability to provide a forum for consultation and consensus-building is already an established part of its competences and can be used very effectively for sharing threat assessments, shaping common perceptions of threat and deciding on the most appropriate response. These functions remain crucial, regardless of whether any response would be NATO-led or even officially involve NATO at all. There are evidently limitations to what NATO can do in terms of consultation and consensus-building with respect to WMD and international terrorism, as previous debates have shown.[27] However, this contribution is likely to remain of prime importance.

Second, deterring terrorist groups through operations such as Operation Active Endeavour will be a relatively low-profile but highly significant role. A NATO presence in areas that have been identified as possible transit routes for WMD or where the prospect of a terrorist attack is high may be enough either to disrupt such activities or prevent them from occurring in the first place. It is evidently preferable for NATO to take a preventive approach by deterring and disrupting these activities rather than having to deal with the consequences that may arise. Crucially, the types of tasks being performed in the Mediterranean are not particularly divisive or controversial so the risks posed to NATO cohesion are minimal.

Third, maintaining a presence in regions of the world where terrorist activities could flourish will remain an important contribution to combating terrorism. NATO's current operations in the Balkans, which have seen its forces acting against terrorist groups with links to al-Qaeda, as well as the command of the ISAF in Afghanistan, are significant in that they will help ensure that the conditions in which terrorism has already emerged, or could potentially emerge, do not continue.

Concentrating NATO's attention on these three roles, rather than focusing on the previously discussed, more controversial and problematic aspects of a potential contribution, would be a logical first step. By doing this, NATO could show the value of its existing roles, which play to its strengths, rather than engage in divisive debates that are likely to highlight its weaknesses. NATO will not be *the* solution to WMD and international terrorism but its ability to be at least a *part* of the solution is the major influence on continued US interest in, and sustained commitment to, NATO. It would appear that, for the time being, the roles outlined above are likely to continue to be the most desirable strategies for NATO.

conclusion

In the decade following the collapse of Communism, the Allies continued to define NATO's core mission as collective defence, but did not always agree on what the thrust of NATO's other missions should be. Before 9/11, differences between the Allies about the appropriate response to WMD and terrorism seemed to be driving a wedge between the United States and the other Allies. On 12 September 2001, however, NATO's original mission of collective defence became central and the Allies were, initially, united in a way that had seemed unlikely in the months before.

Since the war on terrorism began, NATO has placed WMD and international terrorism high on its agenda, which reflects a new consensus about the importance of dealing with these issues. There are, however, many obstacles in NATO's way as it strives to redefine its response to these threats. The outcome of current debates about pre-emption and strategy is of crucial significance for NATO's future. Should NATO be hesitant about, or unable to act in the face of perceived threats to its security, its relevance to combating 'new' security threats will progressively decline. This will have major implications for the United States' view of the value of NATO. This feature of previous debates is more important than ever, because there is now a specific set of circumstances against which to measure NATO's efforts. NATO's ability to address the challenges of the post-9/11 world, in particular WMD and international terrorism, will therefore be one of the determinants of its future vitality.

summary

- The 1991 Gulf War and the collapse of the former Soviet Union raised the profile of WMD. Several new challenges were highlighted and in the early post-Cold War period a number of direct and indirect threats to NATO either emerged or were exacerbated by these events.
- As a result of a series of American initiatives during the 1990s, the Allies debated how NATO should respond to the threat of WMD and, to a far lesser extent, terrorism.
- Although the Allies recognised that WMD could pose a direct threat, they were unable to agree on how NATO should respond, beyond preventative and defensive measures. Differences in threat perception and strategic priorities, concerns about NATO strategy and a lack of consensus about the implications for NATO's relevance of fighting WMD and international terrorism were the most important influences.
- Discussion of NATO's response to terrorism was far less prominent than to WMD. Although the Allies agreed that it was a risk to security, most perceived that NATO was not the best forum for tackling this threat, as they saw terrorism as primarily a domestic security issue rather than an international security priority.
- 9/11 greatly increased the importance of fighting both WMD and international terrorism. As a result, this has become one of NATO's top priorities, in order to respond to changed perceptions of the dangers posed by these threats and to ensure NATO's

relevance. NATO has announced a number of different initiatives designed to enhance its role in combating these threats.

- Despite the increased prominence of WMD and international terrorism, a number of problematic issues remain that may prove very difficult to overcome. NATO may therefore eventually choose to concentrate on existing roles that play to its strengths, rather than develop those that indicate its weaknesses and limitations.

an expanding alliance: nato's post-cold war enlargement process

introduction

The enlargement of NATO's membership has been one of the most prominent items on its agenda in the post-Cold War period. Enlargement is not, however, simply a product of this time, for, as Article 10 of the North Atlantic Treaty states:

> The Parties may, by unanimous agreement, invite any other European State in a position to further the principles of this Treaty and to contribute to the secur-ity of the North Atlantic area to accede to this Treaty. Any State so invited may become a party to the Treaty by depositing its instrument of accession with the Government of the United States of America. The Government of the United States of America will inform each of the Parties of the deposit of each such instrument of accession.[1]

This provision ensured from the outset that there was a possibility for countries which shared NATO's values and objectives to join it. Greece and Turkey became members in 1952, West Germany in 1955 and Spain in 1982. Post-Cold War, NATO has continued to enlarge its membership, in 1999 with the accession of the Czech Republic, Hungary and Poland and in 2004 with the accession of Bulgaria, Estonia, Latvia, Lithuania, Romania, Slovakia and Slovenia. In addition, there are a number of countries that have officially declared their interest in one day joining NATO and other countries that may do so in the future. This, in conjunction with NATO's 'open door' policy, ensures that enlargement will remain a key characteristic of NATO's post-Cold War reform.

This chapter provides an analysis of the evolution of NATO's post-Cold War enlargement process. It initially discusses why and how the enlargement debate emerged in the immediate aftermath of the collapse of Communism and the mechanisms that were put in place to aid aspirant members in their preparations. The chapter continues by providing an analysis of the first round of enlargement in 1999, the reasons for the dramatic shift in opinion regarding the second round of enlargement and the 'big bang' enlargement in 2004. The chapter then addresses the advantages and disadvantages of enlargement and the challenges posed by the process that NATO has to overcome to remain an effective Alliance in both its political and military roles.

the post-cold war enlargement process in context

The collapse of Communism and the eventual break up of the Soviet Union resulted in a power vacuum in Europe and the emergence of a number of weak states that had the potential to produce a range of threats to European stability. Immediately post-Cold War, there was a recognition of the need to put in place structures and mechanisms that would enhance the democratic evolution of former Warsaw Pact countries and maintain peace and stability in Europe. This involved each of the European institutions – NATO, the EU and the OSCE. At about the same time as Western leaders were considering how best to address the challenges of the post-Cold War environment, the newly emerging post-Communist states declared their intention to 'return to Europe': an aim that was first articulated by Vaclav Havel in 1990. 'Returning to Europe' meant that the newly liberated Central and East European states would seek to join the key institutions of the West – NATO and the EU – because of two perceived benefits: from the EU, Central and East European leaders hoped for economic assistance to introduce the standards of living long enjoyed by the West and by joining NATO they hoped for security assurances to guarantee the independence they had achieved from the Soviet Union. Joining the EU and NATO became a foreign policy priority for many Central and East European states.

Although enlargement eventually became a prominent part of NATO's adaptations, it was not a high profile issue in the early post-Cold War period. Discussion of enlargement was problematic whilst the Soviet Union was in existence and even after its dissolution in 1991 the question of its impact on relations with Russia remained troubling. This was primarily because a deterioration of relations between Russia and the West could have had serious implications for European security and stability in this delicate time. In addition, enlargement raised a number of difficult questions for existing members. The cost of enlargement, the impact on collective decision-making and the order in which Central and East European states should be considered for membership were all thorny issues that did not have easy answers. A final influence on the evolution of the NATO enlargement debate concerned the position of the Central and East European states. Although membership of NATO and the EU were both objectives of Central and East European states, their early inclination was to focus on the EU, rather than NATO, as although security concerns remained significant the most pressing issue was economic transformation and a desire for the same assistance and opportunities that the EU had accorded to other states, such as Spain and Portugal, when they joined.

A shift in the prominence and nature of the enlargement debate began to take place from 1993 onward. Although it had been assumed that the EU would have an 'open door' policy, EU members became increasingly reluctant to provide a clear timetable for eastward enlargement. This was partly due to a fear among existing member states that they would lose out, due to the lower cost of labour in Central and Eastern Europe and the inevitable subsidies that new members would qualify for. In addition, the EU was struggling with a very full agenda, which comprised both widening and deepening measures, including the approaching accession of Sweden, Finland and Austria and the challenges posed by the ratification of the Maastricht Treaty, which amongst other issues contained provisions for a CFSP and EMU. For these reasons, no clear timetable for the EU's eastward expansion was forthcoming and in spite of its economic attraction, there was increasingly a perception in Central and East European states that for the moment, EU membership was out of reach. As a result, attention gradually shifted to NATO. The NATO enlargement debate therefore only really began in late 1993.

the beginnings of the enlargement debate

The January 1994 meeting of NATO leaders in Brussels made a first step toward post-Cold War enlargement by affirming, in the Final Communiqué:

the Alliance, as provided for in Article 10 of the Washington Treaty, remains open to membership of other European states in a position to further the principles of the Treaty and to contribute to the security of the North Atlantic area. We expect and would welcome NATO expansion that would reach to democratic states to our East, as part of an evolutionary process, taking into account political and security developments in the whole of Europe.[2]

From January 1994 onward the enlargement of NATO's membership therefore became increasingly realistic.

Once the prospect of enlargement had been confirmed, NATO took a number of steps designed to resolve some of the issues that had presented themselves in the early post-Cold War period. A report was commissioned in 1994 and the 'NATO Study on Enlargement', subsequently published in September 1995,[3] provided a clear set of justifications for more serious consideration of a post-Cold War enlargement process. According to the study, enlargement would help achieve one of NATO's long-standing aims – the enhancement of stability and security in the North Atlantic area – in the following ways: first, the prospect of NATO enlargement would encourage and support democratic reforms in aspirant member states, including civilian and democratic control over the military; second, it would foster, in new members of the Alliance, the patterns and habits of co-operation, consultation and consensus building which characterize relations among current Allies; third, the process would promote good neighbourly relations, which would benefit all countries in the Euro-Atlantic area; fourth, membership of NATO would emphasize the importance of common defence, extend its benefits and increase transparency in defence planning and military budgets and as a result, the instability that might be produced by an exclusively national approach to defence policies would be reduced; fifth, enlargement would reinforce the tendency toward integration and co-operation in Europe, based on shared democratic values, and thereby curb the countervailing tendency toward disintegration along ethnic and territorial lines; last, enlargement would strengthen the Alliance's ability to contribute to European and international security as well as strengthening and broadening the transatlantic relationship.[4] The study also set out the political and military criteria that aspirant members of NATO would have to fulfil to be considered for membership. In essence, they would be judged by the same standards as existing members in areas including democracy, individual liberty and the rule of law, commitment to and respect for OSCE norms and principles and the ability to contribute militarily to collective defence and the

Alliance's new missions.[5] Providing these criteria were fulfilled and the expectations of the positive benefits met, enlargement would be a highly significant contribution to European security and it was within this framework that the NATO enlargement debate progressed.

In spite of what was, for many, a compelling set of reasons in favour of enlargement and the existence of a clear framework within which to proceed, NATO still had to deal with the two problematic issues that had first appeared in the early post-Cold War period. Reaching agreement about the timetable for enlargement, which Central and East European states should be admitted and in which order remained difficult. For a variety of reasons, existing NATO members prioritized different aspirant members and, as a result, reaching a consensus about the progress of enlargement proved difficult in the run-up to the first round. For example, before the first round of enlargement Greece and Italy favoured Romania and Bulgaria as new members, whereas the northern members of NATO favoured the Czech Republic, Hungary and Poland.[6] In addition to intra-NATO differences, the impact of enlargement on NATO–Russia relations continued to be problematic. From Moscow's perspective, enlargement was a threatening development, as the expansion of NATO's territory toward Russia's borders was contrary to its security interests. Russia particularly opposed the potential inclusion of the Baltic states in future rounds of NATO enlargement, as they were once part of the Soviet Union and remained part of Russia's so-called 'near abroad'. Admitting the Baltic states was a 'red line' that Russia considered NATO should not and could not cross. Many in Russia also saw enlargement as demonstrating a continuing distrust toward it, particularly given the extension of a collective defence guarantee to former Warsaw Pact members. Moscow viewed this provision as difficult to justify, if NATO no longer perceived Russia to be a threat. The existence of intra-NATO differences and the potential ramifications of enlargement for NATO–Russia relations caused concerns about enlargement's potentially destabilizing effects both for NATO and for European security and stability more generally. As Chapter Six will demonstrate, the Russian dimension of enlargement eventually resulted in a series of arrangements between NATO and Russia that was in part designed to address this particular problem.

the first round of enlargement

NATO chose the 1997 Madrid Summit as the venue where the first Central and East European states to begin the accession process would be announced. The Czech Republic, Hungary and Poland were deemed to be in an appropriate position to formally begin the process, although this decision had been taken at the last minute, reflecting the somewhat fraught nature of the discussions. Although there was debate about other aspirant members, particularly Slovenia, these three countries were obvious candidates, as none of them had any pressing security issues, their inclusion did not pose a threat to Russia and they already had a relatively high level of political and economic development. In contrast, other aspirant countries, such as Romania and Bulgaria, were thought not to be ready for NATO membership because of weaknesses in their political and military reform processes. There was also a widespread consensus that it was inappropriate for the Baltic states to join NATO in the first round, given the problematic Russian connection and the negative impact this move might have on NATO–Russia relations. Members were in favour of the concept of further enlargement, but considered that careful management was needed in order to avoid divisions in NATO and tensions in Europe.

The first round of enlargement was concluded at the Washington Summit in April 1999, when the Czech Republic, Hungary and Poland formally joined, having successfully completed the accession process and apparently fulfilled the criteria that had been set. Although no new invitations were issued in Washington, the Final Communiqué reaffirmed:

> The Alliance remains open to new members under Article 10 of the Washington Treaty. It expects to extend further invitations in coming years to nations willing and able to assume the responsibilities and obligations of membership, and as NATO determines that the inclusion of these nations would serve the overall political and strategic interests of the Alliance, strengthen its effectiveness and cohesion, and enhance overall European security and stability.[7]

NATO also announced that the progress made by the remaining formal aspirant members would be reviewed at its 2002 summit. By emphasizing that further rounds of enlargement were still on the agenda, NATO could avoid the risk of its continual postponement causing the aspirant members to become increasingly disillusioned with NATO, which might have retarded their military and political reforms and damaged NATO's credibility. The stress placed on the 'open door' policy meant that a further round of enlargement, whether in 2002 or beyond, was inevitable.

the membership action plan

To facilitate further enlargement, the Washington Summit also saw the launch of the Membership Action Plan (MAP), which was designed to aid the preparations of countries wishing to join the Alliance by offering advice, assistance and practical support on all aspects of NATO membership. The MAP incorporates both political and military aspects of reform and encompasses five aspects that prospective members have to address before their membership can seriously be considered: political and economic conditions, defence and military conditions, resources, security and legal issues. The political and economic aspect includes settling any international, ethnic or external territorial disputes by peaceful means, demonstrating a commitment to the rule of law and human rights, establishing democratic control of the armed forces and promoting stability and well-being through economic liberty, social justice and environmental responsibility. The defence and military aspect of the MAP relates to the ability of the country to contribute to collective defence and to the Alliance's new missions. Aspirant members are expected to have a minimal degree of military capability and be able to interoperate with existing members. This provision is designed to ensure that new members are contributors to, and not just consumers of, the security that NATO provides. The resources aspect of the MAP aims to ensure aspirant members commit sufficient resources to defence to allow them to meet the commitments that future membership would bring in terms of collective NATO undertakings, that is, the availability of adequate resources to assume the financial obligations of joining. The security aspect relates to the need for aspirant countries to make sure that procedures are in place to guarantee the security of sensitive information. Last, the legal aspect of the MAP is designed to ensure that the legal arrangements and agreements governing co-operation within NATO are compatible with domestic legislation. Although participation in the MAP is not a guarantee of NATO membership, making the necessary changes at domestic level and meeting the political and military criteria outlined above are key obstacles for prospective members to overcome.

toward a second round of enlargement

Despite the measures taken at the Washington Summit, there was a lull following the first round of enlargement and a more cautious approach to the second than had previously been the case. This caution could seem curious, as in many respects the decision about which countries to invite to begin the accession process should have been easier than in the first round, because the accession of the Czech Republic, Hungary and Poland provided the Allies with evidence of how potential members were likely to perform and how this would affect existing members. Moreover, the MAP would help ensure that potential members were better prepared for the demands of membership, because of the political and military criteria that were set. None the less, a pause, to take stock, was seen as desirable by NATO members. Four influences played a significant role in this. The status of the remaining aspirant members was the first consideration. Some of them still faced a number of political and economic challenges, had more precarious situations with respect to national minorities, posed a security concern for Russia by bringing NATO closer to Russia's borders or had previously been a part of the Soviet Union, which would have crossed one of Russia's 'red lines'.

The second influence was the uncharted territory that NATO had entered. Immediately post-Washington, it was not yet known how successful the first round of enlargement had been and so a trial period was perceived as being a sensible measure. The third influence was that discussion about the first round of enlargement had been fraught and there was consequently little desire to immediately start a fresh series of enlargement talks.

The last – and arguably the most important – influence on the beginnings of the debate over the second round of enlargement was the implications for NATO–Russia relations. It was not simply a question of who to invite and whether they fulfilled the criteria; it was also a question of assessing the implications for NATO–Russia relations of issuing further invitations. In the immediate post-Washington period, this was valid not only for the Baltic states but arguably for all the aspirant members, as the whole enlargement process was problematic, from the Russian perspective. As the following chapter will show, this state of affairs was exacerbated by the fact that relations between Russia and NATO had been in a deep freeze since Operation Allied Force and although there were signs of thawing, it was still a sensitive area. In spite of the difficult state of relations, NATO viewed a second round of enlargement as being inevitable and there was a sense that Russia could not and should not hold the process to ransom. Therefore, the key issue was how best to manage an inevitable, yet potentially damaging, second round. The Allies had to decide what Russia would accept and how further enlargement could be achieved with minimal damage to the NATO–Russia relationship.

Due to these constraints, it was expected that the second round of the enlargement process would be smaller rather than larger. However, it remained the dominant item on NATO's agenda throughout 2000, much of 2001 and was the main reason why the Allies were set to hold a summit in Prague in 2002. The tempo of the debate changed from mid-2001 onward, when a series of highly significant events took place. These changes, in the context of the enlargement debate, served to put into place the new framework within which NATO would shape the second round of its post-Cold War enlargement process.

us endorsement of a robust second round of enlargement

The first change came in mid-2001, primarily as a result of a crucial speech given by President Bush in Warsaw, in which he stated:

> I believe in NATO membership for all of Europe's democracies that seek it and are ready to share the responsibility [...] The question of "when" may still be up for debate within NATO; the question of "whether" should not be [...] The United States will be prepared to make concrete, historic decisions with its allies to advance NATO enlargement. As we plan the Prague summit, we should not calculate how little we can get away with, but how much we can do to advance the cause of freedom.[8]

From June 2001 onward, it became clear that the United States would push for a larger rather than smaller enlargement. Although domestic controversy remained about the implications of enlargement for NATO and the potential costs for the United States, the results of the first round were seen as having been generally positive. In particular, although there were problems with the military goals that they should have met, the Czech Republic, Hungary and Poland had proved to be enthusiastic NATO members and staunch Allies of the US. This augured well for subsequent rounds.

The then NATO Secretary General Lord Robertson strengthened expectations by publicly stating, in the summer of 2001, that NATO would definitely announce a further round of enlargement in Prague. Robertson said:

> NATO hopes and expects, based on current and anticipated progress by the aspiring members, to launch the process of enlargement at the Prague summit in 2002. In other words, the so-called "zero-option" is off the table provided the candidate countries keep up the progress they have demonstrated thus far in the Membership Action Plan.[9]

Given the American push for a significant enlargement and its endorsement by other NATO members, the foundation for the announcement of a larger rather than a smaller enlargement was in place by mid-June 2001.

the impact of 9/11

The next factor that influenced discussions about the second round of enlargement was 9/11. It is a truism that, on 11 September 2001, everything changed. This is as valid for the enlargement debate as it is for other aspects of NATO reform but changes in the enlargement debate had clearly been initiated before these events. In many respects, 9/11 increased an existing momentum rather than initiating a new development. Enlargement was not the main issue in the weeks following 9/11 and there was no immediate and renewed push to discuss the second round, because most attention was focused on the implications of invoking the principle of Article 5 and the initial operations in Afghanistan. As time passed, NATO's missions, and in particular how it could respond to the challenge of international terrorism and the proliferation of WMD, began increasingly to dominate its agenda. The shift from seeing the Prague Summit as being primarily about enlargement to being one that would see the beginnings of transformation was one of the most significant influences on the debate. In spite of the focus on missions and post-9/11 threats to NATO's security, enlargement remained important as a means to tackle the 'new' threats that had emerged. There was a sense among NATO members that strengthening existing partnerships and presenting a united front against the threat of international terrorism would be increasingly important. Enlargement could be one component of a response to the challenges presented by 9/11 and, from late 2001, the debate was therefore subsumed into larger changes.

an improvement in nato–russia relations

The third important influence on the enlargement process was an improvement in NATO–Russia relations. Following 9/11, relations between Russia and the West improved. In some respects, this development preceded 9/11, given the personal rapport between Bush and Putin that had been noted at their first meeting (in Slovenia in June 2001). As new developments between Russia and NATO arose (which will be discussed in the next chapter), it became clear that the Russian attitude toward NATO enlargement had become more relaxed. Russia no longer perceived enlargement as being such a great threat, nor did it see it as being so damaging to Russian interests. Although Russia could not be described as now being in favour of enlargement, the change in Russian attitudes made it unlikely that the prospect of a sizeable enlargement would cause a major conflict between NATO and Russia.

toward the prague summit

These three influences therefore shaped the framework within which decisions about the second round of the enlargement process were made and allowed NATO to reassess the countries that remained aspirant members after the Washington Summit. In the run-up to the 2002 Prague Summit, the Baltic states were seen as being the strongest performers in the MAP and even though they had previously been a part of the Soviet Union, the relaxation of Russian views meant that beginning the accession process was now a realistic prospect. Slovenia had narrowly missed inclusion in the first round of enlargement and, although public opposition to membership had grown, it was perceived as a strong candidate. Slovakia was also seen in the same light, although a complication was the potential election of the autocratic Meciar as president, the only factor that would have caused Slovakia to be barred from NATO membership. Romania and Bulgaria were viewed as having made enough progress to justify serious consideration of their applications and even though their development was not as great as the Baltic states', it could be argued that it would be better to nurture them within NATO rather than keep them out. In addition, there was a perception that there was some strategic significance in including Romania and Bulgaria and a political benefit to bringing them into NATO, as their EU membership in 2004 seemed increasingly unlikely. There was a consensus that Albania, Croatia and the Former Yugoslav Republic of Macedonia should not be offered membership, given the continued instability in the Balkans and the relatively recent nature of their applications. Seven countries – Bulgaria, Estonia, Latvia, Lithuania, Romania, Slovakia and Slovenia – therefore emerged as the countries that were most likely to be invited to begin accession talks at the Prague Summit.

the prague summit

The nature of the discussions leading to the Prague Summit and taking place during it was indicative of the changed status of enlargement, post-9/11. In terms of forging a consensus, the second round of enlargement was the least problematic issue on the agenda. The question of the ongoing commitment of the United States, given its reluctance to engage NATO after 9/11, and the adaptations NATO was making to contribute to the fight against WMD and international terrorism commanded more attention and generated far more discussion than the continuing – and by now relatively uncontroversial – enlargement process. The seven aspirant members of NATO formally joined the accession process and the 'big bang' enlargement, which seemed so unlikely after the Washington Summit, began a new chapter in NATO's post-Cold War history by opening the door not only to former Warsaw Pact adversaries but also to former members of the Soviet Union.

future developments in nato's enlargement process

NATO's open door policy, reiterated at the Istanbul Summit,[10] ensures that further enlargement is likely, meaning that the inherent difficulty of the process – the dual challenges of deciding which countries to include and which to exclude – will remain. There are three aspirant members currently participating in the MAP – Albania, Croatia and the FYROM – and their progress will be reviewed at NATO's next summit.[11] Moreover, a number of countries that are not yet participating in the MAP have expressed their intention to seek NATO membership (for example, Ukraine, in May 2002).

Article 10 of the North Atlantic Treaty does not offer much guidance in defining the limits of NATO membership and simply states that 'any other European State in a position to further the principles of this Treaty and to contribute to the security of the North Atlantic area' may be considered. In the absence of a clear answer from NATO, a more precise indicator of the potential scope of enlargement will be if membership remains predicated on reform. In this sense, future rounds of enlargement will depend as much – if not more – on the applicant countries as they do on current members.

explaining nato enlargement

There are several explanations for why NATO enlarged in 1999 and 2004 and why it is likely to enlarge again in the future. One concerns the crucial role of the United States in initiating and driving forward the process, which is to be expected given its role as NATO's *de facto* leader.[12] Pressures resulting from the delay in expected EU membership for Central and East European states also forced the issue on to NATO's agenda. However, the main motivation for NATO enlargement lies in the perceived benefits for European security. As the early part of this chapter showed, the end of the Cold War necessitated the putting in place of structures and mechanisms that would enhance the democratic evolution of former Warsaw Pact countries and maintain peace and stability in Europe without drawing a new dividing line across the continent. At its most basic, the rationale for enlargement must be seen in terms of the direct impact it can have on the overall stability and security of Europe as well as the benefits it is perceived to have for the Allies.

the stabilization of europe through nato enlargement

Stabilizing Europe (and therefore contributing to European security) through enlargement can be achieved in a number of different ways. The key way is through the political and military criteria that need to be fulfilled by aspirant countries in order to qualify for membership, the most important of which are outlined in the MAP. As a result of the changes that have to be made by prospective members, there is a recognition that NATO members and aspirant countries alike can benefit from the political, economic and military by-products of the enlargement process in areas as diverse as human rights, laws governing language, defence planning and border disputes. The MAP also strengthens the ties between aspirant members and present members of NATO and brings the governments and peoples of aspirant states under close scrutiny. Enlargement is therefore seen to be reinforcing the relatively new democratic forces emerging in the aspirant member states. The integration of Central and East European countries into the Alliance is an important way to foster conditions that will consolidate, stabilize and democratize these post-Communist systems. There are inevitably immediate benefits for the stability and security of Europe but also longer-term benefits, as it is expected that once these changes have been made they will be difficult to reverse.

the facilitation of military operations through nato enlargement

The second way in which enlargement can enhance the security of the Allies is in facilitating military operations, of which encouraging military standardization and interoperability is one important aspect. Chapter One demonstrated how NATO played an important informal military role in the 1991 Iraq War, through the use of its structures and procedures, even though it was not involved formally in the coalition operation. The spread of the use of standardized equipment and the familiarization of new Allies with established structures and procedures can be a highly desirable and useful by-product of enlargement, which can be employed in NATO and non-NATO operations alike. These benefits are often overlooked in the debate over enlargement but have been significant in a series of operations, most recently the ISAF.

The expansion of NATO territory through the admission of new members is a further benefit. The operational benefits of an expanded Alliance have gained particular importance since the beginning of the war on terrorism, given the likely location of future conflicts. These benefits are three-fold.

First, an increase in the number of members means an increase in the number of bases available for the stationing or deployment of NATO forces or assets. Second, a greater number of bases expands NATO's reach and can facilitate access to potential troublespots beyond the Euro-Atlantic area. This strategic operational benefit does not apply equally to all the new or remaining aspirant members but those located in South-East Europe are particularly useful for potential operations in the Balkans or further afield. As Clarke and Cornish observe, Bulgaria and Romania benefited from the consequences of 9/11 because their admission 'could give NATO a coherent and geostrategically significant "southern dimension"'.[13] Romania, for example, occupies a strategic position on the Black Sea and gave the United States permission to use a base in this area during the 2003 Iraq War. Recent US proposals to reposition forces based in Germany to Bulgaria and Romania illustrate the shift in thinking about the location of future conflicts and the implications this will have for the conduct of operations.[14] In this respect, the closer forces can be based to the conflict theatre the easier and more cost-effective future military operations will be.

Third, membership means greater pressure can be placed on states to allow fellow members to use their political, military or geographic assets regardless of whether or not the operation in question is a NATO operation. Pressures resulting from the 'obligations of Alliance' augment the pool of potential political and/or military support for NATO or non-NATO operations. Turkey's refusal to allow the United States to use the strategically important Incirlik base during the 2003 Iraq War demonstrates that the use of bases remains subject to the approval of the host state but it is unlikely that new members will deny the US access to these assets.

The political and military advantages of enlargement outlined above indicate that the process has been driven largely by pragmatic considerations, which benefit existing as much as aspirant members. This is an almost inevitable conclusion to reach, given the pressures resulting from the end of the Cold War and 9/11.

the problems and pitfalls of nato enlargement

Regardless of the motivation behind the process and in spite of the indisputable advantages of enlargement both for NATO and non-NATO members, there are equally significant disadvantages. Critics of enlargement argue that in spite of the political and military advantages, the costs outweigh the benefits. Michael Mandelbaum, for example, spoke for many analysts when he commented, in 1995, 'NATO expansion, under the present circumstances and as currently envisioned, is at best premature, at worst counterproductive, and in any case largely irrelevant to the problems confronting the countries situated between Germany and Russia'.[15] Three potential disadvantages of enlargement have been particularly prominent: the possible destablization of European security and stability, the potential undermining of NATO's cohesion and collective military capabilities and the implications for the nature of NATO. The impact of these perceived problems is important, because if opponents of enlargement are correct, instead of enhancing European security and stability and NATO as an institution it has the potential to have completely the opposite effect.

the possible destabilization of european security and stability

Opponents of enlargement challenge the conventional wisdom that it has a steadying effect on European security and stability and point to three ways in which it could have a negative impact.

One is that enlargement transfers security risks from beyond NATO's borders to within them, in two ways. First, there is no guarantee of the continuation of political or military reform once membership has been achieved. Moreover, should reform stall or even reverse there is no mechanism for suspension or termination of membership. This is important, as democratization is fragile in

some of the countries that joined NATO in 2004. Second, prospective members may solve their internal problems in the short term and
therefore meet the criteria contained in the MAP but may not resolve
them in the long term. Critics point out, in this respect, that NATO
has failed to resolve the tensions and conflict that continue to
characterize the relationship between Greece and Turkey. Often, the
most problematic issues, whether minority rights or border disputes,
are long-standing difficulties that are not easily settled and there is
therefore always potential for them to reoccur. As Rupp comments,

> if NATO expands as currently designed, the organization will be
> required to address security issues that no organization could
> effectively and successfully manage. Each new NATO member will
> bring to the organization known and unknown security issues that
> the organization may become treaty-bound to engage. The list of
> potential conflicts is myriad: Poland-Belarus, Kaliningrad-
> Lithuania, Hungary-Slovenia, Romania-Serbia, and Bulgaria-
> Macedonia, to note but a few. While efforts have been made to
> ameliorate these issues, many of these are age-old conflicts that
> rushed treaties designed to placate Brussels will not settle.[16]

The failure to resolve problems like those identified by Rupp or the
stalling or reversal of reform ensures that, instead of being external,
these issues become internal problems for NATO. In this way, instead
of exporting stability, enlargement actually imports instability.

The second way in which enlargement could undermine
European security and stability is through the implications for the
unsuccessful candidates. Given that enlargement is not limitless, it is
likely that there will always be some aspirant states that will not
achieve the goal of NATO membership. In 1999, for example, the
then President of Georgia, Eduard Shevardnadze, said that he anticipated Georgia would have gained membership within five years.[17] In
2004, five years after Shevardnadze said this, Georgia's membership
of NATO remains at best a distant prospect, if it could be termed a
prospect at all. Thus enlargement produces winners and losers,
which has the potential to weaken emerging democratic forces and
establish new dividing lines in Europe.

The final way in which enlargement could have a negative impact
is the risk of an unnecessary confrontation with Russia, which could
harm future NATO–Russia relations in several ways. First, opponents of enlargement point out that its success to date has hinged on
the co-operation of politicians, such as Vladimir Putin, who have
initiated democratic reforms in Russia and who have wanted to
build a relationship with the West. Even under Putin, however, there

have been problems. One example of the potential damage that enlargement could do to NATO–Russia relations occurred in April 2004, when four Belgian F-16s relocated to a new NATO base in Lithuania to begin patrols of Baltic airspace. The commander of the force described the patrols as 'routine' yet the *Duma* (the Russian Parliament) subsequently adopted a resolution denouncing NATO enlargement generally, and the deployment of the F-16s in particular.[18] Second, the Kosovo conflict provided a relatively recent example of a situation in which Russia and NATO had diametrically opposed positions. As some analysts have pointed out, a similar set of circumstances cannot be ruled out in the future.[19] Third, there is always the possibility that anti-Western parties or politicians, who may not take such a moderate view of the process and implications of enlargement, will come to power in Russia. This appears to be conceivable, for Putin was invited to the Prague Summit but did not attend, as domestic pressures made it inappropriate for him to be seen to be endorsing NATO's enlargement. A downturn in the quality of NATO–Russia relations, resulting in part from enlargement, has the potential to reduce the likelihood of Russia co-operating with the West on other security issues, such as WMD or international terrorism, which may, indirectly, harm European security.

the potential undermining of nato

A second set of arguments against enlargement focuses on the negative implications for NATO. One concern relates to the seriousness of accepting new, and arguably unnecessary, collective defence obligations. The central motivation of many Central and East European states, since membership of NATO became a realistic prospect in the early 1990s has been to benefit from the collective defence guarantee that NATO offers. The comments of the Estonian Ambassador to NATO are indicative in this respect: 'First and foremost, NATO for Estonia is a security issue. We have been trying different options during the previous century. They didn't work. So now, we are trying to get all the security guarantees we can find, and NATO is definitely the only hard security guarantee available'.[20] Given that NATO's most prominent missions are now non-Article 5, rather than Article 5, this view of NATO begs the question as to whether new and aspirant members are seeking to join an Alliance that no longer exists. As one NATO official commented (on condition of anonymity), 'NATO membership [...] is no longer a passport to a strategic vacation. It is now a passport to sharing a collective responsibility for all of the problems of the world. If nations don't wake up to that, the mismatch between expanding the political ambitions of the alliance and the actual capabilities to implement that ambition will grow'.[21] None the less, the expectation, primarily of new members, that NATO will always come to its members' aid, has the potential to cause serious future problems.

First, NATO enlargement has brought it closer to some of Europe's hotspots, which may have serious consequences should regional conflicts spill over into NATO territory. Second, there is a possibility – albeit remote – of Russia acting aggressively toward its former satellites in the future, which would also have important implications for NATO. Third, one of the most basic lessons of NATO's interventions in the Balkans was that European security issues were no longer of vital strategic importance to the United States and so it is far from certain whether a security problem in Europe would provoke a collective response from NATO. It is revealing that NATO has not, as yet, prepared contingency plans for the reinforcement of the defence of new members.[22] The possibility of future conflicts occurring in or near NATO territory could have important implications for NATO's credibility and its cohesion if it appears unwilling to take seriously what some members may consider to be legitimate security issues.

The complication of the decision-making process is a second, and already problematic, concern that is likely to be exacerbated by enlargement. Chapter One showed how the difficulties of decision making negatively affected Alliance cohesion during NATO's Balkan interventions and influenced the decision of the United States not to engage NATO in the immediate response to 9/11. The need for a consensus makes it likely that, the greater the number of members, the greater the difficulty of forging one, whether over the initial response to a situation or over the strategy and tactics that should be employed to deal with it. However, some analysts have suggested that the 2004 enlargement may in fact facilitate decision making, as the accession of several Central and East Europeans states, commonly perceived to be Atlanticist in orientation, may cause a change in the internal dynamics of NATO and shift the balance in the United States' favour. The widespread support in Central and East European NATO states for the US position on the 2003 Iraq War is often cited in this respect. None the less, it is not certain that this assessment will hold true in the future, as it is based on the view that the Central and East European states are homogeneous, which they clearly are not. It is possible that enlargement will exacerbate an existing decision-making problem, thus negatively affecting NATO.

Enlargement may also aggravate a further existing weakness: NATO's collective military capabilities. In theory, the MAP should ensure that new members have a minimal degree of military capability, in order to be able to interoperate with existing members and therefore be contributors to NATO's collective military capabilities, rather than consumers of the security it provides. However, even before enlargement there was no NATO standard of military capability and, given that existing members have struggled to operate together, it is likely that new members, whose capabilities are inferior to those of established members, will add little value. Some analyses suggest the Czech Republic, Hungary and Poland are not expected to reach 'mature capability' before 2009.[23] This weakness will be particularly significant should military reform stall or reverse or other commitments fail to be met. Hungary is a case in point. As Croft comments, 'Hungary agreed to raise its defence spending to 1.8 per cent of GDP by 2001 (well below the NATO median of 2.0 per cent), it actually achieved either 1.7 per cent (according to NATO) or just 1.3 per cent (using SIPRI data)'.[24] Although NATO publicly reprimanded Hungary, there was in reality very little that it could do. The implications of this lack of progress are potentially very great. Lindley-French, for example, argues that enlargement will lead to a four-tier NATO comprising the US, which is vanishing into the military-technical distance, the UK and France, which are in the military mid-Atlantic, the other continental West Europeans and the new members.[25] Opponents of enlargement have argued that it will almost inevitably mean a decrease in NATO's collective military effectiveness. Although NATO took a more robust approach to military reform in the second round of enlargement, partly as a result of the lessons of Kosovo,[26] which resulted in an additional commitment by new members when they signed accession protocols in March 2003, there are still no guarantees that this will ensure that military reform will continue. Enlargement, primarily a political process, therefore has potentially serious implications for NATO's military competence and, as a result, its future military role.

the nature of nato

The potential impact of enlargement on NATO's collective military capabilities leads to a third set of counter-arguments: the implications for the nature of NATO. If opponents of enlargement are correct in assuming that the larger the Alliance becomes the less militarily capable it will be, there is a distinct possibility that enlargement will, inevitably, increasingly politicize NATO, which might ultimately result in its transformation from a military alliance to a political 'talking shop'. This argument has been employed to explain

Russia's changed view of enlargement, as it is argued that Russia now recognizes that the larger NATO grows, the more political it is likely to become, which in turn will make it less of a military threat. Regardless of the merits of this particular argument, the ongoing enlargement process will inevitably change the nature of NATO. The question is how and to what extent.

Critics of enlargement identify a number of different areas in which it may have a negative impact. There is perhaps more weight to these arguments since the decision to have a 'big bang' enlargement in the wake of 9/11. Some argue that the imperatives of the war on terrorism have distorted the criteria for membership, whether political or military, and that the contributions that the members that joined in 2004 could make to the war on terrorism were perceived as more important than the contribution they could make to NATO.[27] Romania, for example, arguably did not fulfil the MAP criteria yet backed the US on the war on terror and is geo-strategically important. If this is the case, then the 'big bang' enlargement may well have addressed short-term objectives without fully considering the medium and long-term implications.

conclusion

NATO gained a new role through post-Cold War enlargement – initiating an essentially political process in order to stabilize Europe both for members and non-members. Enlargement was a risky endeavour, as it had the potential either to contribute to the creation of a new European security order or to the establishment of new dividing lines in Europe. The potential impact on NATO as an insti-tution was equally serious. Thus, although opponents and advocates of enlargement continue to differ on its impact on European secur-ity and on NATO itself, they agree that it will have far-reaching con-sequences. It is revealing that the main focus of the post-9/11 debate about enlargement has not been about the size and composition of NATO, but rather its impact on NATO.

It appears that enlargement is one of the success stories of NATO over the past decade. This is the case both for the new members, for whom enlargement is of considerable historic importance and for NATO itself, as the possibility of its paralysis has not yet come to pass. However, it is still too early to assess the medium to long-term impact of enlargement. As time passes, it will become clear whether the objectives that have been pursued by members as they have endorsed the ongoing enlargement process will be achieved and in particular whether the safeguarding of its collective military capabilities and the avoidance of the transformation from a military alliance into a political 'talking shop' will be compatible with an enlarged NATO. It will then be apparent whether such a significant second round of enlargement created more problems than it solved and raised more questions than it answered.

summary

- Although NATO enlargement is not a new phenomenon, certain characteristics of post-Cold War enlargement differentiate it from previous rounds; most notably the accession of former Warsaw Pact members and former members of the Soviet Union, as well as the size of the 2004 second round.
- When the post-Cold War enlargement debate began in the early 1990s, it encountered a number of problems including the impact on NATO–Russia relations and intra-NATO disagreements. NATO, nevertheless, began preparations and the first round took place in 1999. Additional measures were taken to facilitate further enlargement but for many reasons it was not anticipated that NATO would embark on a second round in the near future.
- From 2001 onwards, there was a shift in the debate, resulting from US endorsement of a second round, the implications of 9/11 and an improvement in NATO–Russia relations. These changes opened the way for a big bang enlargement in 2004. NATO retains an open door policy, so further rounds are inevitable.
- NATO enlargement can be explained by a number of factors, including the benefits for European security and stability and the facilitation of military operations. At the same time, however, there are potentially significant drawbacks to NATO enlargement including the possible destabilization of European security and stability, the potential undermining of NATO and changes to the nature of NATO.
- Although opinions are divided about whether enlargement will ultimately have a positive or negative impact, there is no doubt that it will have far-reaching consequences.

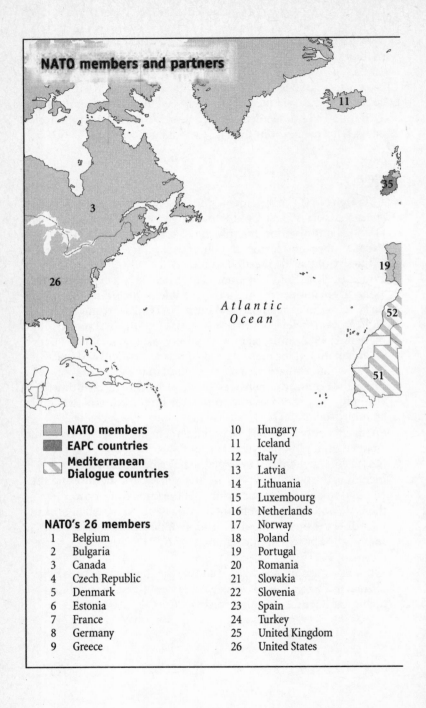

NATO members and partners

11

35

19

52

51

3

26

Atlantic Ocean

	NATO members
	EAPC countries
	Mediterranean Dialogue countries

NATO's 26 members

1	Belgium	10	Hungary
2	Bulgaria	11	Iceland
3	Canada	12	Italy
4	Czech Republic	13	Latvia
5	Denmark	14	Lithuania
6	Estonia	15	Luxembourg
7	France	16	Netherlands
8	Germany	17	Norway
9	Greece	18	Poland
		19	Portugal
		20	Romania
		21	Slovakia
		22	Slovenia
		23	Spain
		24	Turkey
		25	United Kingdom
		26	United States

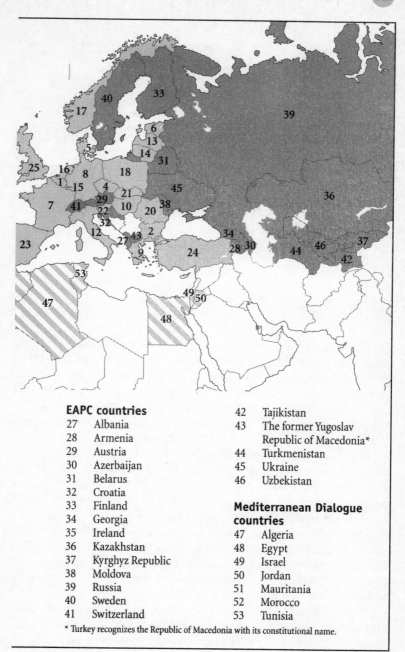

EAPC countries

27	Albania
28	Armenia
29	Austria
30	Azerbaijan
31	Belarus
32	Croatia
33	Finland
34	Georgia
35	Ireland
36	Kazakhstan
37	Kyrghyz Republic
38	Moldova
39	Russia
40	Sweden
41	Switzerland
42	Tajikistan
43	The former Yugoslav Republic of Macedonia*
44	Turkmenistan
45	Ukraine
46	Uzbekistan

Mediterranean Dialogue countries

47	Algeria
48	Egypt
49	Israel
50	Jordan
51	Mauritania
52	Morocco
53	Tunisia

* Turkey recognizes the Republic of Macedonia with its constitutional name.

Map by **MAP**grafix

outreach and partnership: nato's relations with its neighbours

introduction

Partnership and outreach to third countries is the last major area of reform that NATO has embarked on since the end of the Cold War. With the exception of the enlargement process, initially reaching out to, and eventually establishing partnership agreements with, NATO's neighbours to the East and South is very different from the other reforms that NATO has initiated. However, given the absence of similar programmes during the Cold War, the transformation in terms of NATO's roles and responsibilities has been just as profound. Outreach and partnership arrangements with countries to NATO's East, which accounts for most of Central and Eastern Europe and parts of Central Asia, as well as Russia and Ukraine, have absorbed most attention since the early 1990s. A second programme with NATO's Mediterranean neighbours also began during the 1990s, yet was, until recently, far less prominent than the outreach to the East. Changes in the strategic environment resulting from 9/11 have, however, caused the attention devoted to countries to NATO's South to become increasingly important.

The overall aims of NATO's partnership and outreach programmes have remained the same regardless of the geographic focus of the programmes: to promote dialogue, enhance mutual understanding and to initiate and sustain changes in the political and military cultures of Partners. These different measures are all designed to enhance stability and thereby increase NATO's security. As the partnership programmes have developed, however, additional benefits have emerged. Rather than simply being consumers of the benefits of partnership, Partners have progressively become contributors to NATO's post-Cold War operations, particularly the Central and East European countries. Although direct military contributions, in the form of providing forces, have been important, assistance has also included indirect contributions such as the granting of over-flight rights or permission to base forces on national territory. Political support from Partners, such as that offered in the aftermath of 9/11, has also been apparent.[1] All of these contributions can be seen to be a direct result of NATO's partnership programmes. These important by-products of partnership demonstrate how the programmes that NATO has pursued with its neighbours to the East and South since the end of the Cold War are mutually beneficial. At the same time, however, the outreach and partnership programmes have the potential to detract time and attention away from NATO's own internal reforms and harm relations both with Partner and non-Partner countries.

This chapter is divided into three parts. The first provides an overview of NATO's relations with countries to its East. It begins by discussing NATO's initial outreach to the East through the North Atlantic Co-operation Council (NACC) and later the Euro-Atlantic Partnership Council (EAPC) and the Partnership for Peace (PfP) initiative. It then gives an overview of NATO–Russia and NATO–Ukraine relations. The second part discusses NATO's outreach to the South through the Mediterranean Dialogue. It shows how and why more attention has been given to this programme since 9/11 and discusses the different proposals that have recently emerged about how to develop this programme to better address the challenges of the post-9/11 security environment. The final part discusses the challenges that NATO's partnership and outreach initiatives have posed and their potential problems and pitfalls.

the origins of nato's partnership and outreach initiatives

The wave of peaceful revolutions that spread across Central and Eastern Europe, the subsequent breakup of the Warsaw Pact and the eventual dissolution of the Soviet Union set NATO a dilemma regarding its response to the changed strategic environment: whether to continue an inward-looking approach to security, by focusing on the development of its own members or whether to begin a new outward-looking approach, by increasingly focusing on the development of its neighbours to the East. This problem had obviously not existed during the Cold War, when outreach, co-operation and partnership were prevented by the constraints of bipolarity. However, the existence of a number of weak states in Central and Eastern Europe, with the potential to threaten Europe's stability and security, very quickly resulted in recognition of the need to adopt a proactive approach. In many respects, the security vacuum in the early post-Cold War period made NATO's decision to pursue outreach and partnership programmes inevitable, as only this approach could prevent a possible worsening of an already volatile situation. From the outset, therefore, NATO's outreach and partnership programmes must primarily be seen in terms of the benefits they held for NATO although they also offered benefits to NATO's Central and East European neighbours.

The foundations of NATO's present partnership and outreach programmes can be seen as early as June 1990, in the 'Message from Turnberry' in which the NATO Foreign Ministers expressed their determination 'to seize the historic opportunities resulting from the profound changes in Europe to help build a new peaceful order in Europe, based on freedom, justice and democracy. In this spirit, we extend to the Soviet Union and to all other European countries the hand of friendship and co-operation'. They continued by stating, 'true and enduring security in Europe will be best assured through mutual acknowledgement and understanding of the legitimate security interests of all states. We are ready to contribute actively to building confidence and closer relations between all European countries, including the members of the two alliances'.[2]

This early message of friendship was reiterated in July 1990, when the NATO Heads of State and Government, meeting in London, issued a Declaration stating how they intended to modify NATO in order for it to respond to changes in the security environment. NATO, they declared, must become an 'agent of change' that could 'help build the structures of a more united continent, supporting security and stability'. The London Declaration also outlined a framework for a new strategy toward former Warsaw Pact adversaries. NATO invited President Gorbachev and other representatives of Central and East European countries to Brussels, to address the NAC, and also to establish 'regular diplomatic liaison', which would enhance co-operation by allowing NATO 'to share with them our thinking and deliberations in this historic period of change'. This was part and parcel of the wider friendship strategy, as the leaders recognized that

> in the new Europe, the security of every state is insepar-ably linked to the security of its neighbours. NATO must become an institution where Europeans, Canadians and Americans work together not only for the common defence, but to build new partnerships with all the nations of Europe. The Atlantic Community must reach out to the countries of the East which were our adversaries in the Cold War, and extend to them the hand of friendship.[3]

Following the London Declaration, a joint declaration and com-mitment to non-aggression was signed in Paris in November 1990, signalling the formal end of adversarial relations and the intention to refrain from the threat or use of force against the territorial integrity or political independence of any state.

outreach and partnership to the east

As the initial post-Cold War period progressed it became increasingly clear that formalizing and institutionalizing the relationship between NATO and its former adversaries was desirable. In the November 1991 Rome Declaration, NATO declared that it was ready to consider 'a more institutional relationship of consultation and cooperation on political and security issues'. Having laid this foundation, the NACC, which was the first institutionalization of relations between NATO and its Central and East European neighbours, emerged at the end of 1991. The NACC met for the first time in December 1991 and con-sisted of (the then sixteen) NATO members and twenty-two 'former adversaries'. Its composition reflected its role as a means to deal with the legacy of the Cold War. Agreement was reached to meet annually at foreign minister and monthly at ambassadorial level and provision was made for meetings on other issues, including defence planning, and so on. The NACC provided both the political framework for relations between NATO and its former adversaries and a forum for co-operation and dialogue about political and security matters.

In May 1997, the EAPC replaced the NACC and it now maintains the overall political structure for NATO's relations with its Partners. The EAPC differs from the NACC because it is not limited to coun-tries that were 'former adversaries' but also includes West European non-NATO members, such as Sweden and Finland. This reflects the conclusion, which had been drawn in the first half of the 1990s, that a more sophisticated institutional solution had to be found to reflect the contributions of non-NATO members to NATO's post-Cold War operations. The EAPC meets once a month at ambassadorial, twice a year at foreign and defence minister and occasionally at Heads of State and Government level. The majority of EAPC members have also established diplomatic missions at NATO HQ in Brussels, which has facilitated consultation.

The current members of the EAPC are: Albania, Armenia, Austria, Azerbaijan, Belarus, Belgium, Bulgaria, Canada, Croatia, Czech Republic, Denmark, Estonia, Finland, France, Georgia, Germany, Greece, Hungary, Iceland, Ireland, Italy, Kazakhstan, Kyrgyz Republic, Latvia, Lithuania, Luxembourg, Moldova, Netherlands, Norway, Poland, Portugal, Romania, Russia, Slovakia, Slovenia, Spain, Sweden, Switzerland, Tajikistan, The Former Yugoslav Republic of Macedonia, Turkey, Turkmenistan, Ukraine, United Kingdom, United States and Uzbekistan.

An important component of the EAPC is the Partnership Action Plan (PAP), which provides consultation and practical co-operation in areas including regional issues, arms control, etc. Each EAPC PAP lasts for two years and is constructed according to the needs of the country in question. The most recent example is the PAP against Terrorism (PAP-T), which was agreed at the 2002 Prague Summit.

military provisions: partnership for peace

A military dimension developed alongside the political dimension of NATO's partnership programmes during the 1990s. The PfP initiative, first proposed by the then US Secretary of Defense, Les Aspin, in October 1993 and approved by NATO at the January 1994 Brussels Summit is the best example.[4] In contrast to the NACC/EAPC, which were multilateral forums for discussion of political and security issues, the PfP provides a bilateral link between NATO and PfP Partners, enabling Partners to pursue defence and military-related activities and co-operation. In contrast to the political nature of the EAPC, the PfP is designed to initiate and strengthen domestic military reform in Partner countries and strengthen military relations between NATO and PfP Partners. Although the PfP programme was welcomed, many members were also somewhat disappointed with it, as there was a sense that it could delay NATO membership, the ultimate objective of many PfP participants, by providing a 'holding space' and the initiative was sometimes referred to as the 'Policy for Postponement'.

When the PfP was launched in 1994, all states participating in the (then) NACC and CSCE were eligible for membership. The PfP was not limited to 'former adversaries' in the same way as the NACC,[5] ensuring that its membership was diverse. Partners in the PfP have ranged from West European neutrals, such as Switzerland and Sweden, to countries of the Caucasus and Central Asia.

The diversity of countries represented in the PfP programme ensures similar diversity in the reasons why each country is participating. The major interest of the West European neutrals, for example, has been to increase co-operation on military matters with both NATO and non-NATO members. For some East European and Central Asian members the purpose of the PfP has primarily been to initiate and encourage different aspects of domestic military reform. As a result of the varied reasons for participation the programme has had to offer great flexibility to meet its members' expectations. PfP mechanisms allow for each Partner to agree an Individual Partnership Programme (IPP) with NATO. Each IPP is created from the full range of activities, exercises and programmes offered by NATO, including the fight against terrorism, reform of the armed forces and civil emergency planning. Partners select those activities that correspond best to their interests to create their IPP, which is then submitted to NATO as a 'Presentation Document'. The concept of 'self-differentiation' is an important component of the PfP. The IPP is then formally agreed and provides the basis of the Partner's relationship with NATO. An enhanced version of the IPP – the Individual Partnership Action Plan (IPAP) – is also available for those countries that want and are able to deepen their relationship with NATO.

Alongside the IPP and IPAP, the PfP Planning And Review Process (PARP) provides an additional mechanism that allows for an assessment of Partners' capabilities and encourages standardization. This is an optional commitment offered to PfP members. The PARP focuses on defence-related co-operation and has a key operational benefit, as the development of appropriate capabilities increases the level of interoperability between NATO and its Partners, allowing them to participate more easily in NATO operations, should they wish to do so. The Istanbul Summit also saw the beginnings of a 'Partnership Action Plan on Defence Institution Building' to assist Partners in developing democratically responsible defence institutions.[6]

In order to ensure that Partners are able to influence NATO decisions about operations that may involve them, the PfP Partners have permanent representation at NATO HQ in Brussels and also in the International Co-ordination Centre at SHAPE, which provides facilities for co-ordination between NATO and non-NATO members.

the political and military benefits of outreach to and partnership with the east

NATO's outreach and partnership programmes were originally designed to provide help for Central and East countries to address a number of diverse political and military issues and eventually became a key part of preparing Central and East European countries for enlargement. Alongside the benefits that these political and military measures have brought, there is an increasingly important strategic benefit of partnership, which is changing the dynamics of the relationship between NATO and its Partners. As partnership programmes, particularly those relating to military issues, have evolved, Central and East European countries have been increasingly able to contribute to NATO's post-Cold War operations, particularly those in the Balkans. Chapter One demonstrated how the IFOR, SFOR and KFOR were NATO-led, rather than NATO-only operations, given the sizeable contribution of non-NATO nations. It would have been much more difficult to assemble such a diverse mix of forces and conduct these operations without the relationships that had been developed in the NACC/EAPC and PfP frameworks. This demonstrates the strategic value of partnership programmes, in that, by encouraging interoperability and providing mechanisms for participation in NATO operations, the burden of managing European security can be shared.

Although partnership programmes have proved useful in European interventions, their strategic value has recently been demonstrated much farther from NATO's traditional area of operation, most notably in Afghanistan. Partners in Central Asia (for example Uzbekistan) are allowing forces and supplies to be based on former Soviet bases, which has eased logistics. Moreover, some Partners have also granted over-flight rights, which have facilitated the conduct of military operations within the context of the war on terrorism. The partnership agreements forged in the 1990s were important influences on these decisions because, as in the Balkans, it would have been far more difficult to secure these benefits if there had not already been a relationship between these Central Asian states and NATO.

The strategic value of partnership is likely to become even more important as extra-European interventions become more prominent parts of NATO's operations. This is because of the remoteness of these present and future interventions from

NATO members' territory and the need to find solutions to the logistical dilemmas that distance poses. Partnership programmes have had major benefits for the management of Europe but are likely to be of even greater significance for addressing wider security issues.

Since the end of the Cold War, NATO has taken a two-fold approach to outreach and partnership with Central and East European states. The NACC/EAPC has provided a political forum for discussion of security issues and concerns and the PfP has substantiated this by allowing for practical support in developing armed forces, initiating and strengthening military reform and facilitating contributions to NATO operations. Thus, political consultation and military co-operation are mutually reinforcing processes. This approach is significant, as it makes reforms harder to reverse. The result of outreach and partnership has been a significant contribution to stability across the Euro-Atlantic region and therefore an equally significant contribution to NATO's security.

nato–ukraine relations and nato–russia relations

In addition to partnerships with Central and East European countries, NATO has developed distinctive bilateral relationships with Ukraine and Russia. Although Russia and Ukraine were founder members of the NACC, are currently members of the EAPC and participate in the PfP programme, their special status merits a distinct approach, resulting in additional arrangements and provisions. Ukraine is strategically important because it is a buffer between NATO territory and Russia, making its post-Cold War evolution very important and, moreover, it is the most populous country to emerge from the former Soviet Union. Russia is even more important because it is the only country in the Euro-Atlantic area that could, by itself, affect European security and stability; indeed, it is the single most important variable influencing this. As a result of these specificities, relations between NATO and Russia and NATO and Ukraine were formalized, from 1997 onward, in a way that differentiates them from other Central and East European countries.

nato–ukraine relations

NATO–Ukraine relations are influenced by three different dynamics: the objectives of post-Cold War Ukrainian foreign policy, developments in EU-Ukraine relations and developments in Ukraine-Russia relations. The thrust of Ukrainian foreign policy, since the end of the Cold War, has reflected that of other Central and East European states. As we noted in Chapter Five, many of these states saw the end of the Cold War as an opportunity to 'return to Europe'. For Ukraine, this primary objective would be achieved through NATO, that is, a relationship with NATO was the best way to construct links with Europe. Second, EU–Ukraine developments have been an important influence on NATO–Ukraine relations, as the EU has not been particularly willing to address the issue of Ukrainian membership because of political and economic weaknesses in Ukraine and because of the implications for the EU. Although membership of the EU remains a foreign policy priority for Ukraine, as long as it remains a distant prospect, the relationship with NATO will always assume greater importance for Ukrainian policy-makers as a link to Europe. Third, Ukraine–Russia relations are important for NATO–Ukraine relations because of the leverage that Ukraine has with Russia.[7] In many respects, a relationship with NATO has been perceived as a guarantee against any future deterioration of relations between Russia and Ukraine. This assumption of the 'insurance policy' provided by NATO has caused the NATO–Ukraine relationship to gain in significance. Thus, Ukraine's relationship with NATO is its closest with international organizations.[8]

The centrepiece of NATO–Ukraine relations is the Charter on a Distinctive Partnership (CDP), signed at the Madrid Summit in 1997. The CDP signalled a strengthening of ties between Ukraine and NATO by providing a framework for consultation about and co-operation on a number of issues, for example, civil–military relations and defence planning. The CDP also has a crisis consultation mechanism that can be activated when Ukraine perceives a threat to its security. This is not, however, a security guarantee in the Article 5 sense. To manage these issues effectively, a NATO–Ukraine Commission (NUC) was set up as part of the CDP. Representatives from NATO and Ukraine meet at least twice a year to discuss issues including conflict prevention, crisis management and defence reform. In addition, NATO opened a NATO Information and Documentation Centre in Kiev in 1997, the Ukrainian Mission to NATO was launched in 1997 and a NATO Liaison Office was opened in Kiev in 1999.

future prospects for nato–ukraine relations

The mechanisms and agreements outlined above have not only ensured that Ukraine's relationship with NATO is the closest of all its relationships with international organizations but also that it is deeper and more developed than NATO's relationship with any other Central or East European state (except Russia). There is potential, however, for even further deepening. As noted in the previous chapter, Ukraine announced its decision to apply for NATO membership in May 2002. Since the end of the Cold War, Ukrainian élite and public opinion has been divided on the desirability of membership, although it has been suggested that some public opinion polls indicate a growing acceptance of the possibility.[9] Although Ukraine could potentially play an important role in the management of European security, given its geographic position, the prospect of Ukrainian membership poses a number of problems. First, democratic, economic and military reforms have not progressed as quickly in Ukraine as in other Central and Eastern states. In the absence of a quickening of these processes membership will remain out of reach, as Ukraine will not fulfil the political and military criteria set by NATO. Second, Russia is currently hostile to the possibility of Ukrainian membership. Without a substantial change in this position, serious discussion of Ukraine's credentials for NATO membership could antagonize Russia and jeopardize NATO–Russia relations. This is not necessarily an insurmountable problem but remains a consideration. Given these two constraints, the Ukranian objective of NATO membership is likely to remain a medium to long-term development, if it succeeds at all.

This likelihood raises the question of how NATO will manage relations with Ukraine in the mean time. The development of a new strategy will probably become increasingly pressing, if NATO is to avoid Ukraine increasingly perceiving itself as a 'loser' in the enlargement process. At the same time, any deepening of the relationship between NATO and Ukraine, for example an enhanced CDP, could bring with it new, and perhaps unnecessary, expectations, such as a security commitment. Finding the appropriate level and intensity for present and future NATO–Ukraine relationships is likely to absorb much time and attention.

nato–russia relations

Although NATO–Ukraine relations are well developed, the NATO–Russia relationship goes beyond it in importance and intensity. Indeed, NATO's relationship with Russia is its most important partnership. The objectives of the relationship mirror those of other partnership agreements: to promote confidence-building, overcome ongoing suspicions and misconceptions and provide a basis for partnership and co-operation. However, the NATO–Russia relationship has been particularly problematic.

First, it almost goes without saying that the dynamics of NATO–Russia relations are inevitably complicated by an issue that does not exist elsewhere: the legacy of the Cold War and, in particular, that NATO was formed to counter the Soviet threat. Although NATO has consistently denied that its present purpose is to continue to defend against Russia, many in the Russian political and military establishments harbour a continuing distrust of, or could even be termed hostile toward it. Opposition to NATO remains most strong in the Russian military. This problem is exacerbated by the position of some of NATO's most recent members, who, given their experience of Soviet dominance during the Cold War, suspect Russia's motives.

Second, as Ambrosio suggests, no country has been more affected by the end of the Cold War, because of the implosion of the Soviet Union and Russia's subsequent emergence without its former satellite states.[10] In this light, managing relations with Russia has meant a very careful strategy has had to be pursued; one that does not reinforce the perception that the end of the Cold War was Russia's loss and NATO's gain. For obvious reasons, this is particularly important with respect to enlargement.

Third, NATO and Russia have found themselves on opposite sides in post-Cold War conflicts, in Europe and beyond. As later parts of this analysis will show, this has had major implications for their relationship. These influences have caused relations between NATO and Russia to be particularly complex in comparison to other partnership arrangements.

the origins of the nato–russia relationship

The development of a relationship between NATO and Russia was not inevitable. In the early post-Cold War period, Russia's initial objective was to develop a pan-European security system, which would elevate the importance of institutions such as the OSCE. However, there was little support for this among other members of the Euro-Atlantic community, so developing a relationship with NATO became the only realistic alternative.

Developing the institutional set-up and defining the parameters of the NATO–Russia relationship proved problematic, primarily as a result of the lack of a consensus among the Russian élite about the type of relationship that should be pursued (which continues to be matched by a complementary lack within NATO).[11] The influence which Russia should be able to exert over NATO has been a particularly difficult issue; one which has arguably become even more complex since the accession of some Central and East European countries, for whom a more prominent Russian presence is problematic.

Initially, the relationship between NATO and Russia was set within the NACC and PfP. However, neither programme was seen by the Russian élite as befitting its special status and many believed that, by joining the PfP programme, Russia was simply being treated like any other state. For Russia, relations with NATO would have to be conducted within a new, specially created forum, which would symbolize its distinctive role in European security. As the first round of NATO enlargement approached, it became important for NATO to find a way to address Russia's concerns and smooth the way. Treating Russia in a way that reflected its position, as well as finding a way to pacify it with respect to NATO's inevitable enlargement were key considerations in negotiations from the mid-1990s onward.

the permanent joint council

The NATO–Russia Founding Act on Mutual Relations, Co-operation and Security, signed in Paris on 27 May 1997, was the first attempt to address the two concerns outlined above. The Founding Act formally established the NATO–Russia Permanent Joint Council (PJC), which was the first institutionalization of the relationship. The PJC provided a forum for consultation on a range of security issues.

The signing of the Founding Act did not resolve the issue of the degree of Russian influence on NATO decision-making and this would prove crucial to the outcome of the PJC. From a Russian perspective, the PJC would not only reflect its special status but would also be a way that it could meet four objectives: to minimize the military consequences of NATO enlargement, possibly to obtain some guarantees against further enlargement, to enhance its influence on NATO's future transformation and to obtain NATO's support for a new European security system.[12] For Russia, the benefits of the PJC were two-fold: it provided a forum for discussion of its security concerns and an opportunity to have more influence on NATO affairs. From NATO's perspective, the main perceived benefit of the PJC was that the more Russia was involved with NATO the less it would be concerned about it, thus making it more likely to co-operate, not only on security issues but, perhaps more importantly, on enlargement. Russian 'involvement' in NATO issues would be precisely that – involvement rather than influence. For NATO, the PJC was to give Russia 'a voice not a veto'.

The PJC was probably the most that could have been expected from NATO–Russia relations in this period, yet it is important to recognize that it was created because of necessity – the need to appease Russia and manage enlargement – rather than because of a genuine desire for co-operation on either part. Moreover, there appeared to be a gap between the expectations of the PJC and its actual capabilities. It was always probable that, 'when push came to shove', it would prove insufficient.

the impact of operation allied force on nato–russia relations

The limitations of the PJC, particularly with respect to the question of influence, were exposed in 1999 in the run-up to, and during, Operation Allied Force, when Russia vehemently opposed NATO's intervention. The Kosovo crisis, described as the 'most dangerous turn in Russian–Western relations since the early 1980s',[13] had a dramatic impact on NATO–Russia relations. Russia has had links with Serbia for several hundred years, which, for many, explains its support of Serbia and firm opposition to Operation Allied Force. However, Russian opposition to NATO intervention had other fundamental roots. Yeltsin comments, in this respect,

> Did Clinton really think that the problem was our national sympathy for Serbs? Didn't he understand that we were talking about America's approach to the Kosovo problem, about the fate of all Europe, about the fate of the whole world? This was not just a question of some special 'Slavic kinship' attributed to Russian–Serbian relations. We would have reacted the same way if it were a question of any other country – Poland, Spain or Turkey. The country of origin was irrelevant.[14]

Russia's reaction to Operation Allied Force was far more about NATO and its implications for Russia than it was about Serbia. Black comments, in this respect that, 'a real sense of danger emerged after NATO began acting "out of zone" and behaving, according to many Russian observers, as "vigilantes" outside the framework of international law and the strictures of the UN Security Council'.[15] The development of NATO's out-of-area missions and, in particular, self-authorized operations was one of the central issues determining Russia's response to the Kosovo crisis.

Following the commencement of NATO air-strikes against Serbia in March 1999, Russia took a number of steps: it suspended its participation in the PJC and PfP, it withdrew its military mission from NATO, it terminated talks on the establishment of NATO's military mission in Moscow and it ordered the NATO information representative in Moscow to leave the country. This demonstrated that NATO–Russia relations were not on a firm enough footing to withstand disputes and that the PJC really was giving Russia 'a voice' but certainly 'not a veto' on NATO decisions. Operation Allied Force left NATO–Russia relations at a low point.

toward an enhanced nato–russia relationship

After Operation Allied Force, NATO–Russia relations recovered slightly, due to Russian participation in the KFOR, yet remained problematic until 9/11. Following 9/11, the quality of US–Russia and also NATO–Russia relations improved dramatically. President Putin was the first foreign leader to offer his condolences to President Bush on 11 September 2001 and more significantly, on 24 September, he defined his country's post-9/11 strategy: Russia would turn toward the West. In a televised address, Putin outlined five measures that would eventually cause a shift in the quality and intensity of Russia's relations with the United States and with the West in general. The measures were: Russia would pass relevant intelligence to the United States to aid the war on terrorism, it would allow humanitarian flights to the regions where future operations in that war would take place, it would consider allowing the US to use air bases in Central Asia, it would be willing to participate in search and rescue operations if necessary and it would supply arms to the Northern Alliance.[16] This logistical and intelligence co-operation demonstrated a shift in Russia's relationship with the US and the West more generally. In addition, Putin adopted the shrewd strategy of linking Russian problems in Chechnya with al-Qaeda, making Russia part of the war on terrorism rather than a country unaffected by it. The result was that he effectively silenced critics of Russia's military operations in Chechnya.[17]

As a result of changes resulting from 9/11, in particular Russian support for, and co-operation in, the war against terrorism, there was an opportunity to forge a deeper relationship between Russia and NATO. This can be seen as the key benefit of Putin's post-9/11 strategy. Writing in late 2001, Antonenko commented, 'Russia hopes its participation in the anti-terrorist coalition will secure a more decisive role for Russia in its relations with the North Atlantic Alliance, particularly if the alliance makes an anti-terrorist campaign one of its core missions'.[18] This assessment proved to be correct. Discussions of how to build upon the original mechanisms that had been put in place in 1997 were pushed forward by a proposal by the British Prime Minister, Tony Blair, to deepen relations between NATO and Russia within a new institutional framework. The basic idea was that NATO–Russia relations should move beyond discussions, which had been the main function of the PJC. Russia, it was suggested, could participate in decisions in key areas of common interest such as counter-terrorism, peacekeeping operations and other security concerns. It was not, as one British official said, 'about Russia joining NATO or taking part in NATO's integrated military structure' but was a proposal for a relationship that is 'more collaborative, not just a talking point'.[19] This new way of managing NATO–Russia relations prioritized problem-solving rather than discussion.

the nato–russia council

Blair's proposal eventually resulted in the establishment of the NATO–Russia Council (NRC) at the Rome Summit on 28 May 2002. The NRC allows for consultation, consensus-building, co-operation, joint decision-making and joint action and is far more ambitious than the PJC. It meets at least once a month at ambassadorial and military representatives level. The fight against terrorism, crisis management and the non-proliferation of WMD have been identified as key areas of co-operation, although the NRC can address any area of mutual interest. The agenda of the NRC is therefore far more focused than that of the PJC. The NRC is also different in that NATO met with Russia in the PJC after members had already reached a consensus. In contrast, the NRC treats Russia and NATO members equally. As a result of Putin's post-9/11 strategy not only was Russia able to justify its actions in Chechnya, it was also able to ensure the emergence of new, improved collaborative arrangements with NATO that built upon existing structures and potentially enhanced Russia's role.

future prospects for nato–russia relations

When the NRC was established in 2002 there were great hopes for future NATO–Russia relations, given the improvement that had taken place since 9/11. Expectations are now more realistic and some have indicated that Russia and the West have reached 'the end of the honeymoon', given recent Russian developments such as its opposition to the war with Iraq, a more assertive policy toward its former satellite states, a negative attitude toward the EU and NATO enlargement processes and increasingly authoritarian trends in its politics.[20] It appears that the high point of relations between Russia and the West in the immediate aftermath of 9/11 is unlikely to be hit again, which will inevitably affect the NATO–Russia relationship.

There is the possibility of deeper involvement between NATO and Russia either in the form of a revised NRC or even Russian membership of NATO. For the moment, a revised NRC appears unnecessary; the present arrangements are working relatively well so revisiting its nature and objectives seems premature. Russian membership of NATO remains theoretical, because even though there has been some discussion of this Russia has not officially declared its interest in joining. One advocate of Russian membership, James Baker, suggests that it would bring clear benefits to European security. He comments, 'keeping Russia out of NATO increases the risk of Russian expansionism, while making it clear that Russia would be eligible for admission [...] reduces that risk'.[21] This may or may not be the case. However, regardless of the benefits that some perceive may come from potential Russian membership, any discussion has to take into account three different factors. First, Russia fails to meet the political and military criteria set by NATO; without substantial progress in these areas, Russian membership is not viable. Second, many of the new members from Central and East Europe would, in all likelihood, have grave reservations about Russian membership, given present concerns about its motives and intentions. This is a crucial obstacle, as NATO enlargement can only proceed on the basis of a consensus. At present, such a consensus simply does not exist. Third, Russian membership of NATO would undoubtedly change its nature and would transform it into the pan-European security institution that Russia has prioritized since the end of the Cold War. As a result of these influences, Russian membership of NATO is highly problematic and not likely to be resolved in the near future.

Regardless of the possibility of Russian membership of NATO, NATO–Russia relations will remain important for the foreseeable future, not simply because of the implications of any downturn for the stability of the Euro-Atlantic area but also because of the influence that Russia will continue to have on the war on terrorism, resulting from its location, its intelligence capabilities and its links with Central Asian states. It is clear from recent events that NATO–Russia relations are likely to remain unpredictable rather than stable, to be complex rather than straightforward and to oscillate between partnership and conflict. Ensuring that the mechanisms that have been put in place since 2002 are able to cope with these changes in the nature and intensity of

NATO–Russian relations will remain the main challenge facing NATO and Russia.

the mediterranean dialogue

In addition to outreach to and partnership with countries to its east, in the 1990s, NATO initiated outreach to countries to its south. At the Brussels Ministerial Meeting in December 1994, the Alliance launched the 'Mediterranean Dialogue', a programme of outreach and co-operation with six countries on its southern flank: Egypt, Israel, Jordan, Mauritania, Morocco and Tunisia. Algeria joined the Dialogue on 14 March 2000, bringing the number of Partners to seven. The Mediterranean Dialogue aimed to 'contribute to security and stability in the Mediterranean, to achieve better mutual understanding and to correct misperceptions about NATO among Mediterranean Dialogue countries'.[22] The Mediterranean Dialogue therefore attempted to increase the effectiveness of NATO in addressing risks emanating from the south and reflected the growing recognition that the security of the Allies was closely related to developments in the Mediterranean.[23] The broad objectives of the Mediterranean Dialogue and its rationale reflected NATO's outreach initiatives to Central and Eastern Europe.

The thrust of the Mediterranean Dialogue has been regular bilateral discussions – the 26 + 1 formula, and multilateral discussions – the 26 + 7 formula, using the same self-differentiation model as the PfP. The aim is to promote greater understanding of NATO, in addition to discussing the security concerns of the Mediterranean participants. Mediterranean Dialogue countries have participated in NATO's Balkan interventions; for example, Egypt, Jordan and Morocco participated in IFOR and SFOR and Jordan and Morocco participated in KFOR. However, the military dimension of the Mediterranean Dialogue has remained relatively underdeveloped.

divergent perceptions of the dialogue

In contrast to NATO's Central and East European initiatives, the Mediterranean Dialogue has not greatly developed beyond its original mandate. This is not the result of one single factor but rather the combined effect of several different influences, meaning the Mediterranean dimension of outreach and partnership has been less prominent than the Central and East European.

Ever since the start of the Mediterranean Dialogue there has been a lack of uniform commitment from NATO members. Some, particularly the Mediterranean members, prioritized the programme, whereas others, particularly the United States, showed very little interest. This is important, as without the sustained interest of, and input from, the US, the Mediterranean Dialogue was unlikely to progress far. Whilst there was interest in the programme, there was also a lack of agreement among members about how far to develop the Dialogue beyond the general objectives of confidence building, transparency and co-operation. This was as much the case for the Mediterranean members, who had demonstrated enthusiasm for the programme, as it was for other members. There has also, traditionally, been a perceptual difference between the US and the Mediterranean Allies with respect to the Mediterranean region. Policy-makers in the United States primarily think of the Eastern Mediterranean, viewing it as a stepping-stone to the Middle East and the Persian Gulf. European policy-makers, in contrast, think of the Western Mediterranean.[24]

In addition to intra-NATO differences, there has been a lack of a consensus between NATO and the Mediterranean Partners on the starting point of the Dialogue. For most NATO members, its primary objective is to facilitate discussion and dialogue; Mediterranean participants have expected that 'hard' issues would be addressed, for example, the Arab-Israeli conflict.[25]

the impact of external events on the dialogue

External events have also affected the progress of the Mediterranean Dialogue. The 1991 Iraq War focused attention on risks emanating from the South but in the initial post-Cold War period, the challenges of the East were perceived as far more pressing. Events on the European continent and the need to stabilize Europe absorbed vast amounts of NATO's attention throughout the 1990s. The Arab-Israeli peace process has also affected the Mediterranean Dialogue: many of the participating North African and Middle Eastern countries have been either unwilling or unable to co-operate with Israel, even if this 'co-operation' is simply participating in a meeting at which Israel is present. The failure to separate the broader security issues dealt with by the Mediterranean Dialogue from the Arab-Israeli peace process has therefore limited the Dialogue.

Another external agent is the impetus behind the Dialogue. From its inception, the process – to what extent it could, given the constraints outlined above – has been NATO-led. Unlike outreach to and partnership with the East, which in part met the desire from

Central and East European states for NATO engagement and assistance, NATO supplied the Mediterranean Dialogue without much
demand from the Mediterranean Partners.

As a result of these multiple influences, the Mediterranean
Dialogue has been far more limited in scope and ambition than the
EAPC and PfP initiatives and has suffered from a lack of investment
in both resources and attention. The Dialogue has therefore been
exactly that – a political dialogue – rather than the political and military partnership that NATO has forged with countries to its East.

toward a revitalised mediterranean dialogue

Relatively little attention was given to the Mediterranean Dialogue
during the 1990s and early 2000s. However, in recent months it has
received increasing amounts. This is perhaps inevitable, regardless
of 9/11, given the relative stability on the European continent and
the increasing realization that programmes such as the EAPC and
PfP were well established, and had either essentially achieved their
objectives or were well on the way to doing so. The success of
NATO's Eastern initiatives therefore influenced renewed discussion
of the Mediterranean Dialogue.

The second, and far more important, influence is the impact of
9/11. Changed threat perception and, in particular, the increasing
prominence of security challenges from the South has caused it to
become particularly interesting to NATO. The South presents a wide
range of direct and indirect security challenges, including 'hard'
challenges, such as the proliferation of WMD and international terrorism and 'soft' challenges, such as immigration and drug trafficking. The increasing prominence of these issues has indicated that a
greater focus on the South is needed for NATO to continue to
enhance the stability and ensure the security of its members,
reflecting the perception that the main threats to that security no
longer emanate from the East. This is particularly important given
that a number of NATO members – France, Greece, Turkey, Spain
and Italy – are Mediterranean countries and therefore particularly
exposed to these potential risks.

Another change since 9/11 can be linked to NATO adaptation, in
particular to the greater geographic scope of its missions. The
removal of geographic limits and the first extra-European interventions (as discussed in Chapter Two) have direct implications for
NATO's relations with the South. NATO command of the ISAF in

Afghanistan and, in particular, its ongoing role in the Mediterranean through Operation Active Endeavour, could have a direct impact on North African and Middle Eastern countries and could lead to them feeling increasingly threatened by NATO, even if this is not its intention. This is important, as NATO in general, and some of its members in particular, have traditionally had an image problem in North Africa and the Middle East. Specifically, many of those states have been suspicious of NATO and some have perceived it to be searching for a new North African or Middle Eastern enemy. This perception has remained, despite the fact that this is precisely the myth the Mediterranean Dialogue is trying to dispel. In the light of continuing suspicions and the beginning of NATO interventions beyond Europe, a renewed effort to achieve the original objectives of the Mediterranean Dialogue – to dispel myths through the provision of information about NATO and its activities and to reassure North African and Middle Eastern states of NATO's intentions – is arguably more important than it has ever been.

deepening or widening the mediterranean dialogue?

As a result of these influences, attention began to refocus on the challenges of the South and how to rethink the Mediterranean Dialogue to reflect changes both in the strategic environment and within NATO. There have been increasing calls to reassess the Mediterranean Dialogue to make it more effective. A number of proposals have emerged regarding the changes that should be made, consisting of both widening and deepening measures.

The first set of proposals focuses on the lessons learned from NATO's partnership initiatives with Central and East European countries. Some have suggested a direct application of the PfP model to the Mediterranean Dialogue, citing its principal lesson as the prime motivating factor – that changes in individual countries can have a collectively important positive impact. This concept, of deepening the existing Mediterranean Dialogue, is superficially appealing. However, it is difficult to know which aspects of the PfP and how much of its 'menu' is appropriate for inclusion in any new Mediterranean initiative. Moreover, it is highly questionable whether NATO would be able to transfer the mechanisms it used in Central and East Europe to North Africa and the Middle East. Although there were, and remain, important political and cultural differences between NATO members and Central and East European countries, the differences between NATO and North African and Middle Eastern countries are much more profound. It is far from certain whether the benefits of the PfP – encouraging civilian control of the armed forces, to give one example – are transferable to a new context. A new, improved and deepened Mediterranean Dialogue would have to take into account the cultural and political specifics of each participant and the potential limitations that this would mean for NATO initiatives.

The measures outlined above also raise the question of what the ultimate objective of a new Mediterranean initiative would be. Unlike Central and East European countries, for whom engagement and partnership with NATO was perceived as being a first step toward membership, North African and Middle Eastern countries are (for obvious reasons) highly unlikely ever to become members. Determining the long-term objectives of a revised Mediterranean Dialogue would also run contrary to traditional NATO policy, which is to present them ambiguously, if at all. Simply restating that dialogue and co-operation is important is unlikely to be enough to sell a new initiative either to NATO members or to the North African and Middle Eastern states that would be involved.

Widening the Dialogue, through an increase in the number of participants, is the second proposal. Some have gone so far as to suggest that a revised Mediterranean Dialogue should embrace all the countries of the 'Greater Middle East' – essentially from Morocco to Afghanistan – and go beyond its existing narrow confines. This expansive view contains an implicit acknowledgement of the importance of the region to NATO's future security. This measure also presupposes that there is a demand from North African and Middle Eastern countries for engagement with NATO, whether in terms of existing structures or a deeper relationship. There is little evidence at present that the traditionally NATO-driven nature of outreach to the South has been matched by significant changes in the interest either of existing Mediterranean Dialogue members or potential new participants from North Africa and the Middle East. To gain and maintain momentum a new Mediterranean Dialogue will have to be two-way, rather than continuing to be sustained by NATO. Convincing North African and Middle Eastern countries that a new or renewed partnership with NATO is in their interest is a significant obstacle.

The widening and deepening models proposed above represent three schools of thought regarding the future orientation of NATO's outreach to the South: the *maximalists*, the *moderates* and the *minimalists*. The maximalists prioritize the Greater Middle East region and take an expansive view of the potential of a new outreach and partnership programme to the South. The moderates prioritize other regions and countries, for example Caspian Basin countries, such as Azerbaijan and Georgia, with whom there are already some links, rather than the Greater Middle East where there are few or any links. The minimalists prioritize the Balkans and argue that NATO should concentrate on completing unfinished business there, before embarking on new initiatives. Finding common ground among these views is a key challenge for NATO, as the success of any future initiative concerning the South will be dependent on a shared assessment among members about the desirability and feasibility of a new approach.

the 2004 istanbul summit

The June 2004 Istanbul Summit provided some indications of the way forward. Two developments are particularly significant. First, the leaders agreed to enhance NATO's existing Mediterranean Dialogue and make it a genuine partnership.[26] This decision is designed to address the deficiencies and unfulfilled potential of the Dialogue outlined above. Second, they agreed to pursue the 'maximalist' vision of outreach to the Middle East by launching the Istanbul Co-operation Initiative, designed to promote bilateral co-operation between NATO and interested parties in this region.[27] It is anticipated that members of the Gulf Co-operation Council – Bahrain, Kuwait, Oman, Qatar, Saudi Arabia and the United Arab Emirates – will be the first countries to be offered this new initiative. NATO members have therefore agreed to widen *and* deepen existing programmes. However, given the debates that have preceded these moves, it is not certain that progress will be particularly easy nor that the Allies are all convinced of the desirability of these developments, which may restrict the growth and success of the programmes. It could be argued that there was not much substance to NATO's outreach and partnership programmes to the East in the early days but that they evolved into significant programmes, which may indicate that this is also possible in the South. However, the NACC/EAPC and PfP initiatives succeeded because there was a shared perception that dealing with the challenges of the East was both desirable and necessary and so sufficient resources were put in to make them thrive. The lack of progress of the Mediterranean Dialogue and the recent ambivalence of NATO members regarding both a revised Dialogue and the Istanbul Co-operation Initiative indicate that there is not the same sense of urgency about its role in dealing with the South and that they are not willing to commit the same amount of time and level of resources as they did to the countries to the East. NATO's response to the challenges of the South is a 'work in progress'.

the problems and pitfalls of nato's partnership and outreach initiatives

Post-Cold War, NATO has launched, developed and sustained outreach initiatives and partnership programmes to its East and South, with varying degrees of success. These initiatives have not been entirely altruistic endeavours, given that they were originally designed to bring NATO the benefits of enhanced stability, increased security and the military benefits of increased participation of neighbouring countries in NATO's operations.

One of the most significant characteristics of the outreach and partnership initiatives is how NATO has been steadily and deliberately blurring the line between membership and non-membership. This strategy has been advantageous, because of the sense of inclusiveness it has offered and the benefits that can be gained from NATO improving its ability to work with as many countries as possible, regardless of whether or not they are members. Alongside the benefits, partnership has also brought great responsibilities, commitments and complications that are likely to present future challenges to NATO. These can be placed in five 'risk' categories: the overburdening of NATO, the potential damage to Alliance cohesion, the potential damage to NATO's relationship with its Partners, the implications of partnership for NATO's relations with non-Partner members and the implications of partnership and outreach initiatives for the nature of NATO.

the possible overburdening of nato

Partnerships, in particular with Central and East European countries, have meant that as well as ensuring the ongoing political and military progress of its 'old' and 'new' members NATO has taken on the additional burden of ensuring these developments for its non-members. The impact of the stalling or reversal of political and military reform on NATO, its missions and its credibility is far less serious with respect to Partners than for members. However, continued progress is important, because the political and military development of non-members detracts time and resources away from other areas that require just as much, if not more, of NATO's attention.

The complexity of the existing programmes is also perhaps problematic. NATO's partners are not only increasingly diverse geographically, politically and militarily but also in their security interests and co-operation needs. They range, for example, from Switzerland to Jordan to Uzbekistan, all of whom have different requirements and different expectations of their partnership arrangements. NATO has never pursued a 'one size fits all' approach, yet the increasing diversity of its partners may further complicate its programmes. In particular, it is likely to be increasingly difficult to tailor-make bilateral arrangements between NATO and Partners. New initiatives for the Middle East region mean the diversity of NATO's programmes is likely to continue to increase, which may well exacerbate this problem.

potential damage to alliance cohesion

The possibility of NATO increasingly addressing difficult, and perhaps intractable, security concerns in North Africa, the Middle East and beyond not only risks overburdening NATO but also increases the possibility of undermining Alliance cohesion. Generally speaking, there has been a relatively high degree of consensus about the importance of dealing with the challenges of the East and the approaches that should be employed but these features have not characterized discussion of the difficulties of regions beyond Europe. Significantly, the Middle East is arguably the region where the United States and other Allies differ the most, both historically and presently. As Dalia Dassa Kaya comments, 'given their common strategic interests in regional stability, the secure flow of oil, and political and economic reform, one would think that Europe and the United States are bound to cooperate in the Middle East. Yet, cooperation is not inevitable, nor has it been the case historically'.[28] Garton Ash goes one step further by commenting, 'where the cold war against communism in Middle Europe brought America and Europe together, the "war against terrorism" in the Middle East is pulling them apart'.[29] If Garton Ash is correct, these wider differences between America and Europe will inevitably affect NATO's existing, and potential new, initiatives for the Mediterranean and Middle East. Differences are particularly profound with respect to the Arab–Israeli conflict, as there has traditionally been very little agreement between members about the causes of, and solutions to, this. Although greater involvement in North Africa and the Middle East does not automatically mean that NATO should or could adopt a role in the management of the Arab–Israeli conflict, the impact it has had on the success of the Mediterranean Dialogue (and transatlantic relations more generally) indicates that it will be a key – perhaps impossible – obstacle if NATO wants to progress beyond its existing programmes in the South. At the very least, it is a risky strategy for NATO to now focus its attention on issues where the Allies have traditionally differed the most.

potential damage to relations between nato and its partners

Although ever-closer links between NATO and its Partners have proved very useful, the greater the links, the greater the risk that unrealistic expectations are being raised among Partners as to what they will gain from partnership. There have already been concerns whether ever-closer partnership is resulting in the assumption that NATO is making a *de facto* security commitment to its Partners, a commitment which is unlikely to be honoured in a conflict. This has been highlighted in the NATO–Ukraine relationship, given Ukraine's pursuit of an 'insurance policy' relationship, partly to address concerns about the nature of future Ukraine–Russia relations. Raising expectations that are unlikely to be met has serious implications for the quality of relations between NATO and its Partners.

A downturn in relations, due to unfulfilled expectations, is also possible with respect to NATO membership. Although NATO has never presented the PfP programme as the first step on the road, for many it has become exactly that. This is problematic, because as noted previously, many of the present participants in the PfP programme are either unlikely to apply for membership, for example Switzerland, or will only be able to apply in the distant future, if at all. Bhatty and Bronson note that while NATO officials maintain that membership is open to all, they admit, off-the-record, 'there is no possibility of any of these [Central Asian and Caucasian] states ever being permitted to join'.[30] NATO is therefore currently in an unprecedented situation regarding the goal of partnership programmes. This poses a dilemma, not simply because it may be running the risk of raising false expectations about membership, but also because it indicates that it will have to rethink and reorient its partnership programmes. The possible redirection of PfP activities away from membership, whilst retaining the dynamism and vibrancy of the programme will be a key challenge.

potential damage to relations between nato and non-partners

Increasing NATO involvement in the Caucasus and Central Asia, as demonstrated by the June 2004 decision to enhance the EAPC, with a special focus on Partners in the Caucasus and Central Asia,[31] may risk NATO becoming involved in unnecessary confrontations with Russia and with non-Partner countries, such as Iran and China, which have long-established interests in the region. This means NATO risks conflict with countries with which it would otherwise not have been involved. This risk stems from two developments. First, through its Partnership initiatives, NATO now has Central Asian Partners that border China. By gradually approaching, and eventually ending up in, China's backyard, NATO has attracted its attention, to the extent that China began to seek a strategic dialogue in autumn 2002, which resulted in talks between Chinese diplomats and the then NATO Secretary General Lord Robertson.[32] Second, the war on terrorism may provoke even more concern, because of its long-term implications for the deployment of Western forces; even if these movements are not explicitly linked to NATO operations they are likely to have an indirect impact on NATO–China relations. As Medeiros comments, 'from the perspective of a Chinese strategist, the global war against terrorism is an issue of significant concern because it weighs the possibility of the long-term deployment of American and other western forces in Central Asia for a long time'.[33] This is likely, because, as Menon suggests, Central Asia is likely to remain important to the war on terrorism as its environment is ideal for al-Qaeda's purposes.[34] A long-term deployment of Western forces, as well as existing NATO partnership initiatives is likely to heighten concerns about NATO's intentions among non-Partner countries in this region.

In spite of all this, a confrontation with a non-Partner country remains theoretical and many would argue that, rather than feeling threatened by NATO, non-Partner countries like China are simply intrigued. However, given China's response to the spread of the partnership programmes and its concerns about the implications of the war on terrorism there is clearly potential for future problems between NATO and non-Partner countries.

implications for the nature of nato

Breaking down barriers and increasing security through dialogue and co-operation make outreach and partnership essentially political processes, even though there may be military benefits. The increasingly political role that NATO is playing may add momentum to the shift away from its traditional military competences and collective defence role to greater political functions and a collective security role. This increasing politicization, in conjunction with the implications of enlargement and the problem of military capabilities, could signal a change in the balance of NATO's functions and prove to be a significant influence on its nature.

The risks outlined above show that outreach and partnership initiatives are not simply an additional component of NATO's post-Cold War reform but have just as much potential to influence its evolution and vitality as other issues, such as capabilities, that are generally perceived as being far more important. Such initiatives will therefore remain a very significant aspect of post-Cold War NATO reform and one that should justifiably continue to absorb much time and attention.

conclusion

The main conclusion that can be drawn from over a decade of initiatives is that initiating outreach programmes and forging partnerships is a role that plays to NATO's strengths. Moreover, although there are risks associated with these arrangements, the proven benefits by far outweigh them, providing they are well managed. The benefits that can be gained from the forging of relationships between NATO and non-members – whether in the form of dialogue, political or military reform or joint action – are becoming increasingly important. Whilst partnership relationships may not have the same depth and intensity as Alliance relationships, they have undoubtedly been an essential component of the response to the end of the Cold War and the demands of the post-9/11 world.

NATO is well placed to continue to consolidate its existing partnerships and perhaps forge new ones to address post-9/11 problems. The Mediterranean Dialogue – revised or otherwise – has particular potential, if the obstacles that currently exist can be overcome, because relations between the West and the Arab world will continue to be very important in the foreseeable future. In particular, the support of Islamic countries for the war on terrorism will be crucial. There are limits to what NATO can do but it is likely that, as initiatives evolve to respond to the requirements of European and wider security, it will continue to play a valuable role in building partnerships.

summary

- The end of the Cold War provided NATO with an opportunity to establish relationships and partnerships with non-NATO members. Over the course of the post-Cold War period, NATO has forged political and military links with Central and East European countries, Russia, Ukraine and Mediterranean countries, through the NACC/EAPC, PfP programme and the Mediterranean Dialogue. It has also established additional arrangements for its relationships with the Ukraine and Russia, to reflect their special status.

- NATO's partnership initiatives have shared common objectives, including to promote dialogue and enhance mutual understanding and to initiate and sustain changes in the political and military cultures of NATO's Partners. A series of agreements, such as the IPP, has been developed to achieve these objectives.

- Partnership has brought additional benefits for NATO, particularly with respect to the efficient execution of military operations involving Partners and the facilitation of non-NATO operations that have taken place as part of the war on terrorism.

- Relations between NATO and Russia have been problematic, primarily due to the legacy of the Cold War. The initial set-up of NATO–Russia relations proved inadequate in the light of the crisis provoked by Operation Allied Force, although 9/11 signalled a major improvement and allowed new arrangements to emerge. Recent developments between Russia and the West indicate that relations are likely to oscillate between partnership and conflict.

- Until 9/11, NATO's initiatives to the South were low profile and had not developed to the same extent as partnership initiatives to East and Central Europe, because of divergent perceptions of the Mediterranean Dialogue, the impact of external events and the impetus behind the Dialogue. As a result of 9/11, more attention has been given to the challenges of the South, which has resulted in an upgrade of the existing Mediterranean Dialogue and the unveiling of a new initiative for the Middle East.

- Although NATO's partnership initiatives have brought great benefits, there are equally significant potential drawbacks. These include the overburdening of NATO, damage to NATO cohesion, damage to relations between NATO and Partners and non-Partners and negative implications for the nature of NATO. However, the benefits of outreach and partnership appear to outweigh the costs.

an alliance revitalized? future challenges for nato

The multifaceted adaptation process that NATO embarked on in response to the end of the Cold War and 9/11 has ensured it has retained an unrivalled position in the Western security architecture. These changes show that NATO remains an evolving institution, not one that was permanently marginalized by changes in the strategic environment. This is undoubtedly a remarkable achievement, unmatched by any other alliance in history. However, NATO's record with respect to its post-Cold War adaptation is mixed: it has made significant progress in adapting the functional and geographic scope of its military missions but considerably less progress in improving the capabilities needed to perform them. Other aspects of adaptation, such as the enlargement process and the outreach and partnership initiatives have been very successful to date although they will require careful management in the future to avoid potential pitfalls. It is also not inevitable that the issues that have most recently attracted its attention – the challenges posed by WMD and international terrorism – can be successfully addressed in the NATO context. A degree of caution should therefore be exercised when assessing NATO's current achievements and its future prospects.

the future of nato

The course of future NATO reform and the long-term vitality of NATO will ultimately be determined by two influences: the

challenges posed by future international events to its existing structures and capabilities and the quality of relations between the Allies.

It is impossible to assess NATO's response to events that are as yet
unknown. However, it is difficult to imagine a more challenging
scenario than the loss of the threat NATO was originally designed to
counter or, to a lesser extent, a greater crisis of confidence than
NATO experienced in the aftermath of 9/11. Moreover, NATO's past
record in responding to massive changes in the strategic environment post-1989 and post-9/11, through its reform processes, augurs
well for its ability to respond effectively in the future.

The second influence – the quality of relations between the Allies
– is more uncertain. The state of transatlantic relations was a widely
debated subject before 9/11. However, the intensity of the debate
about the perceived emergence of 'continental drift' has increased
since those events and the war with Iraq. The period from 9/11 until
the present has seen some of the greatest highs and greatest lows
between NATO Allies. The high point was undoubtedly
12 September 2001, when NATO invoked the principle of Article 5,
yet only a year later, the run-up to and course of Operation Iraqi
Freedom seemed to signal the lowest point for decades. The Iraq
War continues to feature prominently in discussion of NATO's
future and although it is still too soon to draw any firm conclusions
it is nevertheless possible to make some preliminary assessments
about its impact.

At present, there have been no major shifts in the positions of the
Allies: those who opposed the war remain just as convinced of the
case against it as those who supported it remain convinced of the
case for. However, the stalemate that characterized the discussions
that led to Operation Iraqi Freedom has not resulted in a stalemate
on NATO's role. Proposals for NATO to play a part in Iraq began to
emerge as early as April 2003.[1] Colin Powell asked NATO to consider
expanding its role in December 2003, a move that was not greeted
positively by all the Allies but NATO nevertheless provided
planning, force generation, logistics and communications support
to the Polish-led multinational force. More importantly, in June
2004, following a request by the Iraqi Interim Government, the
Allies agreed to train Iraq's security forces.[2] Many aspects have yet to
be clarified: for example, where the training will take place and how
many troops will be involved; so it is important to exercise a degree
of caution when assessing what this means for NATO. However, it is
a highly significant move, as there is no real need for NATO as an
institution to train Iraq's security forces, for any country or combination of countries could do this; indeed, some are doing so already.

Some have dismissed NATO's decision to train Iraq's security forces, arguing that the US originally had much more ambitious plans for NATO in Iraq but opposition from some Allies ruled them out. Seen in this light, the decision is far less significant. However, the importance of NATO's present or future responsibility in Iraq should not be measured by its scale or prominence. The idea that NATO somehow has something to prove in Iraq and that a high-profile role is just what it needs to demonstrate post-war transatlantic solidarity and counter its critics is misleading and potentially dangerous. Whilst it is true that the decision to train Iraq's security forces is a small step, it is an appropriate and logical response, given NATO's existing commitments, particularly in Afghanistan, which could be negatively affected by the demands of a larger role in Iraq. It should also not be forgotten that agreement about a NATO position in Iraq – small or large – would have been unthinkable in the run-up to the war and for some months afterwards, given the disputes between the Allies. The recent consensus about NATO's role in Iraq may indicate that transatlantic relations are robust enough to withstand the damaging debates that took place over the war. It also arguably indicates a renewed commitment to NATO that demonstrates that it remains sufficiently important to the Allies to be used as the expression of the common interest that they now have in fostering a stable Iraq.

the death of nato?

Crises among the Allies are not simply post-Cold War or post-9/11 phenomena, because there has never been a 'golden age' in transatlantic relations when serious disputes did not occur. In the future, NATO will certainly have to cope with the pressures and strains of international events, because as long as there are disputes in international politics there will be disputes in NATO. In spite of the historical evidence of transatlantic crises and the inevitability of future conflicts, questions about NATO's vitality are likely to remain. Writing in late 2003, Steven E. Meyer, for example, commented,

> NATO's time has come and gone, and today there is no legitimate reason for it to exist. Although the strong differences exhibited in the Alliance over the war against Iraq have accelerated NATO's irrelevancy, the root causes of its problems go much deeper. Consequently, for both the United States and Europe, NATO is at best an irrelevant distraction and at worst toxic to their respective contemporary security needs.[3]

However, it is difficult to provide compelling evidence to support this view in the light of NATO's activities since 9/11, which indicate that, rather than there being no legitimate reason for it to exist, it continues to address the contemporary security needs of the Allies. In addition to its existing missions in the Balkans, NATO has begun roles in the Mediterranean, Afghanistan and Iraq. It has also completed a second round of enlargement and launched new partnership and capabilities initiatives. Since 9/11 and the Iraq War, existing processes have arguably gained strength rather than been weakened as a result of strains within NATO. It is therefore difficult to argue that what we are witnessing is the slow death of a long-outdated or even irrelevant Alliance.

the value of nato

In addition to recent developments in its internal adaptation and external roles, NATO continues to perform a number of crucial functions that should ensure its position in the Western security architecture in the foreseeable future.

First, NATO is the only institutionalization of the transatlantic link. The way in which it ties North America to Europe is important, not only because of the binding nature of the commitment but also because it is the most straightforward and efficient way to organize transatlantic security relations. Without NATO, these relationships would either have to be organised bilaterally or rely on EU–US arrangements, which obviously do not include all the present Allies. This would complicate matters considerably and so it makes sense to organize transatlantic security relations within a fixed framework. NATO is also of value because of the number and breadth of countries that can meet under its auspices. NATO's partnership programmes and forums such as the EAPC bring together a large and diverse range of countries to discuss specific political and military issues.

Second, NATO remains the main forum in which members can discuss and, where possible, co-ordinate transatlantic security policy. Its existence therefore gives the United States a degree of influence over European security that it would not otherwise have and provides other Allies with a greater potential to influence American policy. Some suggest that NATO is primarily a tool for US foreign policy and that the remaining Allies have very little effective influence over the United States. However, this view overestimates the strength of the United States and exaggerates the weakness of other Allies. Moreover, it does not explain some recent developments, for example, the United States' failure to generate a consensus about a greater NATO role in Iraq.

There will be instances where influence will not affect established policy and a consensus will be impossible to achieve. Having a place where different positions can be explained, even if they are not agreed with, remains valuable. The forum that NATO provides remains crucial not simply for building a consensus about NATO policy but also for discussing issues that fall outside its remit. Although some dismiss this role by calling NATO a 'talking shop', this function is arguably more important today than it ever has been, given the complexity of the post-9/11 world, the uncertainty that has accompanied it and the increased potential for disagreement among the Allies.

Third, NATO remains the most effective mechanism for addressing the shared interests of the Allies through political dialogue and consultation *and* military intervention, when necessary. NATO retains a crucial role in encouraging standardization and interoperability among the Allies, even if it cannot ensure it. This applies to NATO-only operations, NATO-led operations and coalition operations where it is the so-called 'invisible hand'. Regardless of the precise configuration, as long as there is a possibility that Europeans and North Americans may fight alongside each other – and they are far more likely to do this with each other than they are with any other countries – this function will remain important. NATO has also encouraged standardization and interoperability among its Partners, the value of which has been shown both in operations in the Balkans and those which have taken place since 9/11.

Fourth, NATO has proven its ability in the fields of crisis management, peacemaking and peacekeeping throughout the 1990s and beyond, in part resulting from the benefits of standardization and interoperability. This does not presuppose that all NATO's post-Cold War operations have been straightforward because they clearly have not. However, NATO is currently a far more experienced and capable peacemaker, peacekeeper and crisis manager than any other international organization. Moreover, it has developed relationships with other international organizations, primarily the UN, and has established and implemented mechanisms for co-operation with the EU. These operational attributes allow NATO to make a unique contribution to European and wider security.

Fifth, NATO is the most effective mechanism for forging and maintaining political and military partnerships with non-NATO members, whether in Eastern Europe, Russia, Ukraine, the Mediterranean or the Middle East. Other organizations, for example, the EU, can also play a role, but for security and defence-related issues, there is currently no other organization that can match the partnership arrangements and input that NATO can offer.

Last, although it is debatable whether NATO has ever truly been a community of values, it cannot be denied that it continues to embody a group of countries that are more like each other than they are like any other group, regardless of the merits or demerits of the 'continental drift' thesis. The broad similarities of the Allies underpin most of the benefits of NATO.

These six characteristics of NATO represent practical and tangible benefits that only it can currently provide. They do not rely on a nostalgia for the NATO of the Cold War to justify its continued existence but point to its present political and military utility. However, membership has costs as well as benefits and NATO can impede its members' actions as much as it can enhance them. However, the benefits do outweigh the costs. For all these reasons, there is a compelling case in favour of NATO remaining the cornerstone of Western security. This assessment does not mean that NATO should be retained at any cost, however. If in the future a more attractive, efficient or effective alternative emerges then NATO could and should come to an end. At present, however, there is no such alternative and little sign of one materializing.

the challenges facing nato

In spite of the ongoing advantages offered by NATO, long-term trends remain that potentially jeopardize its future vitality. These will have to be overcome if NATO is to maintain its current position of strength in the Western security architecture.

avoiding overstretch

The first challenge will be avoiding overstretch. In this, NATO's multifaceted adaptation is both a strength and a weakness; a strength because it demonstrates its flexibility and the range of military and political instruments it has been able to develop in the post-Cold War and post-9/11 contexts and a weakness because of the demands it has placed on NATO. By initiating internal and external reforms as diverse as capabilities initiatives, outreach and partnership programmes and enlargement, the agenda is now very long and a wide range of issues compete for the Allies' attention and NATO's political and military resources.

It is not simply a question of the breadth of NATO reform and the range of issues on the agenda. There are also great demands being placed on NATO within each of these areas. NATO's missions are perhaps the most obvious example, although there are others such as the partnership initiatives and the enlargement process. The kinds of operations that NATO has been engaged in since the end of the Cold War will continue to be necessary. This means that it is likely to continue to be in demand, given its unrivalled experience of planning and performing such operations. For example, as well as proposals for NATO to take a role in Iraq, analysts and officials have also suggested that it should be involved in keeping the peace in the Middle East.[4] The UN Secretary General, Kofi Annan, has recently invited NATO to play an increasing role in Africa, which indicates that the relationship between the UN and NATO may develop further. Although such proposals show that NATO's military role is still required, the downside is that it is not certain whether it can in fact supply what is being demanded today, let alone what will be demanded in the future, as discussions in mid-2004 about increasing the number of NATO troops in Afghanistan indicate. In a speech to the Royal United Services Institute in June 2004, the NATO Secretary General, Jaap de Hoop Scheffer, tackled this issue head on by commenting:

> Our force generation system is far from optimal. We must improve this system so that we can meet future challenges more efficiently. These challenges can be big – a new headquarters, an operational reserve. But they can also be small – a medical facility, a handful of C-130s and medium lift helicopters, a couple of infantry companies, and certain surveillance and intelligence assets. Given the vast quantities of personnel and equipment available to the Alliance overall, we have to ask ourselves why we still cannot fill them. What is wrong with our system that we cannot generate small amounts of badly needed resources for missions that we have committed to politically? [...] I don't mind taking out my begging bowl once in a while. But as a standard operating procedure, this is simply intolerable.[5]

All NATO's current activities represent issues that the Allies consider sufficiently important to merit inclusion on the agenda. However, NATO is arguably facing a problem of overstretch, which could jeopardize the success of its present and future activities. NATO clearly cannot do everything, so debates about how best to use it need to be rooted in realistic expectations of the available capabilities and resources – political or military – of the Alliance. The Allies should avoid the temptation to endow NATO with the responsibility for additional activities that do not necessarily play to its strengths, potentially undermine its effectiveness and jeopardize its cohesion.

The suggestion that NATO should expand its responsibilities in Iraq is perhaps the best contemporary example.

ensuring nato members are equipped to act

The second challenge, which is linked to that outlined above, concerns the tools that NATO needs. Members already possess the assets to manage the political aspects of NATO's activities. NATO also has the military expertise to initiate and sustain reforms in Partner countries and to plan NATO-led or NATO-co-ordinated operations. However, it is clear that NATO does not, at present, enjoy the collective military capabilities to convert political decisions into efficient and effective military operations. NATO should remain, first and foremost, a military alliance but this is increasingly jeopardized by the combined impact of steady improvements in US capabilities, the missed opportunities of previous capabilities initiatives involving the 'old' Allies and the relative weaknesses of the 'new' Allies. In the absence of significant increases in defence spending and major changes in the allocation of defence resources, both of which are unlikely, arguments in favour of specialization become compelling. Without this, the Canadian and European Allies may remain capable of operating with each other, but not with the United States. Increasing emphasis on specialization and fulfilling niche capabilities appears to be the only choice if the Allies are to remain capable of operating alongside the United States, which along with Canada, is, after all, what makes NATO NATO.

Some have expressed reservations about this new emphasis. Deighton reflects, 'the United States has moved toward reinventing NATO in a way that focuses upon its own global fight against terror, implying that the Europeans must intensify their efforts to update their military capabilities; and, further ensure compatibility with the United States' own capabilities'.[6] She continues, 'if in the medium term the "war" against terrorism loses political salience, a re-imagined NATO may have difficulties acting as an international institution and mediating the wider security interests of all its members if it has become a provider of services, including specialised manpower, to the United States'.[7] This is an interesting position to take, not least because many would see the challenges posed by international terrorism as affecting all the Allies and indeed, the international community as a whole, rather than simply the United States, even if the label 'war on terrorism' is, of course, a US one. Moreover, although the capabilities initiatives that NATO has launched have taken place within the context of the 'war on terrorism', this does not imply that improved capabilities would somehow become redundant in a different context or that the current emphasis on them automatically implies a deterioration of NATO's other functions. Any attempts by the Allies to remain militarily compatible with the United States, whether through specialization or any other means, should be seen as aiming to be effective and responsible contributors to international security both in the context of combating international terrorism and outside it, rather than simply becoming pawns in the United States' fight.

responding effectively to the challenge of us unilateralism

The third issue that threatens NATO's future vitality is US unilateralism. Dealing with this challenge has absorbed much time and attention in recent years, particularly since 9/11 and the Iraq War. As it is the only remaining superpower, with a preponderance of diplomatic, economic, military and political might, many see US unilateralism as inevitable. There will certainly be instances where the United States will act according to its own policy preferences and priorities, which may or may not match those of its NATO Allies. This should not be seen as unusual, or always undesirable, because every member will occasionally act unilaterally. US unilateralism is most damaging to NATO in those instances where there is a consensus about the need to act but no collective capability to do so. It is only when the Allies are incapable of contributing in a useful and meaningful way that US unilateralism is both inevitable and detrimental to NATO. The clearest example of this was the initial response to 9/11, which had obvious implications for NATO and provoked a long, agonizing, yet ultimately well-founded debate about its military credibility. If the Allies are serious about addressing the challenge of US unilateralism, then many – although not all – of them will need to take a long, hard look at how their own military weaknesses exacerbate this problem.

It is not simply a question of the military value with which many of the Allies need to equip themselves to have the best chance of addressing the 'inevitability' of US unilateralism, because it can also be addressed politically. US political unilateralism is only inevitable if the Allies cannot provide credible, innovative alternatives to US policy. This will not always be possible but there is no reason to think that US policy-makers will necessarily want to do things 'the American way' if there is an equally, if not more effective alternative, which provides the political legitimacy that comes from working with Allies. This crucial benefit, which has been shown to be so important since the war with Iraq, should be enough to persuade even the most sceptical US policy-maker that Allies matter and can even add value.

conclusion

NATO has faced some formidable challenges in recent years, not least the end of the Cold War and the disappearance of the Soviet Union and it will inevitably face more in the future. None the less, it is well positioned to continue to respond to the complex security problems of the post-9/11 world. NATO is arguably in a better position post- than pre-9/11, as those events refocused the Allies' attention on it in a way that, before then, was unexpected and unlikely.

It is too early to tell whether combating the threats that characterize the post-9/11 strategic environment will be a long-term unifying mission for NATO. The ways in which the Allies respond in the coming years will either be a confirmation of, or challenge to, the conventional wisdom that, at its founding, NATO not only constituted a collective defence alliance against the Soviet threat but also a community of values that underpinned it, regardless of that, or any other threat.

The Allies are currently grappling with some of the biggest strategic changes since the end of World War Two. There is great scope for disagreement in a world where security threats are multiple, diverse and difficult to address. None the less, as Hamilton has observed, 'the test of allies is not the absence of differences, but the ability to manage them in ways that pull [our] respective strengths and perspectives together and point them in a common direction'.[8] The conclusion of this book is that NATO continues to provide the most desirable framework for ensuring the security of North America and Europe and that, as such, its safeguarding and consolidation is crucial. The challenge facing policy-makers on both sides of the Atlantic is to find the best way to enhance and combine the strengths of the Allies without resorting to a division of labour that will progressively undermine the transatlantic security relationship. This is the key to ensuring that NATO will continue to provide an effective solution to the complex security problems of the post-9/11 world and to sustain the long-term vitality of this relationship.

the north atlantic treaty

Washington, DC 4 April 1949

The Parties to this Treaty reaffirm their faith in the purposes and principles of the Charter of the United Nations and their desire to live in peace with all peoples and all governments.

They are determined to safeguard the freedom, common heritage and civilisation of their peoples, founded on the principles of democracy, individual liberty and the rule of law.

They seek to promote stability and well-being in the North Atlantic area.

They are resolved to unite their efforts for collective defence and for the preservation of peace and security.

They therefore agree to this North Atlantic Treaty

article 1

The Parties undertake, as set forth in the Charter of the United Nations, to settle any international dispute in which they may be involved by peaceful means in such a manner that international peace and security and justice are not endangered, and to refrain in their international relations from the threat or use of force in any manner inconsistent with the purposes of the United Nations.

article 2

The Parties will contribute toward the further development of peaceful and friendly international relations by strengthening their free institutions, by bringing about a better understanding of the principles upon which these institutions are founded, and by promoting conditions of stability and well-being. They will seek to eliminate conflict in their international economic policies and will encourage economic collaboration between any or all of them.

article 3

In order more effectively to achieve the objectives of this Treaty, the Parties, separately and jointly, by means of continuous and effective self-help and mutual aid, will maintain and develop their individual and collective capacity to resist armed attack.

article 4

The Parties will consult together whenever, in the opinion of any of them, the territorial integrity, political independence or security of any of the Parties is threatened.

article 5

The Parties agree that an armed attack against one or more of them in Europe or North America shall be considered an attack against them all and consequently they agree that, if such an armed attack occurs, each of them, in exercise of the right of individual or collective self-defence recognised by Article 51 of the Charter of the United Nations, will assist the Party or Parties so attacked by taking forthwith, individually and in concert with the other Parties, such action as it deems necessary, including the use of armed force, to restore and maintain the security of the North Atlantic area.

Any such armed attack and all measures taken as a result thereof shall immediately be reported to the Security Council. Such measures shall be terminated when the Security Council has taken the measures necessary to restore and maintain international peace and security.

article 6[1]

For the purpose of Article 5, an armed attack on one or more of the Parties is deemed to include an armed attack:

- on the territory of any of the Parties in Europe or North America, on the Algerian Departments of France,[2] on the territory of or on the Islands under the jurisdiction of any of the Parties in the North Atlantic area north of the Tropic of Cancer;

- on the forces, vessels, or aircraft of any of the Parties, when in or over these territories or any other area in Europe in which occupation forces of any of the Parties were stationed on the date when the Treaty entered into force or the Mediterranean Sea or the North Atlantic area north of the Tropic of Cancer.

article 7

This Treaty does not affect, and shall not be interpreted as affecting in any way the rights and obligations under the Charter of the Parties which are members of the United Nations, or the primary responsibility of the Security Council for the maintenance of international peace and security.

article 8

Each Party declares that none of the international engagements now in force between it and any other of the Parties or any third State is in conflict with the provisions of this Treaty, and undertakes not to enter into any international engagement in conflict with this Treaty.

article 9

The Parties hereby establish a Council, on which each of them shall be represented, to consider matters concerning the implementation of this Treaty. The Council shall be so organised as to be able to meet promptly at any time. The Council shall set up such subsidiary bodies as may be necessary; in particular it shall establish immediately a defence committee which shall recommend measures for the implementation of Articles 3 and 5.

article 10

The Parties may, by unanimous agreement, invite any other European State in a position to further the principles of this Treaty and to contribute to the security of the North Atlantic area to accede to this Treaty. Any State so invited may become a Party to the Treaty by depositing its instrument of accession with the Government of the United States of America. The Government of the United States of America will inform each of the Parties of the deposit of each such instrument of accession.

article 11

This Treaty shall be ratified and its provisions carried out by the Parties in accordance with their respective constitutional processes. The instruments of ratification shall be deposited as soon as possible with the Government of the United States of America, which will notify all the other signatories of each deposit. The Treaty shall enter into force between the States which have ratified it as soon as the ratifications of the majority of the signatories, including the ratifications of Belgium, Canada, France, Luxembourg, the Netherlands, the United Kingdom and the United States, have been deposited and shall come into effect with respect to other States on the date of the deposit of their ratifications.[3]

article 12

After the Treaty has been in force for ten years, or at any time thereafter, the Parties shall, if any of them so requests, consult together for the purpose of reviewing the Treaty, having regard for the factors then affecting peace and security in the North Atlantic area, including the development of universal as well as regional arrangements under the Charter of the United Nations for the maintenance of international peace and security.

article 13

After the Treaty has been in force for twenty years, any Party may cease to be a Party one year after its notice of denunciation has been given to the Government of the United States of America, which will inform the Governments of the other Parties of the deposit of each notice of denunciation.

article 14

This Treaty, of which the English and French texts are equally authentic, shall be deposited in the archives of the Government of the United States of America. Duly certified copies will be transmitted by that Government to the Governments of other signatories.

chronology of key events

1947

5 June   Marshall Plan is announced by US Secretary of State, George C. Marshall.

1948

22 January   British Foreign Secretary Ernest Bevin proposes the creation of a Western Union comprising Belgium, France, Luxembourg, the Netherlands and the United Kingdom.

22–25 February   A *coup d'état* results in the Communist Party of Czechoslovakia taking control of the government.

17 March   The Brussels Treaty of Economic, Social and Cultural Collaboration and Collective Self Defence is signed by Belgium, France, Luxembourg, the Netherlands and the United Kingdom.

24 June   The Berlin blockade begins.

6 July   Discussions about the formation of a North Atlantic defence organisation begin in Washington, DC between the Brussels Treaty powers, Canada and the United States.

10 December   Negotiations on the North Atlantic Treaty begin in Washington, DC between the Brussels Treaty powers, Canada and the United States.

1949

15 March	Denmark, Iceland, Italy, Norway and Portugal are invited to join the North Atlantic Treaty.
4 April	Belgium, Canada, Denmark, France, Iceland, Italy, Luxembourg, the Netherlands, Norway, Portugal, the United Kingdom and the United States sign the North Atlantic Treaty in Washington, DC.
9 May	The Berlin blockade is lifted.
24 August	The North Atlantic Treaty enters into force.
17 September	The North Atlantic Council meets for the first time.
5 October	The Defence Committee of the North Atlantic Council meets for the first time.
6 October	President Truman signs the Mutual Defence Assistance Act.

1950

25 June	North Korea attacks South Korea.
19 December	US General Dwight D. Eisenhower is appointed as NATO's first Supreme Allied Commander Europe (SACEUR).
20 December	The Brussels Treaty powers agree to merge the military component of the Western Union into NATO.

1951

2 April	Allied Command Europe becomes operational, with Supreme Headquarters Allied Powers Europe (SHAPE) situated at Rocquencourt, near Paris.

1952

18 February	Greece and Turkey join NATO.
12 March	Lord Ismay becomes NATO's first Secretary General.

| 28 April | The North Atlantic Council meets for the first time in permanent session in Paris. |

1955

6 May	The Federal Republic of Germany joins NATO.
6 May	The Brussels Treaty powers, the Federal Republic of Germany and Italy sign the Western European Union treaty. The Western Union becomes the Western European Union.
14 May	Albania, Bulgaria, Czechoslovakia, East Germany, Hungary, Poland and Romania and the USSR form the Warsaw Pact.

1960

| 27 May | A military *coup d'état* takes place in Turkey. |

1961

| 13 August | The East German government begins to construct the Berlin Wall. |

1962

| 18 March | The Evian Accords establish an independent Algeria. |

1963

| 16 January | The NAC announces that the relevant clauses of the North Atlantic Treaty relating to the former Algerian Departments of France became inapplicable as of 3 July 1962. |

1965

| 9 September | Charles de Gaulle declares that France's military integration in NATO will end by 1969. |

1966

| 10 March | Charles de Gaulle formally announces France's intention to withdraw from NATO's integrated military structure. |
| 14 December | The Nuclear Defence Affairs Committee and the Nuclear Planning Group are established by the Defence Planning Committee. |

1967

31 March	SHAPE opens in Mons, Belgium.
21 April	Military regime takes power in Greece.
16 October	NATO's new headquarters open in Brussels.
13–14 December	The Defence Planning Committee adopts a new concept of flexible response.

1970

5 March	The Nuclear Non-Proliferation Treaty comes into force.

1973

3–7 July	The CSCE opens in Helsinki.

1974

25 April	Military *coup d'état* in Greece.
14 August	Greek forces withdraw from NATO's integrated military command.

1980

20 October	Greek forces rejoin NATO's integrated military structure.

1982

30 May	Spain joins NATO.

1989

10 September	Hungary opens its western border allowing thousands of East German refugees to leave the country.
3 October	Thousands of East German emigrants assemble in the embassies of the Federal Republic of Germany in Prague and Warsaw.
9–10 November	Opening of the Berlin Wall.

1990

7–8 June	NATO leaders issue the 'Message from Turnberry'.

6 July	NATO leaders publish the London Declaration on a Transformed North Atlantic Alliance.
2 August	Iraq invades Kuwait.
7 August	Operation Desert Shield begins.
10 August	The North Atlantic Council holds an emergency meeting at the level of Foreign Ministers to discuss developments in the Gulf.
14 September	The Naval On-Call Force Mediterranean is activated and commences operations in the eastern Mediterranean.
3 October	German reunification takes place.
17 December	Turkey requests that NATO deploy aircraft of the ACE Mobile Force – Air to bolster its defence.

1991

13 January	The ACE Mobile Force – Air is deployed to south-east Turkey.
17 January	Operation Desert Storm begins, with a series of air strikes.
24 February	US-led coalition forces begin the ground offensive into Kuwait.
25 February	Warsaw Pact members announce the dissolution of its military structure.
28 February	Coalition forces liberate Kuwait.
5 March	The ACE Mobile Force – Air is withdrawn from Turkey.
7 May	The Yugoslav Defence Minister declares that Yugoslavia is in a state of civil war.
1 July	The Warsaw Pact is officially disbanded.
7–8 November	A summit meeting of NATO Heads of State and Government takes place in Rome. NATO publishes its new Strategic Concept.
9–10 December	Heads of State and Government of EU member states meet in Maastricht and adopt the

Treaty on European Union, which includes provisions for a Common Foreign and Security Policy.

20 December	First meeting of the North Atlantic Co-operation Council.
25 December	The Soviet Union ceases to exist.

1992

21 February	The United Nations Protection Force is established.
4 June	NATO Foreign Ministers meeting in Oslo announce their readiness to support peacekeeping activities under the responsibility of the CSCE on a case by case basis.
19 June	Foreign and Defence Ministers of WEU members meet at Petersberg, near Bonn.
16 July	Operation Maritime Monitor begins.
2 September	NATO announces its readiness to support peace-making activities in the former Yugoslavia.
14 October	The North Atlantic Council authorizes the use of NATO AWACS to monitor the no-fly zone over Bosnia Herzegovina.
16 October	Operation Sky Monitor begins.
6 November	NATO supplies the UNPROFOR with an operational headquarters.
22 November	Operation Maritime Monitor ends. Operation Maritime Guard begins, signalling an expansion of NATO's role.
11 December	NATO Defence Ministers announce that support for UN and CSCE peacekeeping operations should be part of NATO's missions.
15 December	The UN requests access to NATO contingency plans for possible military operations in the former Yugoslavia.

| 17 December | NATO Foreign Ministers announce their readiness to support further action by the UN in the former Yugoslavia and to strengthen NATO's capabilities in this respect. |

1993

14 January	NATO agrees to enforce a no-fly zone over Bosnia Herzegovina if asked to do so by the UN.
10 March	The North Atlantic Council asks NATO military authorities to develop contingency plans for the possible implementation of a UN peace plan for Bosnia Herzegovina.
12 April	Operation Deny Flight begins.
9 August	The North Atlantic Council approves plans for air strikes in Bosnia Herzegovina under the authority of the UN.
20–21 October	NATO Defence Ministers meet in Travemünde, Germany and discuss various subjects including the Partnership for Peace initiative, the Combined Joint Task Force concept and the proliferation of weapons of mass destruction.

1994

10–11 January	The Brussels Ministerial Meeting takes place. NATO launches the Partnership for Peace initiative and all NACC and CSCE countries wanting to participate are invited to join. The CJTF concept is endorsed as a means to support the development of the European Security and Defence Identity. NATO raises the profile of the threat of weapons of mass destruction. NATO leaders affirm that NATO membership remains open to any state in a position to fulfil the principles of the North Atlantic Treaty.
28 February	Four Serb planes violating the no-fly zone over Bosnia Herzegovina are shot down by NATO aircraft.
9 June	NATO publishes the Policy Framework on Proliferation of Weapons of Mass Destruction.

5–6 December	The CSCE is renamed the OSCE.
1 December	The Mediterranean Dialogue is launched.

1995

30 August	Operation Deliberate Force begins.
21 September	'Study on NATO Enlargement' is endorsed by the North Atlantic Council.
1 November	Bosnian Peace Talks start in Dayton, Ohio.
5 December	Operation Joint Endeavour is approved and the North Atlantic Council endorses the deployment of 60,000 troops to Bosnia.
14 December	The General Framework Agreement for Peace – the Dayton Peace Accord – is signed in Paris.
15 December	The IFOR is established by UNSC Resolution 1031.
16 December	The IFOR begins deploying to Bosnia.
20 December	Operation Deny Flight ends.
20 December	Command of the UNPROFOR is transferred to the NATO-led IFOR.

1996

3 June	NATO Foreign Ministers meet in Berlin. Agreement to develop the European Security and Defence Identity using the CJTF concept is reached.
27 June	The IFOR completes the three tasks it was designed to do.
10 December	NATO confirms its readiness to lead a Stabilization Force in Bosnia Herzegovina.
20 December	The SFOR takes over from the IFOR.

1997

7 May	NATO Information and Documentation Centre is opened in Kiev.

27 May	NATO–Russia Founding Act on Mutual Relations, Co-operation and Security is signed in Paris.
30 May	The NACC holds its final meeting and the first meeting of the EAPC is held.
8 July	The Czech Republic, Hungary and Poland are invited to begin accession talks with NATO.
8 July	The Charter on a Distinctive Partnership is signed by NATO leaders and Ukrainian President Kuchma at the Madrid Summit.
26 September	First meeting of the NATO–Russia Permanent Joint Council at Foreign Minister level.
2–3 December	First meeting of the NATO–Russia Permanent Joint Council at Defence Minister level.
4 December	First meeting of the NATO–Russia Permanent Joint Council at Chief of Staff level.

1998

3–4 December	Annual Anglo–French summit held in Saint Malo, France. President Jacques Chirac and Prime Minister Tony Blair issue the Saint Malo Declaration on European Defence.

1999

12 March	The Czech Republic, Hungary and Poland join NATO.
24 March	Start of Operation Allied Force.
23–25 April	The Washington Summit is held in Washington, DC. A new Strategic Concept is approved and the Defence Capabilities Initiative and the Membership Action Plan are launched.
3–4 June	Cologne European Council is held. The EU agrees to transfer most of the functions of the WEU to the EU.
10 June	Operation Allied Force ends.
12 June	KFOR is deployed to Kosovo.

10–11 December	Helsinki European Council is held. The EU announces its intention to create a RRF to perform Petersberg Tasks and the HG is outlined.

2000

14 March	Algeria joins the Mediterranean Dialogue.

2001

22 August	Operation Essential Harvest is launched.
11 September	Terrorists fly three passenger planes into the World Trade Center in New York and the Pentagon in Washington, DC. A fourth plane crashes in a field in Pennsylvania.
12 September	The NAC invokes the principle of Article 5 in response to the terrorist attacks on the United States.
26 September	Operation Essential Harvest ends.
27 September	Operation Amber Fox begins.
2 October	The North Atlantic Council confirms the invocation of Article 5.
4 October	NATO agrees to provide eight measures of an individual and collective nature to support the United States.
7 October	Operation Enduring Freedom begins.
8 October	NATO begins deploying AWACS to the United States.
9 October	Operation Eagle Assist begins.
26 October	Operation Active Endeavour begins.
6 December	NATO publishes 'NATO's Response to Terrorism'.
6 December	The ISAF is established in accordance with the Bonn Agreement.

7 December	The NATO–Russia Permanent Joint Council announces the decision to create a NATO–Russia Council.
15 December	Operation Amber Fox ends.

2002

14 May	The North Atlantic Council, meeting in Reykjavik, removes the geographic limits on NATO's missions.
16 May	Operation Eagle Assist ends.
28 May	The NATO–Russia Council is established.
24–25 September	NATO Defence Ministers are briefed by Donald Rumsfeld about the creation of a NATO strike force.
21–22 November	NATO Heads of State and Government meet in Prague and agree the Prague Capabilities Commitment, the NATO Response Force and a series of WMD and terrorism initiatives.
15 December	Operation Amber Fox ends.
16 December	Operation Allied Harmony begins.

2003

4 February	Operation Joint Endeavour is extended to escort ships in the Strait of Gibraltar.
6 February	Turkey requests that NATO begin planning for defensive measures in the event of a war with Iraq. France, Germany and Belgium block this request.
19 February	The DPC, convened by NATO Secretary General Lord Robertson on 16 February, authorizes defensive measures to assist Turkey.
26 February	Operation Display Deterrence begins.
17 March	Agreement is reached between the EU and NATO on Berlin Plus.
19 March	Operation Iraqi Freedom begins.

31 March	The EU takes over Operation Allied Harmony and re-names it Operation Concordia.
30 April	Operation Display Deterrence ends.
1 May	President Bush announces an end to major combat operations in Iraq.
12 June	NATO defence ministers agree to streamline NATO's command structure.
19 June	Supreme Allied Command Atlantic is decommissioned. Allied Command Transformation is established.
11 August	NATO takes command of the ISAF.
1 September	Allied Command Europe becomes Allied Command Operations.
6 October	NATO announces an expansion of the ISAF's operations from Kabul to Kunduz.
15 October	NATO Response Force is launched at a ceremony in the Netherlands.

2004

16 March	Operation Active Endeavour is expanded to the whole of the Mediterranean.
29 March	Bulgaria, Estonia, Latvia, Lithuania, Slovakia, Slovenia and Romania join NATO.
28–29 June	Istanbul Summit of NATO Heads of State and Government. NATO agrees to conclude the SFOR's mission and hand over responsibility to the EU and agreement is reached to train Iraq's security forces.
1 July	NATO takes command of PRT in Mazar-e-Sharif and Maimana.

member profiles

Belgium (founder member)

Population   10,388,000

Total armed forces

Active   40,800
Reserves   13,750

Army   24,800
Navy   2,450
Air Force   10,250

	2001	2002	2003
GDP (US$)	227bn	277bn	
GDP per capita (US$)	22,060	26,827	
Defence budget (US$)	2.3bn	2.8bn	3.0bn

Bulgaria (2004)

Population	7,814,000

Total armed forces

Active	51,000
Reserves	303,000

Army	25,000
Navy	4,370
Air Force	13,100

	2001	2002	2003
GDP (US$)	13.5bn	15.7bn	
GDP per capita (US$)	1,710	2,021	
Defence budget (US$)	360m	400m	527m

Canada (founder member)

Population	31,478,000

Total armed forces

Active	52,300
Reserves	36,900

Army	19,300
Navy	9,000
Air Force	13,500

	2001	2002	2003
GDP (US$)	704bn	732bn	
GDP per capita (US$)	22,708	23,256	
Defence budget (US$)	7.4bn	7.6bn	9.1bn

Czech Republic (1999)

Population   10,287,000

Total armed forces

Active   57,050 (including 20,400 conscripts)

Army   39,850
Navy   n/a
Air Force   13,100

	2001	**2002**	**2003**
GDP (US$)	57bn	69bn	
GDP per capita (US$)	5,511	6,721	
Defence budget (US$)	1.2bn	1.4bn	1.9bn

Denmark (founder member)

Population   5,314,000

Total armed forces

Active   22,880
Reserves   64,900

Army   14,700
Navy   4,000
Air Force   3,500

	2001	**2002**	**2003**
GDP (US$)	161bn	172bn	
GDP per capita (US$)	30,439	32,435	
Defence budget (US$)	2.1bn	2.24bn	2.6bn

Estonia (2004)

Population   1,383,000

Total armed forces

Active   5,510 (including 1,130 conscripts)

Army   2,550 (including 1,030 conscripts)
Navy   440 (including 230 conscripts)
Air Force   220 (including 50 conscripts)

	2001	2002	2003
GDP (US$)	5.4bn	6.3bn	
GDP per capita (US$)	3,925	4,529	
Defence budget (US$)	67m	99m	158m

France (founder member)

Population   59,729,000

Total armed forces

Active   259,050
Reserves   100,000

Army   137,000
Navy   44,250
Air Force   64,000

	2001	2002	2003
GDP (US$)	1300bn	1600bn	
GDP per capita (US$)	22,115	26,841	
Defence budget (US$)	25.8bn	30.7bn	34.9bn

Germany (1955)

Population   82,148,000

Total armed forces

Active   284,500 (including 94,500 conscripts)
Reserves   358,650

Army   191,350 (including 73,450 conscripts)
Navy   25,650
Air Force   67,500

	2001	**2002**	**2003**
GDP (US$)	1900bn	2200bn	
GDP per capita (US$)	22,700	27,234	
Defence budget (US$)	21.5bn	25.1bn	27.4bn

Greece (1952)

Population   10,624,000

Total armed forces

Active   177,600 (including 98,321 conscripts)
Reserves   291,000

Army   114,000 (including 81,000 conscripts)
Navy   19,000 (including 9,800 conscripts)
Air Force   33,000

	2001	**2002**	**2003**
GDP (US$)	117bn	149bn	
GDP per capita (US$)	11,050	14,069	
Defence budget (US$)	3.4bn	3.6bn	4.0bn

Hungary (1999)

Population	9,849,000

Total armed forces

Active	33,400 (including 22,900 conscripts)
Reserves	90,300
Army	23,600 (including 16,500 conscripts)
Army Maritime Wing	270
Air Force	7,700

	2001	2002	2003
GDP (US$)	52bn	65bn	
GDP per capita (US$)	5,385	6,571	
Defence budget (US$)	823m	1.1bn	1.4bn

Iceland (founder member)

Population	285,000

Total armed forces	0

	2001	2002	2003
GDP (US$)	8bn	8bn	
GDP per capita (US$)	27,209	29,631	
Defence budget (US$)	n/a		

Italy (founder member)

Population 57,438,000

Total armed forces

Active	200,000 (including 20,100 conscripts)
Reserves	63,200
Army	116,000 (including 12,800 conscripts)
Navy	36,000
Air Force	48,000

	2001	**2002**	**2003**
GDP (US$)	1,100bn	1,300bn	
GDP per capita (US$)	19,060	23,300	
Defence budget (US$)	15.9bn	20.2bn	22.3bn

Latvia (2004)

Population 2,366,000

Total armed forces

Active	4,880 (including 1,600 conscripts)
Reserves	13,050
Army	4,000
Navy	620 (including 57 conscripts)
Air Force	250

	2001	**2002**	**2003**
GDP (US$)	7.5bn	8.4bn	
GDP per capita (US$)	3,118	3,533	
Defence budget (US$)	7m	113m	198m

Lithuania (2004)

Population	3,692,000

Total armed forces

Active	12,700 (including 4,700 conscripts)
Reserves	245,700
Army	7,950 (including 3,027 conscripts)
Navy	650 (including 300 conscripts)
Air Force	1,150 (including 150 conscripts)

	2001	2002	2003
GDP (US$)	11.9bn	13.9bn	
GDP per capita (US$)	3,236	3,756	
Defence budget (US$)	167m	273m	359m

Luxembourg (founder member)

Population	441,000

Total armed forces

Active	900
Army	900
Navy	n/a
Air Force	n/a

	2001	2002	2003
GDP (US$)	19bn	24bn	
GDP per capita (US$)	43,527	53,795	
Defence budget (US$)	146m	204m	229m

Netherlands (founder member)

Population 15,975,000

Total armed forces

Active   53,130
Reserves   32,200

Army   23,150
Navy   12,130
Air Force   11,050

	2001	2002	2003
GDP (US$)	384bn	479bn	
GDP per capita (US$)	24,129	29,966	
Defence budget (US$)	5.7bn	6.9bn	7.2bn

Norway (founder member)

Population 4,524,000

Total armed forces

Active   26,600 (including 15,200 conscripts)
Reserves   219,000

Army   14,700 (including 8,700 conscripts)
Navy   6,100 (including 3,300 conscripts)
Air Force   5,000 (including 3,200 conscripts)

	2001	2002	2003
GDP (US$)	164bn	192bn	
GDP per capita (US$)	36,336	42,404	
Defence budget (US$)	3.0bn	3.5bn	4.2bn

Poland (1999)

Population	38,618,000

Total armed forces

Active	163,000 (including 81,000 conscripts)
Reserves	234,000

Army	104,050 (including 58,700 conscripts)
Navy	14,300 (including 7,500 conscripts)
Air Force	36,450 (including 14,800 conscripts)

	2001	2002	2003
GDP (US$)	180bn	188bn	
GDP per capita (US$)	4,656	4,881	
Defence budget (US$)	3.4bn	3.5bn	3.9bn

Portugal (founder member)

Population	10,021,000

Total armed forces

Active	44,900 (including 9,100 conscripts)
Reserves	210,930

Army	26,700
Navy	10,950
Air Force	7,250

	2001	2002	2003
GDP (US$)	111bn	137bn	
GDP per capita (US$)	11,100	13,694	
Defence budget (US$)	1.6bn	1.7bn	1.9bn

Romania (2004)

Population   22,332,000

Total armed forces

Active   97,200 (including 29,600 conscripts)
Reserves   104,000

Army   66,000 (including 18,500 conscripts)
Navy   7,200
Air Force   14,000 (including 3,800 conscripts)

	2001	2002	2003
GDP (US$)	38.8bn	45.7bn	
GDP per capita (US$)	1,732	2,049	
Defence budget (US$)	989m	1.1bn	1.4bn

Slovakia (2004)

Population   5,400,000

Total armed forces

Active   22,000 (including 3,500 conscripts)
Reserves   20,000
Army   13,700 (including 1,800 conscripts)
Navy   n/a
Air Force   7,000 (including 1,700 conscripts)

	2001	2002	2003
GDP (US$)	19.9bn	22.7bn	
GDP per capita (US$)	3,694	4,207	
Defence budget (US$)	345m	464m	624m

Slovenia (2004)

Population 1,998,000

Total armed forces

Active 6,550 (including 1,200 conscripts)
Reserves 20,000

Army 6,550
Navy n/a
Air Force n/a

	2001	2002	2003
GDP (US$)	18.9bn	22.0bn	
GDP per capita (US$)	9,430	11,017	
Defence budget (US$)	275m	274m	387m

Spain (1982)

Population 40,026,000

Total armed forces

Active 150,700
Reserves 328,500

Army 95,600
Navy 22,900
Air Force 22,750

	2001	2002	2003
GDP (US$)	588bn	738bn	
GDP per capita (US$)	14,730	18,445	
Defence budget (US$)	7.1bn	7.8bn	8.5bn

Turkey (1952)

Population   68,652,000

Total armed forces

Active   514,850 (including 391,000 conscripts)
Reserves   378,700

Army   402,000
Navy   52,750
Air Force   60,100

	2001	2002	2003
GDP (US$)	148bn	182bn	
GDP per capita (US$)	2,190	2,656	
Defence budget (US$)	5.7bn	6.5bn	7.8bn

United Kingdom (founder member)

Population   59,702,000

Total armed forces

Active   212,660
Reserves   272,550

Army   116,670
Navy   42,370
Air Force   53,620

	2001	2002	2003
GDP (US$)	1400bn	1600bn	
GDP per capita (US$)	23,842	26,318	
Defence budget (US$)	33.6bn	36.6bn	41.3bn

United States (founder member)

Population	289,696,000

Total armed forces

Active	1,427,000
Reserves	1,237,700

Army	485,000
Navy	400,000
Air Force	367,600
Marine Corps	174,400

	2001	2002	2003
GDP (US$)	10.2tr	10.4tr	
GDP per capita (US$)	35,264	36,058	
Defence budget (US$)	329bn	362.16bn	382.6bn

All figures adapted from International Institute for Strategic Studies, *The Military Balance 2003–04* (Oxford: Oxford University Press, 2004).

MUTUALLY REINFORCING INSTITUTIONS

OSCE

EAPC/PFP

NATO

	Canada	Belarus	Tajikistan [1]
	United States	Kazakhstan	Turkmenistan
		Kyrgyzstan	Uzbekistan

COUNCIL OF EUROPE

Bulgaria	Albania
Iceland	Armenia
Norway	Azerbaijan
Romania	Croatia
Turkey	FYROM [2]
	Georgia
	Moldova
	Russia
	Switzerland
	Ukraine

EU

Belgium	Lithuania
Czech Republic	Luxembourg
Denmark	Netherlands
Estonia	Poland
France	Portugal
Germany	Slovakia
Greece	Slovenia
Hungary	Spain
Italy	United Kingdom
Latvia	

| Austria | Ireland |
| Finland | Sweden |

Cyprus
Malta

Andorra
Bosnia-Herzegovina
Liechtenstein
San Marino
Serbia-Montenegro

Monaco
The Holy See

1. Only member of EAPC
2. Turkey recognises the Republic of Macedonia with its constitutional name

glossary

Allied Command Operations (ACO) One of NATO's two main commands, ACO is responsible for the daily running of NATO's operations, is based at SHAPE and is commanded by the Supreme Allied Commander Europe (SACEUR).

Allied Command Transformation (ACT) The second of NATO's main commands, ACT is responsible for the transformation of NATO's military capabilities and is commanded by the Supreme Allied Commander Transformation (SACT).

Article 4 Fourth article of the North Atlantic Treaty, which provides a consultative mechanism for the Allies to discuss security concerns.

Article 5 Fifth article of the North Atlantic Treaty: NATO's collective defence provision. Article 5 states that an attack on one NATO member shall be considered an attack on them all. The principle of Article 5 was invoked on 12 September 2001 and confirmed for the first time on 2 October 2001 in response to the 11 September attacks on New York and Washington, DC.

Article 5 missions Missions conducted under Article 5 of the North Atlantic Treaty, that is, collective defence missions.

Article 6 Sixth Article of the North Atlantic Treaty, which defines the areas covered by the North Atlantic Treaty. This is, essentially, the territory of NATO members.

Article 10 Tenth Article of the North Atlantic Treaty, relating to NATO's enlargement process. Article 10 states that NATO membership remains open to any state in a position to fulfil the principles of the North Atlantic Treaty.

Berlin Plus A set of discussions following the 1996 Berlin Summit that was designed to tighten the nuts and bolts on the ESDI and CJTF mechanisms. The Berlin Plus arrangements were finally agreed on 17 March 2003.

Charter on a Distinctive Partnership (CDP) An agreement concluded between NATO and Ukraine at the 1997 Madrid Summit. The CDP provides a framework for consultation about, and co-operation on, a number of different issues including civil–military relations and defence planning. The CDP also provides a crisis consultation mechanism that can be activated when Ukraine perceives a threat to its security.

Combined Joint Task Force (CJTF) 'Combined' refers to the co-operation of two or more countries whereas 'joint' refers to two or more services. The CJTF concept is designed to provide versatility and flexibility in the conduct of military operations. This in turn offers the possibility of all-European coalitions of the willing, making the CJTF concept an important contribution to the ESDI.

Common Foreign and Security Policy (CFSP) Pillar Two of the EU's Treaty on European Union – the Maastricht Treaty. The CFSP is designed to embrace all those means by which the EU seeks to exercise influence in foreign affairs.

Conference on Security and Cooperation in Europe (CSCE) A process of dialogue on economic, political and social affairs. This resulted in the 1975 Helsinki Act, which defined a set of fundamental principles on human rights, economic relations and international security and co-operation. In December 1994 the CSCE became the OSCE.

Dayton Peace Accord The General Framework Agreement for Peace – the Dayton Peace Accord – was signed in Paris on 14 December 1995. Negotiations had started on 1 November 1995 to attempt to bring peace to Bosnia Herzegovina. The signing of the Dayton Peace Accord resulted in the deployment of the Implementation Force to Bosnia Herzegovina.

Defence Capabilities Initiative (DCI) A capabilities initiative launched in 1999 by NATO Heads of State and Government to improve NATO's collective military capabilities in order to undertake the full range of missions from peacekeeping to collective defence.

Defence Planning Committee (DPC) One of two senior-level committees in NATO. The Defence Planning Committee's mandate is to provide direction to NATO's military authorities and to manage the force planning process. All NATO members participate in the DPC, except France.

Euro-Atlantic Area An area encompassing the territory of the participants in the EAPC and the NATO Allies.

Euro-Atlantic Partnership Council (EAPC) A multilateral forum for dialogue, consultation and co-operation between NATO and Partner countries throughout the Euro-Atlantic area. The EAPC replaced the NACC and was established in May 1997.

European Security and Defence Identity (ESDI) A series of mechanisms designed to reflect the desire of the European Allies to assume more responsibility in the management of European security and to enable them to do so; the ESDI is intended to enhance the 'European pillar'.

European Security and Defence Policy (ESDP) An EU political project that is designed to provide the EU with a military capability, to bolster the CFSP.

Fundamental security tasks A description of NATO's main tasks. The fundamental security tasks are grouped into five areas: security, consultation, deterrence and defence, crisis management and partnership.

Headline Goal (HG) A set of force goals outlined by the EU at the 1999 Helsinki Summit to ensure appropriate capabilities for the RRF, the military arm of the ESDP.

Implementation Force (IFOR) A NATO-led multinational force created in December 1995 and deployed to Bosnia Herzegovina following UNSC Resolution 1031 of 15 December 1995. The Implementation Force's military mission was three-fold: to secure an end to fighting, to separate the forces of Bosnia Herzegovina's two newly created entities and demobilize their heavy weapons and forces and to transfer territory between these two entities. A Stabilization Force took over the IFOR's mission in December 1996.

Individual Partnership Plan (IPP) A programme agreed between members of the Partnership for Peace (PfP) and NATO. Each IPP is created from a choice of the full range of activities, exercises and programmes offered by NATO.

Individual Partnership Action Plan (IPAP) The IPAP is an enhanced version of the IPP that is offered to PfP members willing and able to deepen their relationship with NATO.

International Security Assistance Force (ISAF) ISAF was created following the Bonn Conference in December 2001, after the Taliban regime had been ousted from Afghanistan. The main task of the ISAF is to assist the Afghan Transitional Authority to maintain security so that the Transitional Authority and UN personnel can operate in a secure environment. NATO took over the command of the ISAF in August 2003.

Kosovo Force (KFOR) A NATO-led multinational force deployed to Kosovo on 12 June 1999 to keep the peace following Operation Allied Force.

Mediterranean Dialogue The framework for NATO's partnership initiative to the South. Launched in December 1994, the Dialogue comprises NATO members and Egypt, Israel, Jordan, Mauritania, Morocco, Tunisia and Algeria. The decision to upgrade the Mediterranean Dialogue was taken at the June 2004 Istanbul Summit.

Membership Action Plan (MAP) A plan launched by NATO at the 1999 Washington Summit to assist the preparations of countries wishing to join. The MAP offers advice, assistance and practical support on political and military aspects of reform.

Mutual Assured Destruction (MAD) A Cold War military doctrine which recognized that the first use of nuclear weapons by the Soviet Union or the United States would result in retaliation of equal or greater force by the other side, which would cause conflict escalation and ultimately result in the total and assured destruction of both.

Non-Article 5 missions The full range of non-collective defence missions, that is, crisis management, peacemaking and peacekeeping operations.

NATO Response Force (NRF) A new force comprising small and highly mobile units, which will be able rapidly to deploy to perform the full range of missions and thus be capable of intervening where NATO interests may be threatened.

NATO–Russia Council (NRC) Established at the Rome Summit on 28 May 2002, the NRC is an enhanced version of the NATO–Russia Permanent Joint Council (PJC). The NRC emerged as a result of changes in the relationship between NATO and Russia following 9/11. The NRC allows for consultation, consensus-building, co-operation, joint decision-making and joint action.

NATO–Russia Permanent Joint Council (PJC) The PJC was established by the Founding Act of 27 May 1997 and was designed to provide a forum for consultation on a range of security issues. The PJC was commonly seen as giving Russia 'a voice not a veto' in NATO's activities.

NATO–Ukraine Commission (NUC) Set up as a part of the Charter on a Distinctive Partnership between NATO and Ukraine, the Commission provides a forum where representatives from NATO and Ukraine can meet to discuss a variety of issues including conflict prevention, crisis management and defence reform.

North Atlantic Co-operation Council (NACC) The NACC was established in December 1991 to facilitate dialogue between the NATO Allies and their former adversaries. The NACC was replaced by the EAPC in May 1997.

North Atlantic Council (NAC) The principal body in NATO that has effective political authority and powers of decision. The NAC comprises the Permanent Representatives of all member countries and meets at least once a week. The NAC also meets at higher levels involving Foreign Ministers, Defence Ministers or Heads of Government.

North Atlantic Treaty NATO's founding treaty, signed in Washington, DC on 4 April 1949. The North Atlantic Treaty is also known as the Washington Treaty.

Nuclear Planning Group (NPG) One of two senior-level committees in NATO. The NPG has authority for all issues concerning NATO nuclear policy. All NATO members, except France, participate.

Operation Active Endeavour NATO's naval operation in the Mediterranean which was undertaken in response to the invocation of Article 5 on 2 October 2001. Operation Active Endeavour began on 26 October 2001 and was expanded to the whole of the Mediterranean on 16 March 2004. Operation Active Endeavour is continuing.

Operation Allied Force The 78-day campaign of air strikes carried out by NATO against Serbia in response to ethnic cleansing in

Kosovo. Operation Allied Force began on 24 March 1999 and ended on 10 June 1999.

Operation Allied Harmony A NATO peacekeeping mission in The Former Yugoslav Republic of Macedonia (FYORM) that was launched on 16 December 2002 following a request from the Macedonian government. Operation Allied Harmony ended on 31 March 2003 and responsibility was transferred to the EU.

Operation Amber Fox An operation launched on 27 September 2001 at the request of the government of the FYROM. Its initial mandate was for three months but was extended until 15 December 2002. Its mission was to contribute to the protection of international monitors from the EU and the OSCE who had been overseeing the implementation of the peace plan in the FYROM.

Operation Concordia The first ESDP military mission in Macedonia, taken over from NATO on 31 March 2003.

Operation Deliberate Force A sustained air strike campaign launched by NATO on 30 August 1995 against Bosnian Serb military targets. Operation Deliberate Force was launched in response to a Bosnian Serb mortar attack on civilians in Sarajevo.

Operation Display Deterrence A series of defensive measures taken by NATO in February 2003 to bolster Turkey's defence in the event of a war with Iraq. Operation Display Deterrence began on 26 February and ended on 30 April.

Operation Deny Flight Operation Deny Flight was conducted from 12 April 1993 to 20 December 1995 and enforced the no-fly zone over Bosnia. It ended when the IFOR assumed responsibility for the implementation of Dayton Peace Accords.

Operation Desert Shield The 1990 US-led military deployment to attempt to persuade Iraq to withdraw from its occupation of Kuwait following the Iraqi invasion of August 1990. Desert Shield ended on 17 January 1991 with the beginning of Operation Desert Storm.

Operation Desert Storm The military actions carried out by the international coalition formed as a response to Iraq's invasion of Kuwait in August 1990. Operation Desert Storm began on 17 January 1991 and ended on 28 February 1991 with the withdrawal of Iraqi forces from Kuwait.

Operation Eagle Assist The defensive air patrols undertaken by NATO AWACS in the United States in the aftermath of 9/11.

Operation Eagle Assist began on 9 October 2001 and ended on
16 May 2002.

Operation Enduring Freedom The US-led military response to the
11 September 2001 terrorist attacks on the United States. It was
originally called Operation Infinite Justice but this name was
changed due to concerns that the religious terminology might
offend Muslims. Operation Enduring Freedom began on
7 October 2001.

Operation Essential Harvest A NATO mission requested by the
Macedonia government in 2001. Operation Essential Harvest was
launched to disarm ethnic Albanian groups and destroy their
weapons. Operation Essential Harvest began on 22 August 2001
and ended on 26 September 2001.

Operation Iraqi Freedom The 2003 US-led coalition operation to
oust the Iraqi President, Saddam Hussein. Operation Iraqi Freedom
began on 19 March 2003. President Bush declared an end to major
combat operations on 1 May 2003 but fighting continues.

Operation Maritime Guard A NATO operation in support of
UNSC Resolution 787 aimed at enforcing the UN embargoes in the
former Yugoslavia. Operation Maritime Guard began on
22 November 1992.

Operation Maritime Monitor A NATO operation conducted from
16 July to 22 November 1992 that preceded Operation Maritime
Guard. Its mission was to monitor the UN arms embargo and economic sanctions on the Adriatic.

Operation Sky Monitor A NATO operation to provide the UN with
additional air space monitoring assistance through an extension of
the role that NAEW aircraft had been playing in Operations
Maritime Guard and Maritime Monitor. Operation Sky Monitor
began on 16 October 1992.

Operation Southern Guard NATO's response to Iraqi aggression in
1990. Its mission was to be ready to counter any threat that might
develop in the Southern Region of Allied Command Europe as a
result of the Gulf crisis. As the crisis escalated, Operation Southern
Guard was divided into two sections – Operation Dawn Set and
Operation MedNet – designed to enhance defence and early warning
for South Eastern Turkey and monitor air and sea routes in the
Mediterranean.

Organization for Security and Co-operation in Europe (OCSE) A regional security organization with 55 participating states from Europe, Central Asia and North America. The OSCE deals with a wide range of security-related issues including arms control, preventive diplomacy, human rights, democratization, election monitoring and economic and environmental security. The OSCE was known as the CSCE from 1972 to 1994.

Partnership for Peace A programme launched in 1994 to provide a bilateral link between NATO and PfP participants and allow them to pursue a variety of defence and military-related activities and co-operation.

Petersberg Tasks A range of military missions from humanitarian and rescue tasks and peacekeeping tasks to tasks of combat forces in crisis management, including peacemaking. The Petersberg Tasks were established at the Ministerial Council of the Western European Union (WEU) held at the Petersberg Hotel, near Bonn, in June 1992.

Prague Capabilities Commitment (PCC) NATO's current capabilities initiative, designed to improve the collective military capabilities of the Allies. The PCC is based on NATO members making national commitments and agreeing to specific deadlines. Four operational capability areas are prioritised: ensuring secure command, communications and information-superiority, improving interoperability of deployed forces and key aspects of combat effectiveness, ensuring rapidly deployable and sustainable forces and defending against chemical, biological, radiological and nuclear attacks.

Provincial Reconstruction Teams (PRT) Teams of civilian and military personnel seeking to facilitate the development of a secure environment and aid reconstruction in Afghanistan's provinces.

Revolution in Military Affairs (RMA) The major change in the nature of warfare, brought about by the innovative application of new technologies. The result is a fundamental change in the character and conduct of military operations.

Saint Malo Declaration An Anglo–French Declaration on European Defence resulting from the December 1998 meeting between Jacques Chirac and Tony Blair. The Saint Malo Declaration provided the basis for the emergence of ESDP by endorsing the concept of the EU having the capacity 'for autonomous action, backed up by credible military forces, the means to decide to use them and a readiness to do so, in order to respond to international crises'.

Stabilization Force (SFOR) A smaller NATO-led force that took over from the IFOR in 1996. The SFOR will be taken over by the EU in 2004.

Strategic Concept A statement of NATO's approach to security and defence. It expresses NATO's enduring purpose, nature and fundamental security tasks. It also identifies the key features of the security environment, specifies the elements of the Alliance's broad approach to security and provides guidelines for the further adaptation of its forces. NATO's current Strategic Concept was produced in 1999 by NATO Heads of State and Government meeting in Washington, DC.

Supreme Allied Commander Atlantic (SACLANT) Until 2003, SACLANT headed Allied Command Atlantic (ACLANT) in Norfolk, Virginia, USA. Following decisions taken by NATO Defence Ministers in 2003, ACLANT was replaced by ACT and Supreme Allied Commander Transformation (SACT). ACT HQ remains in Norfolk, Virginia.

Supreme Allied Commander Europe (SACEUR) One of two top-level commanders in NATO's integrated military structure. SACEUR heads SHAPE in Mons, Belgium and is also Commander US European Command.

Supreme Allied Commander Transformation (SACT) Created in 2003, Supreme Allied Commander Transformation (SACT) is the commander of ACT and also Commander, Joint Forces Command.

Supreme Headquarters Allied Powers Europe (SHAPE) The head-quarters of ACO, located in Mons, Belgium.

United Nations Protection Force (UNPROFOR) UNPROFOR was formed on 21 February 1992 and initially had a mandate to ensure demilitarization of designated areas in Croatia. It was later extended to Bosnia Herzegovina.

Warsaw Pact A mutual assistance pact between Albania, Bulgaria, Czechoslovakia, East Germany, Hungary, Poland, Romania and the USSR established by the Treaty on Friendship, Co-operation and Mutual Assistance on 14 May 1955. The Warsaw Pact was the nominal counterweight to NATO.

Weapons of Mass Destruction (WMD) An elastic term referring to a wide range of weapons including chemical, biological, nuclear and radiological weapons.

Western European Union (WEU) A collective defence group created by the Brussels Treaty of Economic, Social and Cultural Collaboration and Collective Self-Defence of 1948, signed by Belgium, France, Luxembourg, the Netherlands and the United Kingdom and later by West Germany, Greece, Italy, Portugal and Spain. The WEU was effectively made redundant by the creation of NATO in 1949, yet was reactivated following the end of the Cold War to serve as the EU's defence arm. The WEU and the EU merged in 1999 and the EU adopted most of the WEU's functions.

notes

introduction

1. The term 'Europe' is an extremely elastic one and can be employed to describe a multitude of entities. For the purposes of this book, however, the terms 'Europe' or 'European Allies' generally refer to the European members of NATO, unless specifically indicated otherwise. Canada is in a unique position as it is the only non-European member of NATO apart from the United States.

2. Nanette Gantz and John Roper, *Towards a new partnership. US-European relations in the post-Cold War era* (Paris: Institute for Security Studies, 1993): 1.

3. Ernest Bevin to George Marshall, 15 December 1947. Cited in Theodore C. Achilles, 'The Omaha Milkman. The role of the United States in the negotiations' in André De Staercke *et al.*, *NATO's Anxious Birth. The Prophetic Vision of the 1940s* (London: C. Hurst and Company, 1985): 30.

4. Theodore C. Achilles, 'US Role in the Negotiations that Led to Atlantic Alliance. Part 1', *NATO Review* 27, No. 4 (1979): 12.

5. Stanley Sloan, 'US Perspectives on NATO's future', *International Affairs* 71, 2 (1995): 220.

6. The terrorist attacks of 11 September 2001 are now commonly referred to as 9/11. This abbreviation will be used throughout this book.

7. John Roper, 'NATO's New Role in Crisis Management', *The International Spectator* XXXIV, (2) (1999): 58. Ochmanek also observes, 'NATO is the institution best-suited to harmonizing and executing policies on security issues that affect the United States and Europe. Its members share habits of co-operation based on the experience of having worked together for decades to address common security challenges. Moreover, once a consensus

is reached at the policy level, NATO's unique system of multi-national headquarters, command and control centers, and common doctrine and training allows allied forces to carry out agreed policies in a well-coordinated fashion'. David A. Ochmanek, *NATO's Future: Implications for U.S. Military Capabilities and Posture* (Santa Monica: RAND, 2000): 38.

8.   Stuart Croft, Jolyon Howorth, Terry Terriff, Mark Webber, 'NATO's Triple Challenge', *International Affairs* 76, 3 (2000): 495.

9.   See, for example, Stephen M. Walt, 'The Ties That Fray: Why Europe and America are Drifting Apart', *The National Interest*, Winter 1998/99; Robert Kagan, 'Power and Weakness', Policy Review no. 113, June/July 2002; Jessica T. Mathews, 'Estranged Partners', *Foreign Policy*, November/December 2001. For a critique of the 'continental drift' thesis, see Antony J. Blinken, 'The False Crisis Over the Atlantic', *Foreign Affairs*, May/June 2001.

10.   Dieter Mahncke, 'The Role of the USA in Europe: Successful Past but Uncertain Future?', *European Foreign Affairs Review* 4, 3 (Autumn 1999): 353.

11.   'Lift' referred to lifting the arms embargo against the Bosnian government and 'strike' referred to the launching of air strikes against the Bosnian Serbs.

basic information

1.   Cited in Josef Joffe, 'The Alliance Is Dead. Long Live the New Alliance', *New York Times*, 29 September 2002.

2.   Paul Cornish, *Partnership in Crisis: The US, Europe and the fall and rise of NATO* (London: Cassell, 1997): 22.

3.   See Paragraph 10 of the Alliance's Strategic Concept Approved by the Heads of State and Government participating in the meeting of the North Atlantic Council in Washington D.C. on 23rd and 24th April 1999.

4.   For detailed information on NATO's structure, see *NATO Handbook* (Brussels: NATO HQ, 2001).

chapter one

1.   Manfred Wörner, 'The Atlantic Alliance in a New Era', *NATO Review* 39, 1 (February 1991): 5.

2.   See Robert D. Hormats, 'Redefining Europe and the Atlantic Link', *Foreign Affairs* 68, 4 (Fall 1989): 86. See also David M. Abshire, 'Don't Muster Out NATO Yet: Its Job Is Far from Done', *Wall Street Journal*, 1 December 1989.

3.   Howe defines the 'petro-weapon' as 'the manipulation for political purposes of the price of petroleum from the Persian Gulf and access to it'. See Jonathan T. Howe, 'NATO and the Gulf crisis', *Survival* 33, 3 (1991): 248.

4.   UNSC Resolution 661, 6 August 1990.

5.   UNSC Resolution 662, 9 August 1990.

6.   UNSC Resolution 678, 29 November 1990.

7.   Howe: 250.

8.   Ibid: 252.

9.   Jeffrey McCausland, *The Gulf Conflict: A Military Analysis*, Adelphi Paper 282 (London: International Institute for Strategic Studies, 1993): 19.

10.   The debate primarily stemmed from domestic debates in Germany, in particular Germany's constitutional prohibition of military deployments beyond the NATO area and the opposition of the Social Democrats, who urged Chancellor Kohl to turn down Turkey's request. The Social Democrats argued that Turkey had provoked Iraq by allowing the United States to use Turkish bases, which in their view therefore invalidated any German response in the context of the Article 5 collective defence clause. In response to Germany's hesitation, a senior Turkish official commented, 'the reluctance [of NATO] is very difficult to understand. It is shaking belief in Turkey that NATO will come to Turkey's assistance in an emergency. If they don't send the force it will mean a complete revision of policies towards NATO'. Cited in Hugh Pope, 'Gulf Crisis: "Reluctant" NATO worries allies in Turkey', *The Independent*, 27 December 1990.

11.   McCausland: 20.

12.   The American deployment of forces began on 6 August 1990 and by January 1991 the number of American troops totalled half a million. Britain's contribution consisted of 43,000 troops, 75 warplanes, and 15 ships. This was the largest European military contribution to the coalition and Britain's largest foreign deployment since World War Two.

13.   'European Theater Remains One of Conflict and Transition', prepared statement of Gen. George A. Joulwan, Commander-in-Chief, US European Command, to the House National Security Committee, 2 March 1995, in *Defense Issues* 10, 40 (1995): 7. Cited in Philip H. Gordon, 'Recasting the Atlantic Alliance', *Survival* 38, 1 (Spring 1996): 55.

14.   William J. Taylor, Jr. and James Blackwell, 'The ground war in the Gulf', *Survival* 33, 3 (May/June 1991): 233.

15.   Stephen Badsey, 'The Doctrines of Coalition Forces' in John Pimlott and Stephen Badsey (eds), *The Gulf War Assessed* (London: Arms and Armour, 1993): 61.

16. Julian Thompson, 'The Military Coalition' in James Gow (ed.), *Iraq, the Gulf conflict and the World Community* (London: Brassey's, 1993): 146.

17. Badley: 132.

18. In August 1990, Osman Olcay commented that NATO was 'a defensive alliance never designed to cope with the kind of crisis we are now facing'. Cited in Robert Fox, 'Self-confidence high in Turkey', *The Daily Telegraph*, 14 August 1990.

19. Jacques Poos, Foreign Minister of Luxembourg, proclaimed, 'this is the hour of Europe, not the hour of the Americans'. Cited in Charles Grant, *Strength in Numbers: Europe's Foreign and Defence Policy* (London: Centre for European Reform, 1997): 7.

20. Paragraph 1, 'The Situation in Yugoslavia', Statement by the Heads of State and Government participating in the meeting of the North Atlantic Council, Rome, 7–8 November 1991.

21. In retrospect, Owen comments 'if the EC had launched a political initiative in August 1991 to address the key problem facing the parties to the dispute […] if in addition NATO had been ready to enforce that cease-fire as well as provide peacekeeping forces for immediate deployment […] the Serbo-Croat war would have been stopped in its tracks'. David Owen, *Balkan Odyssey* (London: Victor Gollancz, 1995): 342.

22. Of the PfP countries, Albania, Austria, Bulgaria, the Czech Republic, Estonia, Finland, Hungary, Latvia, Lithuania, Poland, Romania, Russia, Sweden, and Ukraine contributed forces. Egypt, Jordan, Malaysia, and Morocco also participated.

23. See Paragraph 8, Istanbul Summit Communiqué, issued by the Heads of State and Government participating in the meeting of the North Atlantic Council, 28 June 2004.

24. For an analysis of the background to the Kosovo war see, Tim Judah, 'Kosovo's Road to War', *Survival* 41, 2 (1999).

25. See Paragraph 9, Istanbul Summit Communiqué, ibid.

26. Gregory L. Schulte, 'Former Yugoslavia and the New NATO', *Survival* 39, 1 (1997): 20.

27. See Statement by the North Atlantic Council, Press Release (2001) 124, 12 September 2001.

28. The most striking example of this was a report in the *Guardian* on 13 September, which described how 'NATO is now drawing up an emergency plan for a massive attack on Afghanistan if proof emerges that Osama bin Laden, the wanted Saudi-born terrorist, sheltered by Afghanistan, was responsible for the attacks'. See Julian Borger, Richard Norton-Taylor, Ewen MacAskill and Ian Black, 'US Rallies the West for Attack on Afghanistan', *The Guardian*, 13 September 2001.

29. A NATO spokesman quickly denied the story and said that the Guardian story was based on 'unfounded speculations' and that

'NATO is not planning the invasion of Afghanistan, or of any other country, as suggested by the Guardian's article'. See NATO Press Release (2001) 125. 13 September 2001.

30. See Statement to the Press by NATO Secretary General Lord Robertson on the North Atlantic Council Decision on Implementation of Article 5 of the Washington Treaty following the 11 September Attacks against the United States, 4 October 2001.

31. Cited in 'NATO Agrees to All of U.S. Aid Requests', *International Herald Tribune*, 5 October 2001.

32. On 4 February 2003, Operation Active Endeavour was extended to include escorting non-military ships travelling through the Strait of Gibraltar and to secure the safe transit of selected NATO ships. The operation was expanded to the whole of the Mediterranean on 16 March 2004.

33. See, for example, Antony J. Blinken and Philip H. Gordon, 'NATO is Ready to Play a Central Role', *International Herald Tribune*, 18 September 2001.

34. Anatol Lieven, 'The End of NATO', *Prospect*, December 2001.

35. Cited in Robin Wright, 'NATO Promises Cohesive Stand Against Terrorism', *Los Angeles Times*, 7 December 2001.

36. See Paragraph 5, Istanbul Summit Communiqué, ibid.

37. See Marc Champion, 'Eight European Leaders Voice Their Support for US on Iraq', *Wall Street Journal*, 30 January 2003.

38. 'New Allies Back US on Iraq Policy', *International Herald Tribune*, 6 February 2003.

39. David S. Yost, *NATO Transformed: The Alliance's New Roles in International Security* (Washington, DC: United States Institute of Peace Press, 1998): 62.

40. Cited in Kori Schake, 'NATO after the Cold War, 1991-1995: Institutional Competition and the Collapse of the French Alternative', *Contemporary European History* 7, 3 (1998): 397.

41. Cited in Thomas Freedman, 'NATO or BATO?', *New York Times*, 15 June 1999.

42. Schake: 405.

43. 'General wanted to call the shots in Kosovo', Public Information Office, Regional Headquarters AFSOUTH, 27 January 2000.

44. As Lesser comments, 'the geopolitics of NATO's southern periphery at the opening of the 21st century suggest a future dominated by security challenges that cut across traditional regional lines. European, Middle Eastern, and Eurasian security will be increasingly interwoven, with implications for the nature of risks facing the Alliance'. Ian O. Lesser, *NATO Looks South. New Challenges and New Strategies in the Mediterranean* (Santa Monica: RAND, 2000): 4.

chapter two

1. Elizabeth D. Sherwood, *Allies in Crisis. Meeting Challenges to Western Security* (Yale University Press: New Haven, 1990): 1.

2. Richard L. Kugler, *U.S.-West-European Cooperation in Out-of-Area Military Operations. Problems and Prospects* (Santa Monica: National Defense Research Institute, RAND: 1994): 1–2.

3. There was clearly not always a consensus over issues affecting the Allies within the North Atlantic area, which means that the transatlantic security discourse of the Cold War cannot be neatly divided into consensus 'in area' and conflict 'out of area'. There was, in fact, considerable conflict between the Allies over the Soviet threat. However, as Freedman comments, 'the frequency of controversies over developments outside of the Atlantic region (even when broadly interpreted) has been sufficient to make this a distinctive feature of the relationship. Arguably, it is *the* key divergence, for by contrast the security arrangements within Europe still appear to be remarkably stable'. Lawrence Freedman, 'The Atlantic Crisis', *International Affairs* 58, 3 (1982): 407–408.

4. Theodore C. Achilles, 'US Role in Negotiations the Led to Atlantic Alliance. Part 2', *NATO Review* 27, 5 (1979): 17. Author's emphasis.

5. Cited in Paul E. Gallis, *NATO: Issues for Congress*, CRS Report for Congress, 31 August 2001: 2.

6. Lawrence Freedman, *The Troubled Alliance: Atlantic relations in the 1980s* (London: Heinemann, 1983): 3.

7. Sherwood: 1.

8. Two examples of extra-European threats to Alliance security that intensified the perception that events outside Europe posed serious challenges to a variety of national and Western interests in the wider world were the Iranian Revolution of 1979 and the Soviet intervention in Afghanistan. On this, see Peter Foot, 'Western Security and the Third World' in Freedman: 137.

9. Secretary General Manfred Wörner, Speech to the North Atlantic Assembly, 29 November 1990.

10. Kori Schake, 'NATO after the Cold War, 1991–1995: Institutional Competition and the Collapse of the French Alternative', *Contemporary European History* 7, 3, (1998): 383.

11. Senator Richard G. Lugar, 'NATO: Out of Area or Out of Business: A Call for U.S. Leadership to Revive and Redefine the Alliance', text of speech to the Overseas Writers' Club, Washington, DC, 24 June 1993.

12. Richard Kugler commented, for example, 'Exactly what out-of-area challenges lie ahead are unknowable. However, the need to prepare for them is a critical item on NATO's security agenda. If the Western alliance expects to remain secure and to achieve its

high-priority goals for the transformation of Europe into a peaceful and democratic continent, then it will need to expand its planning beyond the protection of its own borders. In essence, it will need to become strongly capable of projecting security and military power outward in peace, crisis, and war'. Richard L. Kugler, *U.S.-West European Cooperation in Out-of-Area Military Operations. Problems and Prospects* (Santa Monica: RAND, 1994): 161.

13. Paragraph 11, Final Communiqué, Ministerial Meeting of the North Atlantic Council, Oslo, 4 June 1992.

14. Paragraph 4, Final Communiqué, Ministerial meeting of the North Atlantic Council, Brussels, 17 December 1992.

15. David S. Yost, *NATO Transformed: The Alliance's New Roles in International Security* (Washington, DC: United States Institute of Peace Press, 1998): 233.

16. Cited in Stephen S. Rosenfeld, 'NATO's Last Chance', *The Washington Post*, 2 July 1993. Robert Manning, of the Council on Foreign Relations, also commented 'in the Balkans, one must strain hard to get even in the parking lot of the ballpark of a vital American interest'. Robert Manning, 'Bumbling Around in the Balkans', *Washington Post*, 15 February 1999.

17. This assessment only holds true in terms of military capabilities. The number of European troops deployed in the Balkans has consistently been larger than the number of US troops. This issue caused particular tension between the Allies during the 2000 US presidential campaign when George W. Bush stated, 'I'm aware of the commitments the president has made, I'd be mindful of those commitments, for example in the Balkans, but I would hope to be able to convince our friends and allies to start being the peacekeepers in that region, as opposed to us'. Bush's objective of increasing the NATO Allies' contribution to NATO's operations in the former Yugoslavia was greeted with almost universal disapproval in Europe primarily because at the time European troops accounted for more than 80 per cent of NATO's forces in the Balkans.

18. Former senior US officials Ashton Carter and William Perry in 1997 rated the 'Kosovos, Bosnias, Somalias, Rwandas, and Haitis' as 'a "C-list" of important contingencies that indirectly affect US security but do not directly threaten U.S. interests'. Ashton B. Carter and William J. Perry, *Preventive Defense. A New Security Strategy for America* (Washington, DC: Brookings Institution Press, 1999): 11.

19. Gompert and Kugler, for instance, comment, 'with the Soviet Union gone and regional threats on the rise, the proper object of [NATO] strategy is to protect more distant interests – Persian Gulf oil, for instance – not Western Europe's borders'. David Gompert and Richard Kugler, 'Free-Rider Redux. NATO Needs

to Project Power (and Europe Can Help)', *Foreign Affairs* 74, 1 (1995): 7. Gompert and Kugler later remark: 'A NATO power projection capability is the only realistic solution to the West's common security needs [...] This new way of viewing and using NATO as a Western force projection coalition would also give the alliance a strategic purpose not dependent on an increasingly implausible Russian threat to Europe'. Ibid: 11–12.

20. David A. Ochmanek, *NATO's Future. Implications for U.S. Military Capabilities and Posture* (Santa Monica: RAND, 2000): 38.

21. Ronald D. Asmus, Robert D. Blackwill, F. Stephen Larrabee, 'Can NATO Survive?', *The Washington Quarterly* 19, 2 (1996): 88.

22. Ibid: 83.

23. Secretary of State Madeleine K. Albright, Statement to the North Atlantic Council, Brussels, 8 December 1998.

24. Cited in John-Thor Dahlburd 'NATO Ponders New Role as it Nears 50', *Los Angeles Times*, 9 December 1998.

25. The eventual wording contained in Paragraph 15 of the new Strategic Concept stated, 'The United Nations Security Council has the primary responsibility for the maintenance of international peace and security and, as such, plays a crucial role in contributing to security and stability in the Euro-Atlantic area'. Paragraph 15, The Alliance's Strategic Concept, Approved by the Heads of State and Government participating in the meeting of the North Atlantic Council in Washington D.C. on 23rd and 24th April 1999.

26. Paragraph 6 of the new Strategic Concept states, for example: '[...] Based on common values of democracy, human rights and the rule of law, the Alliance has striven since its inception to secure a just and lasting peaceful order in Europe. It will continue to do so. The achievement of this aim can be put at risk by crisis and conflict affecting the security of the *Euro-Atlantic area*. The Alliance therefore not only ensures the defence of its members but *contributes to peace and stability in this region*'. Paragraph 6, The Alliance's Strategic Concept, Approved by the Heads of State and Government participating in the meeting of the North Atlantic Council in Washington D.C. on 23rd and 24th April 1999. Author's emphasis.

27. The lack of a definition of the Euro-Atlantic area is significant, as NATO officials have previously referred to the Euro-Atlantic region as encompassing all the members of the Euro-Atlantic Partnership Council (EAPC). In addition to West European members of the EAPC – Austria, Finland, Sweden and Switzerland – and countries on NATO's immediate eastern and southern periphery, this somewhat expansive view would include Armenia, Azerbaijan, Belarus, Bulgaria, Estonia, Georgia, Kazakhstan, Kyrgyz Republic, Latvia, Lithuania, Moldova,

Romania, Russia, Slovakia, Slovenia, Tajikistan, Turkmenistan, Ukraine and Uzbekistan. The formula 'the Euro-Atlantic area' is therefore not as Euro-centric as it first appears.

28. Paragraph 20, The Alliance's Strategic Concept, ibid.

29. Asmus and Weisser argued in December 2001, for example, 'If threats to NATO can come from beyond Europe, the alliance must be able to respond beyond Europe, too'. Ronald D. Asmus and Ulrich Weisser, 'Refit NATO to Move Against Threats From Beyond Europe', *International Herald Tribune*, 6 December 2001. Senator Lieberman, in a speech at the February 2002 Wehrkunde conference, and later before the Senate Armed Services Committee remarked: 'For years, physical defense of member nations' home soil, as defined under Article V, has been the core of our alliance. That changed with Bosnia and then Kosovo, as NATO applied necessary force just outside of its immediate borders for the common good of stability in Europe. The awful events of September 11th prompted another evolution, as NATO invoked Article V, responding to the attacks on American soil by supporting a war against an enemy half a world away from America. Technology has collapsed geographical distinctions to the point that today, a plot conceived in North Africa, South America or Southeast Asia can pose just as serious a threat to NATO members' security as an aggressive military movement by a nearby nation. NATO must accept this new reality and embrace a more expansive geographical understanding of its mission'. Remarks by Senator Joe Lieberman at the 38th Annual Wehrkunde conference, 3 February 2002; Lieberman statement on 'The Future of NATO'. Opening Statement Before the Senate Armed Services Committee, 28 February 2002.

30. General Klaus Naumann, 'Crunch Time for the Alliance', *NATO Review* 2, Summer 2002.

31. Final Communiqué, Ministerial Meeting of the North Atlantic Council Held in Reykjavik, 14 May 2002.

32. Lord Robertson re-emphasized the greater reach of NATO's future missions at the June meetings of NATO defence ministers by commenting, 'we have made it clear that we must be ready to deal with threats whenever they occur and wherever they occur, and the language in there is very explicit, very deliberate and is designed to make sure people understand that an attack on the Alliance and the Alliance's interests is something that will be responded to from wherever it comes and we need to have the means to do that'. Secretary General Lord Robertson, Transcript of Press Conference following the meeting of the North Atlantic Council, 6 June 2002.

33. Cited in Donald H. Rumsfeld, 'Transforming the Military', *Foreign Affairs* 81, 3 (2002): 31.

34.   Hans Binnendijk and Richard Kugler, 'Transforming European Forces', *Survival* 44, 3 (2002): 121.

35.   Michael Clarke and Paul Cornish, 'The European defence project and the Prague Summit', *International Affairs* 78, 4 (2002): 782.

36.   Binnendijk and Kugler: 123.

chapter three

1.   David S. Yost, 'The NATO Capabilities Gap and the European Union', *Survival* 42, 4 (2000–2001): 97.

2.   Some analysts have put the percentage of deployable European forces at less than 10. See Michael Clarke and Paul Cornish, 'The European defence project and the Prague summit', *International Affairs* 78, 4 (2002): 778.

3.   'The Role of NATO in the 21st Century', speech by NATO Secretary General Lord Robertson at the Welt am Sonntag Forum, Berlin, 3 November 2003.

4.   Paragraph 313, House of Commons Defence Committee, *Lessons of Kosovo* (London: House of Commons, 2000). See also Department of Defense, *Kosovo/Operation Allied Force After-Action Report to Congress* (Washington, DC: Department of Defense, 2000).

5.   'Rebalancing NATO for a Strong Future', Remarks by NATO Secretary General, Lord Robertson, Defence Week Conference, Brussels, 31 January 2000.

6.   Deputy Secretary of State Strobe Talbott, Speech to the Royal Institute for International Affairs, London, 7 October 1999.

7.   Cited in Michael O'Hanlon, 'Rumsfeld's Defence Vision', *Survival* 44, 2 (2002): 108.

8.   Adapted from 'International comparisons of defence expenditure and manpower, 1985, 2001, 2002', *The Military Balance 2003–4* (Oxford: Oxford University Press, 2004): 335–336.

9.   Schake comments in this respect, 'with the deployment of NATO's Implementation Force to the former Yugoslavia in 1995, the European debate became less about excluding US and NATO influence and more about ensuring US and NATO support for WEU operations'. Kori Schake, *Constructive Duplication: Reducing EU reliance on US military assets* (London: Centre for European Reform, 2002): 16.

10.   See Paragraph 4, Declaration of the Heads of State and Government participating in the meeting of the North Atlantic Council, Brussels, 10–11 January 1994.

11.   French Foreign Minister Hervé de Charette declared, for example, 'for the first time in the history of the Atlantic alliance, Europe can express its defence identity', Cited in 'Defence deal keeps all the parties happy', *The Independent*, 4 June 1996.

12. The timing of the Pörtschach statement and the subsequent Franco-British defence 'breakthrough' is significant, as the St. Malo declaration pre-dates Operation Allied Force. This demonstrates that European governments were already considering developing an autonomous European security and defence regardless of the controversial conduct of the Kosovo conflict.

13. Paragraph 2, Franco-British Joint Declaration on European Defence, Saint Malo, 4 December 1998.

14. Paragraph 2, Franco-British Joint Declaration, ibid. Author's emphasis.

15. UK Defence Secretary Geoff Hoon confirmed the Blair government's views of the capabilities benefits of the EU's initiatives in 2000 by stating, 'Helsinki is all about enhancing military capability. It is not about political niceties. We are setting real world, measurable targets for improvements in military capability [...] If hanging a "European" tag on it is what it takes to make it happen, then so be it'. Secretary of State for Defence Geoff Hoon, Address to the Brookings Institution, Washington, DC, 26 January 2000.

16. See Paragraph 5, *Defence Capabilities Initiative*, 25 April 1999.

17. See Paragraph 4, Statement on Capabilities issued at the Meeting of the North Atlantic Council in Defence Ministers Session, 6 June 2002.

18. Cited in Bradley Graham, 'NATO Ministers Back U.S. Plan for Rapid Reaction Force', *Washington Post*, 25 September 2002.

19. General George A. Joulwan commented in this respect: 'Can we develop in NATO a force that would be capable of rapid deployment, that would have the ability to respond to a crisis and be able to integrate with U.S. forces and have the technical capabilities to do that? What I gather Rumsfeld will put on the table is a way to do that'. Cited in Elaine Sciolino, 'U.S. Pressing NATO for Rapid Reaction Force', *New York Times*, 18 September 2002.

20. SACEUR General James L. Jones, 'NATO launches Response Force', SHAPE news release, 15 October 2003.

21. Kori Schake, *Constructive Duplication: Reducing EU Reliance on US Military Assets* (London: Centre for European Reform, 2002): 16.

22. Binnendijk and Kugler comment for example, 'the focus of the ERRF is on Petersberg tasks such as peacekeeping and limited crisis interventions on Europe's periphery; it is not intended for intense combat in distant areas'. Hans Binnendijk and Richard Kugler, 'Transforming European Forces', *Survival* 44, 3 (2002): 121.

23. *IGC 2003 – Defence*, CIG 57/1/03 REV 1, Brussels, 5 December 2003: 4.

24. See Paragraph 19, Istanbul Summit Communiqué, issued by the Heads of State and Government participating in the meeting of the North Atlantic Council, 28 June 2004.

chapter four

1. See, for example, Paragraph 2 of the 1994 Alliance Policy Framework on Proliferation of Weapons of Mass Destruction issued at the Ministerial Meeting of the North Atlantic Council, Istanbul, 9 June 1994.

2. For one example, see Richard G. Lugar, 'Redefining NATO's Mission: Preventing WMD Terrorism', *The Washington Quarterly*, Summer 2002.

3. Paragraph 12. 1991 Strategic Concept, Agreed by the Heads of State and Government participating in the meeting of the North Atlantic Council in Rome on 7–8 November 1991.

4. Paragraph 49. Ibid.

5. Paragraph 12. Ibid.

6. Paragraph 17. Declaration of the Heads of State and Government Participating in the Meeting of the North Atlantic Council, Brussels, 10–11 January 1994.

7. Ibid.

8. Ibid.

9. See Alliance Policy Framework, ibid.

10. Paragraph 11, Final Communiqué, Ministerial Meeting of the North Atlantic Council, Berlin, 3 June 1996.

11. Secretary of State Madeleine K. Albright. Statement at the North Atlantic Council Ministerial Meeting. NATO Headquarters, Brussels, 16 December 1997. Albright's emphasis.

12. Paragraph 22, The Alliance's Strategic Concept Approved by the Heads of State and Government participating in the meeting of the North Atlantic Council in Washington D.C. on 23–24 April 1999.

13. Paragraph 56, The Alliance's Strategic Concept. Ibid.

14. See Crispin Hain-Cole, 'The Summit Initiative on Weapons of Mass Destruction: Rationale and Aims', *NATO Review* 47, 2, 1999.

15. Paragraph 24, The Alliance's Strategic Concept. Ibid.

16. See Joanna Spear, 'Weapons of Mass Destruction' in Robert D. Blackwill and Michael Stürmer (eds), *Allies Divided. Transatlantic Policies for the Greater Middle East* (Cambridge, MA: MIT Press, 1997): 247.

17. Cited in Keith B. Richburg, 'U.S. Keeps NATO Outside', *International Herald Tribune*, 27 September 2001.

18. NATO's Response to Terrorism, Statement issued at the Ministerial Meeting of the North Atlantic Council held at NATO Headquarters, Brussels, 6 December 2001.

19. Paragraph 5. Ibid.

20. Nora Bensahel, *The Counterterror Coalitions. Cooperation with Europe, NATO and the European Union* (Santa Monica: RAND, 2003): 24.

21.   Paragraph 4, Prague Summit Declaration, issued by the Heads of State and Government participating in the meeting of the North Atlantic Council in Prague, 21 November 2002.

22.   See Paragraph 13, Istanbul Summit Communiqué, issued by the Heads of State and Government participating in the meeting of the North Atlantic Council, 28 June 2004.

23.   Section V of the National Security Strategy of the United States states, 'We must adapt the concept of imminent threat to the capabilities and objectives of today's adversaries. Rogue states and terrorists do not seek to attack us using conventional means. They know such attacks would fail. Instead, they rely on acts of terror and, potentially, the use of weapons of mass destruction – weapons that can be easily concealed, delivered covertly, and used without warning. The targets of these attacks are our military forces and our civilian population, in direct violation of one of the principal norms of the law of warfare. As was demonstrated by the losses on September 11, 2001, mass civilian casualties are the specific objective of terrorists and these losses would be exponentially more severe if terrorists acquired and used weapons of mass destruction. The United States has long maintained the option of preemptive actions to counter a sufficient threat to our national security. The greater the threat, the greater is the risk of inaction – and the more compelling the case for taking anticipatory action to defend ourselves, even if uncertainty remains as to the time and place of the enemy's attack. To forestall or prevent such hostile acts by our adversaries, the United States will, if necessary, act pre-emptively'. The National Security Strategy of the United States (Washington, DC: The White House, 2002).

24.   Press conference by US Secretary of Defense, Donald Rumsfeld, NATO Headquarters, 6 June 2002.

25.   Transcript of Press Conference given by NATO Secretary General, Lord Robertson, NATO HQ, Brussels, 6 June 2002.

26.   Stephens succinctly summarizes the difficulties of pre-emption by commenting, 'just how far can the definition of self-defence be stretched? Who is to be arbiter of whether a threat is real or imagined? Where do the boundaries lie in the light of Mr Bush's comment that "if we wait for threats to fully materalise, we will have waited too long"? Would it be enough for a hostile state to develop a nuclear or ballistic missile programme to invite US military intervention? Where do we draw the line between pre-emptive action against an obvious and imminent menace and what one senior US official has called "preventative retaliation" to head off a more distant threat?' Philip Stephens, 'The American way of defence', Financial Times, 13 June 2002.

27.   In 2001, for example, Lord Robertson termed NATO 'an essential forum' for discussion of missile defence. It very quickly became clear, however, that the Bush Administration's interpretation of

'consultation' and 'discussion' essentially meant 'my-way-or-take-the-highway'. Lord Robertson effectively acknowledged this in March 2001 by commenting: 'There is a recognition in the alliance that the decision [about missile defence] has been taken and the administration will not be talked out of it and that we should have a healthy discussion about how and when'. Cited in Steven Mufson 'Seeking "Common Framework"', *The Washington Post*, 10 March 2001.

chapter five

1.   Article 10, North Atlantic Treaty, 4 April 1949.
2.   Declaration of Heads of State and Government, Ministerial Meeting of the North Atlantic Council/North Atlantic Co-operation Council, NATO Headquarters, Brussels, 10–11 January 1994.
3.   See NATO, *Study on Enlargement* (Brussels: NATO, 1995).
4.   Paragraph 3, Chapter 1, ibid.
5.   Paragraphs 68–78, Chapter 5, ibid.
6.   Sean Kay, 'NATO Enlargement' in *NATO and the Future of European Security* (Lanham: Rowman and Littlefield, 1998): 92.
7.   Paragraph 39, The Alliance's Strategic Concept Approved by Heads of State and Government participating in the meeting of the North Atlantic Council in Washington, DC, 23 and 24 April 1999.
8.   President George W. Bush, Remarks at University Library, Warsaw, Poland, 16 June 2001.
9.   Lord Robertson, 'NATO: Managing the Challenges of Today, and Tomorrow', Speech at the Mayflower Hotel, Washington, DC, 20 June 2001.
10.   Paragraph 25, Istanbul Summit Communiqué, issued by the Heads of State and Government participating in the meeting of the North Atlantic Council, 28 June 2004.
11.   Paragraph 25, ibid.
12.   On this, see Ronald D. Asmus, *Opening NATO's Door: How the Alliance Remade Itself for a New Era* (New York: Columbia University Press, 2002) and James Goldgeier, *Not Whether But When: The US Decision to Enlarge NATO* (Washington, DC: The Brookings Institution, 1999).
13.   Michael Clarke and Paul Cornish, 'The European defence project and the Prague Summit', *International Affairs* 78, 4 (2002): 779.
14.   General Charles Wald commented, for example, 'around 98.4 per cent of our U.S. forces are mostly in Germany and Central Europe and that is not necessarily where the security problem is anymore [...] The security problem is generating itself further to

the east and further to the south'. Cited in 'Balkans Hope to Land U.S. Bases', *Deutsche Welle*, 23 July 2003.

15. Michael Mandelbaum, 'Preserving the New Peace: The Case Against NATO Expansion', *Foreign Affairs* 72, 3, (1995): 9.

16. Richard Rupp, 'NATO 1949 and NATO 2000: From Collective Defense toward Collective Security', *Journal of Strategic Studies* 23 (2000): 171.

17. See Robin Bhatty and Rachel Bronson, 'NATO's Mixed Signals in the Caucasus and Central Asia', *Survival* 42, 3 (2000): 131.

18. See Steven Lee Myers, 'Fighter jet roar stirs joy and anger', *New York Times*, 3 April 2004.

19. Oksana Antonenko, 'Russia, NATO and European Security after Kosovo', *Survival* 41, 4 (1999–2000): 124.

20. Video Interview with Ambassador Harri Tiido, Head of the Mission of the Republic of Estonia to NATO, NATO HQ, 27 October 2003.

21. Cited in Glenn Kessler, 'NATO Seeks to Soothe Russia', *Washington Post*, 3 April 2004.

22. Neil Barnett, Luke Hill, Jirí Kominek, Elisabeth Konstantinova, David Mulholland, Radu Taylor, 'NATO Expansion: The Newcomers', *Jane's Defence Weekly*, 15 October 2003.

23. Jirí Šedivy, 'The Puzzle of NATO Enlargement', *Contemporary Security Policy* 22, 2 (2001): 1.

24. Stuart Croft, 'Guaranteeing Europe's security? Enlarging NATO again', *International Affairs* 78, 1 (2002): 106.

25. Julian Lindley-French, 'Dilemmas of NATO Enlargement' in Jolyon Howorth and John T. Keeler, *Defending Europe: The EU, NATO, and the Quest for European Autonomy* (London: Palgrave Macmillan, 2003): 183.

26. See Timothy Edmunds, 'NATO and its New Members', *Survival* 45, 3 (2003): 155.

27. Clarke and Cornish comment that a new criterion was introduced with 9/11: 'what could the applicants bring to NATO's support for the US in the "war against terrorism"?', Michael Clarke and Paul Cornish, 'The European defence project and the Prague summit', *International Affairs* 78, 4 (2002): 779.

chapter six

1. The Euro-Atlantic Partnership Council released a statement on 12 September 2001 condemning the terrorist attacks on the United States. Press Release (2001) 123, 12 September 2001.

2. '*Message from Turnberry*', Ministerial Meeting of the North Atlantic Council, Turnberry, United Kingdom, 7–8 June 1990.

3. Paragraph 4, London Declaration On A Transformed North Atlantic Alliance, issued by the Heads of State and Government

participating in the meeting of the North Atlantic Council, 5–6 July 1990.

4. See Partnership for Peace: Invitation and Framework Document. Issued by the Heads of State and Government participating in the meeting of the North Atlantic Council, Brussels, 10–11 January 1994.

5. Current non-NATO members of the PfP are Albania, Armenia, Austria, Azerbaijan, Belarus, Croatia, Finland, Georgia, Ireland, Kazakhstan, Kyrghyz Republic, Moldova, Russia, Sweden, Switzerland, Tajikistan, The Former Yugoslav Republic of Macedonia, Turkmenistan, Ukraine and Uzbekistan.

6. See Paragraph 28, Istanbul Summit Communiqué, issued by the Heads of State and Government participating in the meeting of the North Atlantic Council, 28 June 2004.

7. Taras Kuzio, 'Kiev craves closer ties with NATO', *Jane's Intelligence Review*, 1 October 2000.

8. Ibid.

9. Yaroslav Bilinsky, *Endgame in NATO's Enlargement. The Baltic States and Ukraine* (Westport: Praeger, 1999).

10. Thomas Ambrosio, 'From Balancer to Ally? Russo-American Relations in the Wake of 11 September', *Contemporary Security Policy* 24, 2 (August 2003): 3.

11. F. Stephen Larrabee, *NATO's Eastern Agenda in a New Strategic Era* (Santa Monica: RAND, 2003): 169.

12. Oskana Antonenko, 'Russia, NATO and European Security after Kosovo', *Survival* 41, 4 (Winter 1999–2000): 129.

13. Ibid: 124.

14. Boris Yeltsin, *Midnight Diaries* (London: Weidenfeld and Nicolson, 2000): 256–257.

15. J. L. Black, *Russia Faces NATO Expansion. Bearing Gifts or Bearing Arms?*, (Lanham: Rowman and Littlefield, 2000): 238.

16. Cited in Kara Bosworth, 'The Effect of 11 September on Russia–NATO Relations', *Perspectives on European Politics and Society* 3, 3 (2002): 365.

17. Angela Stent and Lila Shevtsova, 'America, Russia and Europe: a Realignment?' *Survival* 44, 4 (Winter 2002–2003): 124.

18. Oksana Antonenko, 'Putin's Gamble', *Survival* 43, 4 (Winter 2001): 55.

19. Cited in Bosworth: 373.

20. *Strategic Survey 2003/2004* (Oxford: Oxford University Press, 2004): 116–129.

21. James Baker III, 'Russia in NATO?', *The Washington Quarterly* 25, 1 (2002): 99.

22. 'The Alliance's Mediterranean Dialogue'. *NATO Handbook* (Brussels: NATO, 2001): 92.

23. The WEU, the EU and the OSCE also launched Mediterranean initiatives, often with different groups of countries. The absence

of links between these different institutions and the
Mediterranean initiatives that they started is striking. On this, see
Martin Ortega, *The Future of the Euro-Mediterranean Security
Dialogue*, Occasional Paper 14 (Paris: Western European
Union/Institute for Security Studies, 2000).

24. Ronald D. Asmus, F. Stephen Larrabee, Ian O. Lesser,
     'Mediterranean security: new challenges, new tasks' *NATO
     Review* 44, No. 3 (1996).

25. Mohamed Kadry Said, 'Assessing NATO's Mediterranean
     Dialogue', *NATO Review*, 1 (2004).

26. See Paragraph 36, Istanbul Summit Communiqué, ibid.

27. Ibid.

28. Dalia Dassa Kaya, 'Bound to Cooperate? Transatlantic policy in
     the Middle East', *The Washington Quarterly* 27, 1 (Winter
     2003–4): 79.

29. Timothy Garton Ash, 'Anti-Europeanism in America', *New York
     Review of Books*, 13 February 2003.

30. Robin Bhatty and Rachel Bronson, 'NATO's Mixed Signals
     in the Caucasus and Central Asia', *Survival* 42, 3 (Autumn 2000):
     141.

31. See Paragraph 31, Istanbul Summit Communiqué, ibid.

32. See 'China seeks dialogue with NATO', BBC News online, 14
     November 2002.

33. Cited in Lisa Rose Weaver, 'China homes in on NATO',
     CNN.com, 25 November 2002.

34. Rajan Menon, 'The New Great Game in Central Asia', *Survival* 45,
     2 (2003): 189.

conclusion

1. See, for example, Philip H. Gordon, 'Give NATO a Role in Post-
    war Iraq', *Brookings Daily War Report*, 10 April 2003.

2. See 'Statement on Iraq', issued by the Heads of State and
    Government participating in the meeting of the North Atlantic
    Council in Istanbul, 28 June 2004.

3. Steven E. Meyer, 'Carcass of Dead Policies: The Irrelevance of
    NATO', *Parameters* (Winter 2003–2004): 83.

4. For one example, see Steven Everts, 'Why NATO should keep the
    Mideast peace', *Financial Times*, 29 July 2003.

5. NATO Secretary General Jaap de Hoop Scheffer, 'NATO's
    Istanbul Summit – New Missions, New Means', speech at the
    Royal United Services Institute, 18 June 2004.

6. Anne Deighton, 'The Eleventh of September and beyond:
    NATO', *The Political Quarterly* 73, 1 (2002): 131.

7. Ibid: 132.

8. Daniel S. Hamilton, 'Should NATO's new function be counter-
    terrorism?', *NATO Review* No. 2 (Summer 2002).

the north atlantic treaty

1. The definition of the territories to which Article 5 applies was revised by Article 2 of the Protocol to the North Atlantic Treaty on the accession of Greece and Turkey signed on 22 October 1951.

2. On 16 January 1963, the North Atlantic Council noted that in so far as the former Algerian Departments of France were concerned, the relevant clauses of this Treaty had become inapplicable from 3 July 1962.

3. The Treaty came into force on 24 August 1949, after depositions of the ratifications of all signatory states.

bibliography

David M. Abshire, 'Don't Muster Out NATO Yet: Its Job Is Far from Done', *Wall Street Journal,* 1 December 1989.

Theodore C. Achilles, 'US Role in the Negotiations that Led to Atlantic Alliance. Part 1', *NATO Review* 27, 4 (1979).

——. 'US Role in the Negotiations that Led to Atlantic Alliance. Part 2', *NATO Review* 27, 5 (1979).

Madeleine K. Albright, Statement to the North Atlantic Council, Brussels, 8 December 1998.

Thomas Ambrosio, 'From Balancer to Ally? Russo-American Relations in the Wake of 11 September', *Contemporary Security Policy* 24, 2 (August 2003).

Oksana Antonenko, 'Putin's Gamble', *Survival* 43, 4 (2001).

——. 'Russia, NATO and European Security after Kosovo', *Survival* 41, 4 (Winter 1999–2000).

Ronald D. Asmus, *Opening NATO's Door. How the Alliance Remade Itself for a New Era* (New York: Columbia University Press, 2002).

Ronald D. Asmus, Robert D. Blackwill, F. Stephen Larrabee, 'Can NATO Survive?', *The Washington Quarterly* 19, 2 (1996).

Ronald D. Asmus, F. Stephen Larrabee, Ian O. Lesser, 'Mediterranean security: new challenges, new tasks', *NATO Review* 44, 3 (1996).

Ronald D. Asmus and Ulrich Weisser, 'Refit NATO to Move Against Threats From Beyond Europe', *International Herald Tribune,* 6 December 2001.

Neil Barnett, Luke Hill, Jiří Kominek, Elisabeth Konstantinova, David Mulholland, Radu Taylor, 'NATO Expansion: The Newcomers', *Jane's Defence Weekly,* 15 October 2003.

Nora Bensahel, *The Counterterror Coalitions. Cooperation with Europe, NATO and the European Union* (Santa Monica: RAND, 2003).

Robin Bhatty and Rachel Bronson, 'NATO's Mixed Signals in the Caucasus and Central Asia', *Survival* 42, 3 (2000).

Yaroslav Bilinsky, *Endgame in NATO's Enlargement. The Baltic States and Ukraine* (Westport: Praeger, 1999).

Hans Binnendijk and Richard Kugler, 'Transforming European Forces', *Survival* 44, 3 (2002).

J. L. Black, *Russia Faces NATO Expansion. Bearing Gifts or Bearing Arms?* (Lanham: Rowman and Littlefield, 2000).

Robert D. Blackwill and Michael Stürmer (eds), *Allies Divided. Transatlantic Policies for the Greater Middle East* (Cambridge, MA: MIT Press, 1997).

Antony J. Blinken, 'The False Crisis Over the Atlantic', *Foreign Affairs* (May/June 2001).

Antony J. Blinken and Philip H. Gordon, 'NATO is Ready to Play a Central Role', *International Herald Tribune*, 18 September 2001.

Julian Borger, Richard Norton-Taylor, Ewen MacAskill and Ian Black, 'US Rallies the West for Attack on Afghanistan', *The Guardian*, 13 September 2001.

Kara Bosworth, 'The Effect of 11 September on Russia–NATO Relations', *Perspectives on European Politics and Society* 3, 3 (2002).

Ashton B. Carter and William J. Perry, *Preventive Defense. A New Security Strategy for America* (Washington, DC: Brookings Institution Press, 1999).

Marc Champion, 'Eight European Leaders Voice Their Support for US on Iraq', *Wall Street Journal*, 30 January 2003.

Michael Clarke and Paul Cornish, 'The European defence project and the Prague Summit', *International Affairs*, 78, 4 (2002).

Paul Cornish, *Partnership in Crisis: The US, Europe and the fall and rise of NATO* (London: Cassell, 1997).

Stuart Croft, 'Guaranteeing Europe's security? Enlarging NATO again', *International Affairs* 78, 1 (2002).

John-Thor Dahlburd 'NATO Ponders New Role as it Nears 50', *Los Angeles Times*, 9 December 1998.

Dalia Dassa Kaya, 'Bound to Cooperate? Transatlantic policy in the Middle East', *The Washington Quarterly* 27, 1 (Winter 2003–4).

Department of Defense, *Kosovo/Operation Allied Force: After-Action Report to Congress* (Washington, DC, 31 January 2000).

Anne Deighton, 'The Eleventh of September and beyond: NATO', *The Political Quarterly* 73, 1 (2002).

Timothy Edmunds, 'NATO and its New Members', *Survival* 45, 3 (2003).

Steven Everts, 'Why NATO should keep the Mideast peace', *Financial Times*, 29 July 2003.

Robert Fox, 'Self-confidence high in Turkey', *The Daily Telegraph*, 14 August 1990.

Lawrence Freedman, 'The Atlantic Crisis', *International Affairs* 58, 3 (1982).

——. *The Troubled Alliance: Atlantic relations in the 1980s* (London: Heinemann, 1983).

——. 'NATO or BATO?', *New York Times*, 15 June 1999.

Paul E. Gallis, *NATO: Issues for Congress*, CRS Report for Congress, 31 August 2001.

Nanette Gantz and John Roper, *Towards a new partnership: US-European relations in the post-Cold War era* (Paris: Institute for Security Studies, 1993).

Timothy Garton-Ash, 'Anti-Europeanism in America', *New York Review of Books*, 13 February 2003.

Paul R.S. Gebhard, *The United States and European Security*. Adelphi Paper 286 (London: International Institute for Strategic Studies, 1994).

James Goldgeier, *Not Whether But When: The US Decision to Enlarge NATO* (Washington, DC: The Brookings Institution, 1999).

David Gompert and Richard Kugler, 'Free-Rider Redux. NATO Needs to Project Power (and Europe Can Help)', *Foreign Affairs* 74, 1 (1995).

Philip H. Gordon, 'Give NATO a Role in Post-war Iraq', *Brookings Daily War Report*, 10 April 2003.

———. 'Recasting the Atlantic Alliance', *Survival* 38, 1 (1996).

James Gow (ed.), *Iraq, the Gulf Conflict and the World Community* (London: Brassey's, 1993).

Bradley Graham, 'NATO Ministers Back U.S. Plan for Rapid Reaction Force', *Washington Post*, 25 September 2002.

Charles Grant, *Strength in Numbers: Europe's Foreign and Defence Policy* (London: Centre for European Reform, 1997).

Daniel S. Hamilton, 'Should NATO's new function be counter-terrorism', *NATO Review* 2, Summer 2002.

Robert D. Hormats, 'Redefining Europe and the Atlantic Link', *Foreign Affairs* 68, 4 (1989).

House of Commons Defence Committee, *Lessons of Kosovo* (London: House of Commons, 2000).

Jonathan T. Howe, 'NATO and the Gulf crisis', *Survival* 33, 3 (1991).

Jolyon Howorth and John T. Keeler, *Defending Europe: The EU, NATO, and the Quest for European Autonomy* (London: Palgrave Macmillan, 2003).

IGC 2003 – Defence, CIG 57/1/03 REV 1, Brussels, 5 December 2003.

International Institute for Strategic Studies, *The Military Balance 2003–04* (Oxford: Oxford University Press, 2004).

———. *Strategic Survey 2003/2004* (Oxford: Oxford University Press, 2004).

Josef Joffe, 'The Alliance Is Dead. Long Live the New Alliance', *New York Times*, 29 September 2002.

Tim Judah, 'Kosovo's Road to War', *Survival* 41, 2 (1999).

Lawrence S. Kaplan, *NATO and the United States: The Enduring Alliance* (Boston: Twayne Publishers, 1988).

Sean Kay, *NATO and the Future of European Security* (Lanham: Rowman and Littlefield, 1998).

Glenn Kessler, 'NATO Seeks to Soothe Russia', *Washington Post*, 3 April 2004.

Richard L. Kugler, *U.S.–West-European Cooperation in Out-of-Area Military Operations. Problems and Prospects* (Santa Monica: RAND, 1994).

Taras Kuzio, 'Kiev craves closer ties with NATO', *Jane's Intelligence Review*, 1 October 2000.

F. Stephen Larrabee, *NATO's Eastern Agenda in a New Strategic Era* (Santa Monica: RAND, 2003).

Ian O. Lesser, *NATO Looks South. New Challenges and New Strategies in the Mediterranean* (Santa Monica: RAND, 2000).

Anatol Lieven, 'The End of NATO', *Prospect*, December 2001.

Richard G. Lugar, 'Redefining NATO's Mission: Preventing WMD Terrorism', *The Washington Quarterly*, Summer 2002.

——. 'NATO: Out of Area or Out of Business: A Call for U.S. Leadership to Revive and Redefine the Alliance', text of speech to the Overseas Writers Club, Washington, DC, 24 June 1993.

Mohamed Kadry Said, 'Assessing NATO's Mediterranean Dialogue', *NATO Review*, 1 (2004).

Robert Kagan, 'Power and Weakness', Policy Review 113, June/July 2002.

Taras Kuzio, 'Kiev craves closer ties with NATO', *Jane's Intelligence Review*, 1 October 2000.

Dieter Mahncke, 'The Role of the USA in Europe: Successful Past but Uncertain Future?', *European Foreign Affairs Review* 4, 3 (Autumn 1999).

Michael Mandelbaum, 'Preserving the New Peace: The Case Against NATO Expansion', *Foreign Affairs* 72, 3 (1995).

Robert Manning, 'Bumbling Around in the Balkans', *Washington Post*, 15 February 1999.

Jessica T. Mathews, 'Estranged Partners', *Foreign Policy*, November/December 2001.

Jeffrey McCausland, *The Gulf Conflict: A Military Analysis*. Adelphi Paper 282 (London: International Institute for Strategic Studies, 1993).

Rajan Menon, 'The New Great Game in Central Asia', *Survival* 45, 2 (2003).

Steven E. Meyer, 'Carcass of Dead Policies: The Irrelevance of NATO', *Parameters*, Winter 2003–2004.

Steven Mufson, 'Seeking "Common Framework"', *The Washington Post*, 10 March 2001.

Steven Lee Myers, 'Fighter jets' roar stirs joy and anger', *New York Times*, 3 April 2004.

General Klaus Naumann, 'Crunch Time for the Alliance', *NATO Review* 2 (Summer 2002).

NATO, *Alliance Policy Framework on Proliferation of Weapons of Mass Destruction* issued at the Ministerial Meeting of the North Atlantic Council, Istanbul, 9 June 1994.

NATO, *Defence Capabilities Initiative*, 25 April 1999.

NATO, *Final Communiqué, Ministerial Meeting of the North Atlantic Council*, Brussels, 17 December 1992.

NATO, *Final Communiqué, Ministerial Meeting of the North Atlantic Council*, Oslo, 4 June 1992.

NATO, *Final Communiqué, Ministerial Meeting of the North Atlantic Council*, Reykjavik, 14 May 2002.

NATO, *Istanbul Summit Declaration*, issued by the Heads of State and Government participating in the meeting of the North Atlantic Council, Istanbul, 28 June 2004.

NATO, *London Declaration On A Transformed Atlantic Alliance*, issued by the Heads of State and Government participating in the meeting of the North Atlantic Council, London, 10–11 January 1990.

NATO, *NATO Handbook* (Brussels: NATO, 2001).

NATO, *North Atlantic Treaty*, 4 April 1949.

NATO, *NATO's Response to Terrorism*, Statement issued at the Ministerial Meeting of the North Atlantic Council, Brussels, 6 December 2001.

NATO, *Partnership for Peace: Invitation and Framework Document*, issued by the Heads of State and Government participating in the meeting of the North Atlantic Council, Brussels, 10–11 January 1994.

NATO, *Prague Summit Declaration*, issued by the Heads of State and Government participating in the meeting of the North Atlantic Council, Prague, 21 November 2002.

NATO Press Release (2001) 125, 13 September 2001.

NATO, 'Rebalancing NATO for a Strong Future', Remarks by NATO Secretary General Lord Robertson, Defence Week Conference, Brussels, 31 January 2001.

NATO, *Statement on Capabilities*, issued at the Meeting of the North Atlantic Council in Defence Ministers Session, 6 June 2002.

NATO, *Statement by the North Atlantic Council*, Press Release (2001) 124, 12 September 2001.

NATO, *Statement to the Press*, by NATO Secretary General Lord Robertson on the North Atlantic Council Decision to Implement Article 5 of the Washington Treaty following the 11 September attacks against the United States, 4 October 2001.

NATO, *Study on Enlargement* (Brussels: NATO, 1995).

NATO, *The Alliance's Strategic Concept*, Approved by Heads of State and Government participating in the meeting of the North Atlantic Council, Washington, DC, 23–24 April 1999.

NATO, *The Situation in Yugoslavia*, statement by the Heads of State and Government participating in the meeting of the North Atlantic Council, Rome, 7–8 November 1991.

NATO, *Transcript of Press Conference*, following the meeting of the North Atlantic Council, 6 June 2002.

Joseph S. Nye, 'The US and Europe: continental drift?', *International Affairs* 76, 1 (2000).

David A. Ochmanek, *NATO's Future. Implications for U.S. Military Capabilities and Posture* (Santa Monica: RAND, 2000).

Michael O'Hanlon, 'Rumsfeld's Defence Vision', *Survival* 44, 2 (2002).

Martin Ortega, *The Future of the Euro-Mediterranean Security Dialogue*, Occasional Paper 14 (Paris: Western European Union/Institute for Security Studies, 2000).

David Owen, *Balkan Odyssey* (London: Victor Gollancz, 1995).

John Pimlott and Stephen Badsey (eds), *The Gulf War Assessed* (London: Arms and Armour, 1993).

Hugh Pope, 'Gulf Crisis: "Reluctant" NATO worries allies in Turkey', *The Independent*, 27 December 1990.

John Roper, 'NATO's New Role in Crisis Management', *The International Spectator* XXXIV, 2 (1999).

Stephen S. Rosenfeld, 'NATO's Last Chance', *The Washington Post*, 2 July 1993.

Donald H. Rumsfeld, 'Transforming the Military', *Foreign Affairs* 81, 3 (2002).

Richard Rupp, 'NATO 1949 and NATO 2000: From Collective Defense toward Collective Security', *Journal of Strategic Studies* 23 (2000).

Kori Schake, *Constructive Duplication: Reducing EU reliance on US military assets* (London: Centre for European Reform, 2002).

——. 'NATO after the Cold War, 1991–1995: Institutional Competition and the Collapse of the French Alternative', *Contemporary European History* 7, 3 (1998).

Gregory L. Schulte. 'Former Yugoslavia and the New NATO', *Survival* 39, 1 (1997).

Elaine Sciolino, 'U.S. Pressing NATO for Rapid Reaction Force', *New York Times*, 18 September 2002.

Secretary of State for Defence, *Kosovo. Lessons from the Crisis* (London: House of Commons, 2000).

Jiří Šedivy, 'The Puzzle of NATO Enlargement', *Contemporary Security Policy* 22, 2 (August 2001).

Stanley Sloan, 'US Perspectives on NATO's future', *International Affairs* 71, 2 (1995).

SHAPE, 'NATO launches Response Force', 15 October 2003.

Elizabeth D. Sherwood, *Allies in Crisis. Meeting Challenges to Western Security* (Yale University Press: New Haven and London, 1990).

André de Staercke *et al.*, *NATO's Anxious Birth: The Prophetic Vision of the 1940s* (London: C. Hurst and Company, 1985).

Angela Stent and Lila Shevtsova, 'America, Russia and Europe: a realignment?', *Survival* 44, 4 (2002–2003).

Philip Stephens, 'The American way of defence', *Financial Times*, 13 June 2002.

Strobe Talbott, Speech to the Royal Institute for International Affairs, London, 7 October 1999.

William J. Taylor Jr, and James Blackwell, 'The ground war in the Gulf', *Survival*, 33, 3 (1991).

United States Government, *The National Security Strategy of the United States* (The White House: Washington, DC, 2002).

Stephen Walt, 'The Ties That Fray: Why Europe and America are Approaching a Parting of the Ways', *The National Interest*, 54 (Winter 1998/1999).

Lisa Rose Weaver, 'China homes in on NATO', CNN.com, 25 November 2002.

Manfred Wörner, 'The Atlantic Alliance in a New Era', *NATO Review* 39, 1 (1991).

Robin Wright, 'NATO Promises Cohesive Stand Against Terrorism', *Los Angeles Times*, 7 December 2001.

Boris Yeltsin, *Midnight Diaries* (London: Weidenfeld and Nicolson, 2000).

David S. Yost, *NATO Transformed: The Alliance's New Roles in International Security* (Washington, DC: United States Institute of Peace Press, 1998).

——. 'The NATO Capabilities Gap and the European Union', *Survival*, 42, 4 (Winter 2000–2001).

index

Note: Page numbers in **bold** refer to diagrams, page numbers in *italics* refer to tables. See pp. xii–xiv for the abbreviations used in this book.